INTERNATIONAL QUANTITY FOODS

INTERNATIONAL
◆ *Quantity Foods* ◆

◆ *Pamela Goyan Kittler*, M.S. ◆

FOOD AND NUTRITION CONSULTANT

◆ *Kathryn Sucher*, Sc.D., R.D. ◆

ASSOCIATE PROFESSOR,
SAN JOSE STATE UNIVERSITY

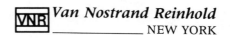
VNR *Van Nostrand Reinhold*
NEW YORK

Library of Congress Catalog Card Number 89-22498

ISBN 0-442-31862-6

Printed in the United States of America

Van Nostrand Reinhold
115 Fifth Avenue
New York, New York 10003

Van Nostrand Reinhold International Company Limited
11 New Fetter Lane
London EC4P, 4EE, England

Van Nostrand Reinhold
480 La Trobe Street
Melbourne, Victoria 3000, Australia

Nelson Canada
1120 Birchmount Road
Scarborough, Ontario M1K 5G4, Canada

All photographs by Peter de Lory

16 15 14 13 12 11 10 9 8 7 6 5 4 3 2 1

Library of Congress Cataloging-in-Publication Data

Kittler, Pamela Goyan, 1953–
    International quantity foods / Pamela Goyan Kittler, Kathryn Sucher.
      p. cm.
    ISBN 0-442-31862-6
    1. Quantity cookery.   2. Cookery, International.   I. Sucher, Kathryn.   II. Title.
TX820.K53   1990
641.5'7—dc20
                                        89-22498
                                            CIP

◆ *Contents* ◆

v

◆ *Preface* ◆

American cuisine includes the foods and cooking styles of many nations. Even the dishes we consider distinctly American, such as hamburgers, hot dogs, French fries, and apple pie, originated with foods brought to this country by early settlers from around the world. More recent immigrants continue to introduce us to many new and sometimes exotic foods. In addition to our traditional American foods, today our meals are just as likely to include falafel, pizza, sushi, or tacos.

This book is an introduction to the many different ethnic cuisines common in the United States. The chapters are arranged alphabetically from the Caribbean to West Africa. The recipes were selected and designed specifically for use by commercial and institutional food services.

Each chapter presents information about the characteristic cooking style of a particular nation or region, including ingredients, methods of preparation, and meal patterns. Some chapters discuss important ways in which the ethnic cuisine has influenced American cooking, especially in the development of regional styles. Every chapter concludes with traditional menus and recipes. Some recipes have been modified to suit the particular needs of the food service industry. Nutritional information is also provided.

The recipes in this book are simple, yet authentic. They were adapted from a variety of sources, including many of the traditional ethnic cookbooks cited in the reference section. Consideration was given to both availability of ethnic ingredients and acceptability of certain foods—no recipe requires durian, tripe, or iguana meat! Whenever possible, the glossary at the back of this book includes suggested substitutes for some of the ethnic ingredients.

In the interest of authenticity, ingredients such as sweet butter or fresh herbs are often listed in the recipes. If these items are not standardly available in your particular food service operation, conventional substitutions (such as margarine or dry herbs) will not seriously alter the flavor of the dish. Those few instances where substitutions should not, or cannot, be made are clearly noted.

The nutritional values for each recipe were approximated using "The Food Processor" (ESHA Corporation, 1984), "Nutritionist III" Version 4 (N-square Computing, 1988), and a variety of international food composition references.

When values were in question, due to unavailable or questionable data on an ingredient or cooking technique, the value is left blank or put in parentheses.

Unfortunately, we can provide only a "taste" of these ethnic cuisines; each is deserving of a book in itself. Our hope is that the information on ingredients and preparation methods will familiarize you with traditional ethnic cooking styles, and that the recipes will whet your appetite for further exploration.

◆ *Acknowledgments* ◆

This book would not have been possible without the expertise and advice shared by Panfilo Belo, Ph.D., Doris Becker, Bob Caron, Norma Jean Downes, M.S., R.D., Julie Dutcher, M.S., R.D., Darcie Ellyne, Robbie Fanning, Ben Helprin, M.F.A., Laura McEwen, Lucy McProud, Ph.D., R.D., Kristin Nelson, Miriam Saltmarch, Ph.D., Sonia Scanlon, M.S., R.D., Jewel Swindle, M.S., R.D., and Marianne Wilcox, R.D.

In addition, we wish to thank our family and friends for taste-testing these recipes during development: the Anderson family, the Cocotas family, the Crummy family, the Cumberland Elementary School staff, the Hungerford family, the Johnson family, the Kittler family, the Quillinan family, David Stone, the Swanson family, the Thomas family, the Tupper family, and the students of spring semester 1989 Nutrition and Food Science 111A quantity cooking laboratory.

INTERNATIONAL QUANTITY FOODS

◆ *1* ◆ COOKING FROM THE
◆ *Caribbean* ◆

Puerto Rican pionoñes (fried plantain rings filled with pork) served with red beans and rice.

The earliest settlers of the Caribbean Islands cultivated sweet potatoes, cassava, and corn; harvested papaya and guava; and hunted iguana. They fished offshore, gathered shellfish on the beaches, and trapped wild duck and other fowl. They flavored their food with allspice and chili peppers.

After Columbus arrived in the Caribbean on his first voyage to the New World, explorers from Portugal, England, France, the Netherlands, and Denmark, as well as from Spain, came to the region in search of spices. Many of these explorers settled in the islands, bringing with them familiar European livestock such as cattle, goats, and hogs. Plants that flourished in the tropical climate included figs, oranges, lemons, bananas, coffee, breadfruit, mangoes, and nutmeg. Wheat, rice, olives, grapes, and sugar cane were also introduced but with less initial success. By the 16th century, enough sugar cane was finally produced to provide an exportable surplus.

With the development of the sugar industry and the production of sugar products such as molasses and rum, slaves were brought from Africa to work on the sugar plantations. They brought their native foods, including okra, taro, and ackee. When slavery was outlawed, plantation owners imported cheap labor from both China and India. As a result, rice and curry dishes became an integral part of island cooking, and Chinese food became popular.

The Caribbean Islands can be divided into four groups, each heavily influenced by a different colonial heritage: the Spanish group comprises Cuba, Puerto Rico, and the Dominican Republic; the French group includes Haiti, Guadeloupe, Martinique, and St. Bartholomew; the British group is made up of Jamaica, Barbados, and Grenada; and the Dutch group includes Aruba and Curaçao.

Most countries have their own specialties. Jamaica is known for its spicy vegetable soup known as pepperpot, and for ackee and salt fish; Haiti for its banana-stuffed chicken dish called *poulet rôti à la créole*; the Dominican Republic for *sancocho* (a meat and vegetable stew); Curaçao for its orange-flavored liqueur of the same name; Dominica for its "mountain chicken" (a large, tasty frog); and Barbados for its unusual seafood dishes made with flying fish, green turtles, and sea urchins.

Puerto Rican cuisine is notable for its use of *sofrito*, a combination of onions, garlic, cilantro, sweet peppers, and tomatoes that are lightly fried in lard colored with annatto seeds. Sofrito serves as a base for many dishes, as well as an all-purpose sauce. The Spanish-influenced chicken *adobo* is also typical of Puerto Rican cookery. In this dish, black pepper, oregano, garlic, salt, olive oil, and lime juice are rubbed onto chicken several hours before cooking.

Cuba is unique in the Caribbean for its use of black beans; they are cooked with rice and are used in black bean soup. A traditional Cuban dish is *picadillo*, a beef hash flavored with olives and raisins, which are traditional Spanish ingredients, and tomatoes and chili peppers, which are native ingredients. Picadillo is served with fried plaintains, black beans, rice, and fried eggs. Another specialty that combines ingredients from different cultures is *chicharrónes de pollo*, small pieces of chicken marinated in lime juice and soy sauce, then fried in lard.

Despite these variations, many foods of the Caribbean are remarkably similar for an area with so many different culinary influences. Because a good deal of contact has been maintained between the islands, ingredients and cooking methods are much the same throughout the region. For example, beans are a staple and are prepared in a similar manner throughout the islands. They are cooked with lard and salt, and are usually flavored with onion, sweet peppers, and tomatoes, then served with rice. However, dishes prepared on one island may taste different from those same dishes cooked on another island. For example, corn cakes fried in butter on a French-influenced island will taste different from corn cakes fried in lard on a Spanish-influenced island.

Ingredients

MILK AND MILK PRODUCTS
Fresh, evaporated, and condensed milk are used in some dishes and are often added to coffee. Milk- or cream-based desserts, such as custards and ice cream, are popular. But milk is often costly and is not available to all Caribbean Islanders.

MEAT AND MEAT ALTERNATIVES
Beans are a major protein source in the Caribbean. Kidney or red beans are favored in Puerto Rico, as well as in Jamaica and Haiti, where they are called

peas. Black beans are preferred in Cuba. Other legumes, such as black-eyed peas, are also common.

Fish and shellfish are featured in many dishes and come in an almost endless variety, although dried salt cod is the most popular. Mackerel, crab, lobster, tuna, shrimp, grouper, snapper, flying fish, and conch are commonly eaten, as are turtle, frog, and iguana. Pork is favored on islands where the Spanish dominated. Jamaicans have acquired a taste for beef, and kid (goat) is sometimes served. Throughout the islands eggs are widely consumed, especially at breakfast.

FRUITS AND VEGETABLES

Citrus fruits, bananas, pineapples, and other tropical fruits are routinely exported to temperate climates and are thus well known throughout the world. These, however, are only a small sample of the tremendous variety of fascinating fruits that abound in tropical areas. The Caribbean is host to many, some native and others coming originally from South America, Africa, and India. The *guanabana*, or *soursop*, has a white aromatic flesh and is eaten plain or used to make sherbet or beverages. The papaya, light orange inside, has a delicate flavor reminiscent of melon. Tamarind is a dark brown pod whose pulp provides a sour taste in beverages and chutneys. The pink or white flesh of guavas is well suited for jams and jellies, or it can be eaten fresh. The mango is a large, juicy fruit with fragrant flesh and tastes similar to peaches. Breadfruit is a large, green fruit containing soft, white flesh reminiscent of bread when roasted and is used as a vegetable. The *ackee* from Africa is cleaned and the edible part, which resembles scrambled eggs, is cooked with fish and vegetables. Plaintains look like green bananas and must be cooked before they can be eaten. *Carambola* is a ribbed yellow fruit with a crisp, tart flesh. *Granadilla* or passion fruit, persimmons, *sapodillas*, *mameys*, cashew apples, and uglis are a few of the other fruit delicacies to be found.

Many root vegetables grow in the Caribbean including white (or English) potatoes, sweet potatoes, taro (commonly called *dasheen* or *eddo*), *cassava* (known also as *yuca*, *manioc*, or *tapioca*), and *malanga* (also called *yautia* or *tannier*). These starchy vegetables form a cornerstone of island diets.

Other frequently used vegetables include *chayote* (christophine), a type of squash; peppers, both hot and sweet; onions; tomatoes; avocados; and greens such as kale and taro leaves, known as *callaloo*.

BREADS AND CEREALS

Rice is frequently eaten in the Caribbean. Cornmeal and wheat flour are used for most breads. Fried corn cakes and fritters are popular. A specialty of the region is cassava bread, made from grated cassava that is mixed with brown sugar and coconut, then fried.

OTHER INGREDIENTS

Butter is widely used in islands influenced by the French, whereas lard is the fat of choice in those islands influenced by the Spanish. Coconut, corn, and olive oils are also used for some dishes, and many foods are fried. Nuts are used in some dishes, coconut in its many forms being by far the most common, with peanuts second. The creamy liquid squeezed from fresh grated coconut is used in cooking in much the same way that milk and cream are used.

Coffee, introduced by early European settlers, flourished in Jamaica, where today it is grown for export. Many coffee drinkers consider Jamaican Blue Mountain beans among the finest in the world. Coffee is a popular beverage in the Caribbean, and is often served with milk. It is consumed at meals, as a snack, and even as a dessert, flavored with orange rind, cinnamon, whipped cream, coconut cream, or rum. Fruit drinks and ices are also enjoyed. The most common alcoholic drink is rum, and nearly every island makes its own variety. In addition, local brews are made from oranges, rice, or spices. The best known is ginger beer, which is traditional at Christmas in much of the Caribbean.

Seasonings

Although Columbus failed to find the East Indian spices he was in search of when he arrived in the Caribbean, Spaniards later discovered small, round berries, which they thought to be peppercorns, and accordingly named them *pimenta*. In Europe these were ground and, because their flavor combined the aroma of nutmeg, cinnamon, and cloves, were called allspice. However, a more significant contribution from the Caribbean to cuisines worldwide was the chili pepper. Unrelated to the black pepper that had been brought to Europe from the Far East, chili peppers soon made their way around the world, adding new heat to chutneys, relishes, and barbecued, stir-fried, and curried dishes. Today, peppers of this family come in many sizes, shapes, colors (from purple to green, yellow, white, and red), and degrees of hotness.

Cilantro, or fresh coriander leaves, has a unique flavor and is one of the most widely used herbs. Basil, thyme, chives, and sorrel (a sour herb) are also used. Lemon, lime, and garlic flavor many Caribbean foods, and *annatto*, a reddish seed also known as *achiote*, is used to color foods orange. Sweet spices such as cinnamon, cloves, ginger, nutmeg, and mace, as well as vanilla and rum, are added to baked goods and desserts. Seasonings from other cuisines, such as soy sauce and curry powder, have also been adopted.

Preparation

Although many of the fruits, fish, and seafoods found in the Caribbean do not require much preparation, certain foods must be carefully processed. The cassava root, from which tapioca is derived, is poisonous unless thoroughly cooked or the juice expelled. It is peeled, grated, squeezed, or pressed to

Chicharrónes de pollo (fried chicken marinated in lime juice, rum, and soy sauce), a Cuban specialty.

remove the juice, and dried in the sun. It can also be baked and then ground into flour to make a hard, crusty bread. The expressed cassava juice is boiled to make *cassarep*, a thick, black, seasoned syrup used in making many dishes, such as pepperpot, a meat and vegetable stew. The ackee, a reddish fruit brought from Africa, must be selected and cleaned with care. Both immature and overripe fruits are poisonous, and the membrane surrounding the seeds is toxic. Part of the shell of the cashew apple, used in making preserves and candies, contains a poison that is destroyed by heat, so the fruits are soaked in salt water, peeled, boiled, and drained before being used.

Most foods, however, are simply fried or boiled. Grilling is common and originated with the Arawak Indians who called it *barbacoa*, from which we get the word *barbecue*. Pirates who once frequented the Caribbean smoked meat — usually pork — over a slow fire as a means of preserving it. This method is called *boucan*, and the pirates became known as *boucaniers*, or buccaneers.

Traditional cooking methods easily accommodated the new foods that kept appearing throughout Caribbean history. In addition, some dishes were introduced that became popular more or less intact. Thus, European dishes such as *escabeche* (pickled fish, seafood, or poultry), *morillas* (a type of blood sausage), and fried corn cakes can be found. African foods include *foofoo* (okra and plaintain), *coocoo* (cornmeal and okra bread), and salt cod fritters. Called *bacalaitos* in Puerto Rico, these cakes have a different name on nearly every island, from *arcat de marue* to "stamp and go." Asian dishes are found mostly in those countries that were dominated by the British, Dutch, or French. Curried foods (called *kerry* on the Dutch-influenced islands and *colombo* on the French-influenced islands) and variations of rice pilaf are common. Chinese cooking is very popular.

Meal Patterns

Caribbean meals typically emphasize starchy vegetables; these are served with some meat, poultry, or fish, usually fried. Ethnic heritage sometimes influences the menu; for example, a poor native Indian may exist mostly on yuca, chili peppers, tomatoes, and a bit of fish. Most meals are multicultural, however, and mix African, European, and native Indian foods.

In many Caribbean countries, breakfast consists of coffee with milk and bread. Eggs, cereal, and fruit are added if affordable. The most popular lunch menu includes rice and beans with meat. In rural areas, a starchy vegetable with dried salt cod is also common. The dinner meal is similar to lunch, although extra meats, vegetables, and milk may be added, followed by fruit, ice cream, or pastries for dessert. Fruit is eaten often as a snack.

```
+  ───────────     +        +  ───────────     +

        M  E  N  U                      M  E  N  U
    *Puerto Rican Dinner*               *Cuban Dinner*

         Surullitos                  Sopa de Frijol Negro
        (corn sticks)                  (black bean soup)
          Pionoñes                 Chicharrónes de Pollo
  (plantain rings with pork)      (marinated fried chicken)
    Red Beans and Rice                  Baked Papaya
          Sofrito
     (spicy tomato sauce)
       Pelo de Angel*
      (candied squash)


 Serving suggestions: Offer fruit    Serving suggestions: Offer steamed
    juice or coffee with milk.           rice and fruit juice or
                                             strong coffee.
   *Fried bananas flavored with
   brown sugar and rum can be
    substituted, if desired.

+  ───────────     +        +  ───────────     +
```

M   E   N   U   *Puerto Rican Dinner*

◆ Surullitos (Corn Sticks)

FRY: 3–5 minutes
DEEP-FAT FRY:
 350°F
YIELD: 48 portions
PORTION: 2 corn
 sticks

3 qt. water
2 T. salt

2 lb. yellow cornmeal
1 lb. Cheddar cheese, shredded

1. Boil water and salt. Slowly pour in cornmeal, stirring constantly. Stir for 2 to 3 minutes until mixture is thick. Remove from heat.
2. Add cheese to cornmeal and mix. Cool.
3. With moistened hands, press 2 tablespoons of corn mixture into 3″ × 1″ sticks. (May be refrigerated for 24 hours at this point.)
4. Deep-fat fry until golden brown. Drain. May be served hot or at room temperature.

CALORIES: 246
CHOLESTEROL: 20 mg
VITAMIN A: 305 IU

CARBOHYDRATE: 20 g
CALCIUM: 141 mg
VITAMIN C: 0 mg

PROTEIN: 7 g
SODIUM: 667 mg

FAT: 25 g
IRON: 1 mg

9 ◆ COOKING FROM THE CARIBBEAN

◆ *Pionoñes (Plantain Rings with Pork)*

FRY: 6–8 minutes
DEEP-FAT FRYER:
  350°F
YIELD: 50 portions
PORTION: 2 rings

1½ c. annatto oil (page 12)
10 lb. pork, ground
2 lb. onions, chopped
1 lb. sweet peppers, chopped
3 T. garlic, chopped
10 lb. tomatoes, peeled, seeded, and
  chopped
3 T. salt or to taste

1 lb. green olives stuffed with
  pimento, finely chopped
½ lb. raisins
1 c. vinegar
25 lb. plantains, large and ripe
  (about 1 lb. each)
1½ c. vegetable oil
30 eggs, beaten

1. Cook pork in annatto oil thoroughly. Add onions, sweet peppers, and garlic. Cook until they are softened.
2. Add tomatoes and salt. Simmer until all of the liquid in the pan evaporates and the mixture thickens.
3. Stir in green olives, capers, and vinegar. Adjust seasoning. Chill.
4. Peel plantains and cut each lengthwise into ⅛- to ¼-inch slices. Fry until plantains are soft and lightly browned. Do not overcook. Drain and cool.
5. Form 1- to 1½-inch balls of the meat mixture. Carefully wrap a plantain strip around each, securing with a toothpick.
6. Dip these into the eggs and then deep-fat fry until the pionoñes are golden brown. Drain and serve immediately.

CALORIES: 669   CARBOHYDRATE: 67 g   PROTEIN: 19 g   FAT: 64 g
CHOLESTEROL: 213 mg CALCIUM: 65 g   SODIUM: 1367 mg   IRON: 3 mg
VITAMIN A: 2515 IU   VITAMIN C: 46 mg

◆ *Red Beans and Rice*

YIELD: 50 portions
PORTION: 1–1½ c.

6 lb. dried red or pinto beans
2 gal. water
2 T. salt
1 c. vegetable oil

3 c. sofrito (recipe follows)
5 lb. white rice
1 gal. reserved bean liquid
  (plus water if necessary)

1. Rinse beans. Combine with salt and water. Bring to a boil, cover, and simmer 1½ hours, until beans are tender. Do not overcook. Drain beans and reserve liquid.
2. Heat oil and stir in sofrito, rice, and bean liquid. Cover and simmer for 20 minutes or until rice is cooked. Stir in beans and adjust seasoning.

CALORIES: 380   CARBOHYDRATE: 65 g   PROTEIN: 12 g   FAT: 14 g
CHOLESTEROL: 8 mg   CALCIUM: 64 mg   SODIUM: 519 mg   IRON: 4 mg
VITAMIN A: 243 IU   VITAMIN C: 13 mg

♦ Sofrito (Spicy Tomato Sauce)

YIELD: 1 qt.

1 lb. salt pork, finely diced
¼ c. annatto oil (page 12)
1 lb. onions, chopped
2 T. garlic, minced
1 lb. smoked ham, cubed
1½ lb. sweet peppers, chopped

3 lb. tomatoes, peeled, seeded, and diced (and drained if canned)
2 T. fresh coriander, chopped
1 tsp. oregano
4 tsp. salt
¼ tsp. pepper

1. Render fat from the salt pork and discard the pork. Add annatto oil.
2. Add onions and garlic and sauté until soft. Add smoked ham, sweet peppers, tomatoes, coriander, oregano, salt, and pepper. Simmer for 15 to 20 minutes, stirring often.

Note: If carefully sealed, sofrito can be stored in the refrigerator for 1 or 2 weeks.

♦ Pelo de Angel (Candied Squash)

YIELD: 50 portions
PORTION: ¼ c.

7–8 lb. chayote squash, peeled and julienned

1½ lb. sugar
1 qt. water

Simmer squash in sugar and water for approximately 20 minutes, or until soft and translucent. Chill.

CALORIES: 62	CARBOHYDRATE: 16 g	PROTEIN: <1 g	FAT: <1 g
CHOLESTEROL: 0 mg	CALCIUM: 18 mg	SODIUM: 2 mg	IRON: <1 mg
VITAMIN A: 283 IU	VITAMIN C: 7 mg		

Cuban Dinner

◆ *Sopa de Frijol Negro (Black Bean Soup)*

YIELD: 50 portions
PORTION: 1 c.

5 lb. dried black beans
1½–2 gal. chicken stock
¾ c. annatto oil (recipe follows)
1 lb. onions, chopped
1 lb. sweet peppers, chopped
2 T. garlic, minced

3 lb. ham, diced
3 lb. tomatoes, seeded and chopped
¾ c. vinegar
1 T. cumin
½ T. pepper or to taste

1. Rinse dried beans, cover with water by 2 inches. Bring to a boil and simmer 2–3 hours. When beans are very tender, drain (reserve liquid) and cool to room temperature. Mash beans in a mixer or put through a sieve. Add chicken stock. (Or add stock and lightly purée in a food processor.)
2. Sauté onions, sweet peppers, and garlic in oil until soft. Stir in ham, tomatoes, vinegar, cumin, and pepper. Cook over high heat until thick (approximately 10 minutes).
3. Add bean mixture and simmer until soup is heated through.

Annatto Oil
1 c. vegetable oil   ½ c. annatto seeds

Heat oil to 350°–375°F. Add annatto seeds and fry for about 1 minute. Remove from heat and cool. Strain oil. If properly sealed, oil can be stored for several months.

CALORIES: 198   CARBOHYDRATE: 15 g   PROTEIN: 14 g   FAT: 15 g
CHOLESTEROL: 17 mg   CALCIUM: 38 mg   SODIUM: 850 mg   IRON: 2 mg
VITAMIN A: 172 IU   VITAMIN C: 10 mg

♦ Chicharrónes de Pollo (Marinated Fried Chicken)

FRY: 5–10 minutes
DEEP-FAT FRY:
350°F
YIELD: 50 portions
PORTION: 4 pieces

2½ c. rum
2½ c. soy sauce
2½ c. lime juice
1 T. chopped garlic

45–50 lb. chicken
2 lb. flour
1 T. salt or to taste
2 tsp. pepper or to taste

1. Heat rum in a pan. Turn off heat, ignite rum. Carefully shake pan. When flames have died, add soy sauce, lime, and garlic.
2. Cut each chicken into 16 small pieces. (Split wings, thighs, drumsticks, and breasts in half.) Combine with rum and soy sauce mixture. Marinate chicken in refrigerator for at least 4 hours, turning twice.
3. Remove chicken from marinade and pat dry. Coat with seasoned flour.
4. Deep-fat fry until chicken is thoroughly cooked.

CALORIES: 473
CHOLESTEROL: 166 mg
VITAMIN A: 130 IU

CARBOHYDRATE: 6 g
CALCIUM: 35 mg
VITAMIN C: <1 mg

PROTEIN: 55 g
SODIUM: 1088 mg

FAT: 35 g
IRON: 3 mg

♦ *Baked Papaya*

BAKE: 45–60
minutes
OVEN: 350°F
YIELD: 50 portions
PORTION: ½
papaya

25 papaya (ripe but still firm),
  peeled, halved, and seeded

12 oz. butter
1 lb. sugar

Place papaya halves, cut-side up, in baking dish. Add water to a depth of ½ inch. Dot each half with approximately 1 teaspoon butter and 2 teaspoons sugar. Bake until tender.

CALORIES: 142
CHOLESTEROL: 15 mg
VITAMIN A: 3269 IU

CARBOHYDRATE: 24 g
CALCIUM: 38 mg
VITAMIN C: 56 mg

PROTEIN: 1 g
SODIUM: 60 mg

FAT: 8 g
IRON: <1 mg

◆ *2* ◆ C O O K I N G   F R O M
◆ *Central America* ◆

Fiambre, traditional festive Guatemalan salad.

The area now known as Central America (encompassing Guatemala, Nicaragua, Honduras, Belize, Costa Rica, El Salvador, and Panama) was originally inhabited by numerous Indian tribes, including the Mayans, who had a highly developed culture and cuisine. Spaniards arrived in the 1500s, bringing with them new customs and foods, some of which grew well and were embraced by the Indians. The Spaniards planted bananas and sugar cane on huge plantations and imported slaves from Africa to tend them. Thus, the cuisine of Central American countries today combines native techniques and ingredients with those from Europe and Africa.

The Mayans cultivated beans, chili peppers, corn, peanuts, pineapples, squash, tomatoes, and other foods. They raised domesticated turkeys and kept bees for honey. Mayans also managed herds of deer that were used for food, hunted other game, and gathered fruits and vegetables.

Among the foods brought by the Europeans, rice and pork are two that have become an integral part of Central American cuisine. Other popular nontraditional foods not associated with Latin American cooking include salami and sauerkraut, brought by later European immigrants. In general, this cuisine is not as spicy as that of Mexico; its seasoning is more delicate. Achiote, chili peppers, cilantro, coconut milk, and orange juice flavor many dishes. Each country has its characteristic cooking traditions.

In Guatemala, seasonings are mild and bean dishes are favorites. Some of the more unusual dishes eaten in this area are fried iguana, boiled iguana eggs, and baked parrot. Honduran cooking is more like that of Mexico, and seafood is a specialty, including conch and sea turtle. In El Salvador, hot *papusas* — corn dough filled with meat, black beans, or cheese — are a specialty. Nicaragua is known for its tripe soup and tamales. Pork and beef dishes are also featured. Rice is commonly eaten in Costa Rica; a typical dish is *casado*, a fish, meat, or chicken dish that includes rice, beans, and cabbage. Because of its canal, Panama has many more foreign visitors than other Central American countries, and therefore the country experiences a stronger foreign influence. One of the favorite dishes is *sancocho*, a stew containing pork, beef, ham, tomato, potato, squash, sausage, and green bananas.

In addition to national specialties, the cooking of Central America can also be divided between coastal lowland cuisines and those of the interior highlands. The cooking along the north coast is similar to that of the Caribbean in both available foods and number of foreign influences. But the cuisine of the central region is more affected by native Indian cooking. Today, the influence of the United States can be seen in the common use of canned and processed foods and ready-to-eat breakfast cereals.

Ingredients

MILK AND MILK PRODUCTS

Milk is not widely consumed as a beverage, but evaporated milk and cream are very popular in the dishes of some regions. Both aged and fresh cheese (similar to crumbly farmer's cheese) are eaten.

MEAT AND MEAT ALTERNATIVES

Legumes are important in the cuisine of Central America. Beans can be part of a meat or poultry dish or they can be a specialty on their own. Black beans, kidney beans, red beans, white beans, fava beans, and chickpeas are used often.

Pork is available throughout the region. All parts are consumed, including the knuckles, tripe, and *chicharrónes* (pork skin). Sausages are made, such as *longanzina* (mildly spiced pork sausage) and Spanish-style *chorizo*. Beef is also eaten, usually in the more cosmopolitan cooking of the cities. Chicken, turkey, and duck are especially popular. Eggs are commonly served.

Fish and shellfish, including shrimp, clams, flounder, mackerel, shark, sole, tarpon, and mussels, are eaten primarily in the coastal regions. Conch, sea snail, and turtle soups are served in the seaports of Honduras. Sea turtle eggs are also popular. Minnows, perch, trout and other freshwater fish are available throughout the area, but are commonly consumed only in those regions where seafood is eaten.

Game is also hunted, particularly deer. Small animals such as iguanas and other lizards are also sometimes eaten.

FRUITS AND VEGETABLES

Tropical fruits are abundant, including *granadilla* (passion fruit), guava, mangoes, oranges (both sweet and sour varieties), pineapples, tangerines, bananas, and papaya. Some of the less familiar kinds are breadfruit (which has a soft, breadlike pulp when cooked), *mameys* (whose sweet, yellowish flesh is reminiscent of pumpkin), *nances* (similar to small, yellow cherries), and *zapote* or *sapodilla* (a member of the persimmon family). Temperate fruits such as grapes and apples are also available.

Native vegetables including *chayote* squash, corn, potatoes, sweet peppers, chili peppers, tomatoes, yams, and green beans are popular. Plaintains, avocados, *cassava* (the root that tapioca is made from), onions, carrots, cabbage, and many other vegetables are also extensively used. Watercress, peas, asparagus, hearts of palm, *pacaya* buds (palm flowers), beets, cucumbers, cauliflower, tomatillos, eggplant, and leeks are also eaten.

BREADS AND CEREALS
Rice and corn are the predominant grains of the region. Fresh *masa* (a dough made from dried corn soaked in slaked lime) and *masa harina* (the flour made from dehydrated masa) are used to make *tortillas* (round, unleavened, flat bread) and *tamales* (steamed dough packets, unfilled or stuffed with meats or vegetables). Wheat flour breads are common, especially those known as *pain Française*, French bread dough baked as rolls; banana bread; and coconut bread. Wheat flour is occasionally used to make tortillas.

OTHER INGREDIENTS
Lard is the most commonly used fat, although butter, vegetable shortening, and vegetable oils such as corn oil are used in some recipes.

Nuts from various palm trees are used in soups and salads. *Pepitas* are toasted squash seeds, often ground, which add a nutty flavor to foods. Coconut meat and coconut milk are added to many dishes.

Hot chocolate and coffee, which is grown in Central America, are the favorite hot beverages. *Refrescos*, or cold drinks, are made with tropical fruit flavors such as passion fruit, mango, pineapple, and tangerine. In Nicaragua, *tiste* is made from roasted corn, cocoa powder, sugar, cold water, and cracked ice. *Chicha* may be brewed from grain or fruit juice, and rum is made locally. Beer is widely available.

Seasonings
Cilantro (fresh coriander) and *epazote* are important herbs in Central American cuisine. Chili peppers add heat to many dishes, but are not used with such a free hand as in Mexico or the southwestern United States. Garlic, onions, cinnamon, cloves, nutmeg, thyme, vanilla, and even Worcestershire sauce are also used for flavoring. *Achiote* (annatto) is used to color foods orange. Honey and sugar are used as sweeteners (simple sugar syrup is sometimes called "honey" as well), and sour orange juice gives a tang to foods. Cocoa is popular and is added to sauces, beverages, and some desserts.

Preparation

The cooking of Central America features many soups and stews. *Sopa de pesce* is a hearty seafood soup from Honduras. Stew is often sold as a snack by street vendors. Palm nut soup is served in Costa Rica. *Mondongo*, a tripe soup, is popular in Nicaragua, and *pozol* (corn soup) and *olla de carne* (meat stew with cassava and plaintain) are examples from Costa Rica.

Meat may also be braised, fried, or steamed. *Gallo in chicha*, or chicken in fruit wine, is popular, made with chicken pieces marinated in chicha, fried, and then simmered for hours in a sauce of chicha and spices. Pork may also be marinated before being fried. Fish can be steamed in banana leaf packets or corn husks, used as filling for tamales, or included in soups and stews. Ground meat is made into seasoned patties or fried with vegetables. Stuffed foods and sandwiches are eaten almost daily. *Pupusas* are tortillas filled with a cheese stuffing, a chicharrónes mixture, or black bean paste, before they are cooked. *Chiles rellenos*, or stuffed peppers, are made in Costa Rica. *Empanadas*, pastry filled with meat, and *arreglados*, bread filled with meat and vegetables, are sold on the streets. Tamales in Nicaragua are filled with pork seasoned with sour orange juice and spices; even the masa (dough) is made with orange juice. Tamales from other regions use tomato fillings, or chicken with cocoa and other seasonings, and in the highlands of Guatemala, potato or plantain dough is used in place of masa. Coconut milk tortillas (made with wheat flour) may be served with meat or fruit preserves. Turkey sandwiches, made on French bread with pickled vegetables, are popular in El Salvador.

Beans are prepared in many ways. They can be fried, mixed with rice, mashed, and then deep-fried, or boiled and served with chopped onion and sour cream. Raw, cooked, or pickled vegetables are served with most meals. Plaintains, potatoes, and cassava are steamed, mashed, or fried. Fried plaintain is a very common accompaniment, and vegetable fritters are a specialty. Salads are popular, made from avocados, tomatoes, carrots, hearts of palm, cabbage, onions, and other vegetables. *Fiambre*, a Guatemalan specialty, is an elaborate salad with numerous vegetables, meats (including pork, beef, chicken, and sausages), and garnishes (such as asparagus, cheese, eggs, pacaya buds, and salami). Related to salads are pickled vegetables. Sauerkraut is sometimes added to stuffed foods or sandwiches. Pickled condiments, such as *escabeche*, commonly contain vegetables flavored with chili peppers or onions.

Custards, ice cream (which comes in many tropical fruit flavors), and guava paste are common for dessert. Some more elaborate sweets are also made. Cakes or fritters in syrup are popular, such as *borracho* (a rich sponge cake with honey-rum syrup) and *buñuelos* (corn or wheat dumplings in sugar or honey syrup). Bananas, papayas, and pineapple are sold by street vendors as snacks, as are ices made with fruit syrups. Candies, especially those made with coconut, are favorites with coffee.

Meal Patterns

Meal patterns vary from one area to another, though generally three meals a day are eaten, often with at least one between-meal snack. It is not uncommon for the midday meal to be as large as, or larger than, the evening meal. A late afternoon coffee break, similar to English tea time, is taken in some urban areas. Appetizers are commonly served before meals and with drinks. They consist of tiny ears of corn, slivers of charcoal broiled steak, wedges of meat- or cheese-filled pastry, soft-boiled turtle eggs, and many other tidbits. Stews are usually served with rice, tortillas, or rolls. Beans, rice, a vegetable, and condiments accompany the entrée, or the main dish may have substantial garnishes such as avocado salad, fried plantains, hard-boiled eggs, and pickled vegetables. Hot sauces and chili peppers are common condiments. Frequently eaten snacks are tamales, stuffed tortillas, fruit, and ice cream. In poorer areas, rice and beans may be the staples of the diet, eaten only twice a day, supplemented with available vegetables and occasional meat, poultry, or fish.

Marinated pork (adobado de carne de cerdo) with fried black beans.

```
┌─────────────────────────────────┐
│  ◆                           ◆  │
│  ─────────                      │
│         M E N U                 │
│                                 │
│     Central American            │
│        Dinner I                 │
│                                 │
│      Sopa de Pesce              │
│       (fish soup)               │
│   Adobado de Carne de Cerdo     │
│      (marinated pork)           │
│     Fried Black Beans           │
│       Tomato Salad              │
│      Coconut Candy              │
│                                 │
│ Serving suggestions: Offer      │
│   steamed rice with the         │
│   entrée and fruit              │
│     juice and coffee.           │
│                                 │
│  ◆                  ─────────  ◆│
└─────────────────────────────────┘
```

◆ *Sopa de Pesce (Fish Soup)*

YIELD: 50 portions
PORTION: 1 c.

1 gal. coconut milk
½ lb. onions, chopped
⅔ lb. sweet peppers, chopped
8 lb. tomatoes, chopped
1 oz. parsley, chopped
2 T. salt
1 T. pepper
2 tsp. crushed red pepper
5 qt. fish stock

5–6 lb. small clams, rinsed
2 lb. crabmeat
5 lb. large shrimp, peeled and deveined
5 lb. plantains, peeled and cubed
1 #2 can tomato paste
10 oz. bread crumbs, dry
5–10 limes, sliced

1. Combine coconut milk, onions, sweet peppers, tomatoes, parsley, salt, and crushed red pepper. Bring to a boil.
2. Add fish stock, whole clams, crabmeat, shrimp, plantains, and tomato paste. Bring to a boil. Reduce heat and simmer for 30 minutes.
3. Slowly add bread crumbs to thicken the soup. Serve hot, garnished with a slice of lime.

CALORIES: 370
CHOLESTEROL: 88 mg
VITAMIN A: 1476 IU

CARBOHYDRATE: 24 g
CALCIUM: 198 mg
VITAMIN C: 29 mg

PROTEIN: 23 g
SODIUM: 860 mg

FAT: 25 g
IRON: 4 mg

◆ *Adobado de Carne de Cerdo (Marinated Pork)*

YIELD: 50 portions
PORTION: 5 oz.

1 oz. garlic cloves
3 T. cumin
3 T. thyme
3 T. oregano
1½ T. paprika
1 T. cloves
½ T. allspice

1½ T. pepper
3 T. salt or to taste
17 lb. boneless pork sliced into ½"
   steaks (approximately 3 per lb.)
1¾ qt. sour orange juice (see note)
2½ c. vegetable oil

1. Purée garlic, cumin, thyme, oregano, paprika, cloves, allspice, pepper, and salt in a blender or food processor. Rub into pork steaks and marinate, covered, in orange juice overnight in the refrigerator.
2. Grill or fry the pork in hot oil. Cook approximately 6 or 7 minutes on each side, or until no longer pink in the center.

Note: Sour orange juice comes from the bitter Seville orange. To make a substitute, mix 2 parts sweet orange juice with 1 part lemon juice.

CALORIES: 370	CARBOHYDRATE: 4 g	PROTEIN: 45 g	FAT: 19 g
CHOLESTEROL: 143 mg	CALCIUM: 35 mg	SODIUM: 491 mg	IRON: 3 mg
VITAMIN A: 205 IU	VITAMIN C: 12 mg		

◆ *Fried Black Beans*

YIELD: 50 portions
PORTION: 3 oz.

6 lb. black beans
1 gal. water
1 lb. onions, chopped
1½ T. garlic, finely chopped

1 T. salt
1 lb. onions, chopped
1 c. vegetable oil

1. Soak beans in water for at least 8 hours. Add onions, garlic, and salt. Bring to a boil and simmer 1 hour, or until beans are very tender. Purée beans in food processor or blender.
2. Sauté onions in ½ cup oil until light brown and slightly crispy. Drain. Mix with bean purée.
3. Heat remaining ½ cup oil over low heat. Add bean purée and mix well. Cook until mixture thickens and can hold a shape. Form into thick sausages.

CALORIES: 156	CARBOHYDRATE: 22 g	PROTEIN: 8 g	FAT: 9 g
CHOLESTEROL: 0 mg	CALCIUM: 46 mg	SODIUM: 142 mg	IRON: 2 mg
VITAMIN A: 21 IU	VITAMIN C: 2 mg		

♦ Tomato Salad

YIELD: 50 portions
PORTION: 4 oz.

10 lb. tomatoes, seeded and cubed
4 lb. sweet onions, cubed
1 T. garlic, finely chopped,
    or to taste

½ T. cayenne or to taste
1½ T. salt
1¼ qt. vinegar
2½ c. water

Combine all ingredients and chill for 8 hours in refrigerator.

CALORIES: 31
CHOLESTEROL: 0 mg
VITAMIN A: 761 IU

CARBOHYDRATE: 9 g
CALCIUM: 24 mg
VITAMIN C: 22 mg

PROTEIN: 1 g
SODIUM: 212 mg

FAT: <1 g
IRON: 1 mg

♦ Coconut Candy

BAKE: 30 minutes
OVEN: 350°F
YIELD: 48 portions
PORTION: two 2"
    squares

24 c. grated coconut, unsweetened
4 lb. dark brown sugar
2¼ qt. coconut milk (whole milk
    may be substituted)

24 eggs, beaten
8 oz. butter, melted

Combine coconut, sugar, and coconut milk. Simmer over low heat until liquid becomes syrupy and slightly thick, approximately 30 minutes. Cool slightly; add eggs and butter. Pour into 2 greased 12" × 18" × 2" cake pans. Bake until toasted on top.

CALORIES: 550
CHOLESTEROL: 147 mg
VITAMIN A: 275 IU

CARBOHYDRATE: 61 g
CALCIUM: 62 mg
VITAMIN C: 1.6 mg

PROTEIN: 5 g
SODIUM: 214 mg

FAT: 34 g
IRON: 3 mg

♦   ♦

M E N U

Central American Dinner II

*Fiambre
(Guatemalan salad)*

Serving suggestions: This dish is a meal in itself. Offer French bread and fruit wine or fruit juice.

♦   ♦

◆ *Fiambre (Guatemalan Salad)*

YIELD: 50 portions
PORTION: 2 c.

3 lb. green beans, cut
2 lb. carrots, julienned
3 lb. cauliflowerettes
5 lb. frozen peas, thawed
1½ lb. canned beets, julienned
3 lb. cabbage, shredded
1½ lb. boneless beef chuck, cut into bite-size pieces
1 c. orange juice
1 T. lemon juice
3 lb. chicken, cooked and sliced into ½" strips
1½ lb. pork, cooked and cubed
2 lb. chorizo, cooked and cut into ½" slices
3 qt. chicken stock
1 qt. vinegar
4 oz. sugar

½ lb. scallions, chopped
2 oz. parsley, chopped
1 lb. capers
½ lb. pimentos
2" piece ginger root
1 T. garlic, chopped
1 c. olive oil
2–3 lb. leaf lettuce, washed
6 oz. radishes, sliced
1 lb. salami, sliced thin
1 lb. ham, baked and julienned
12 eggs, hard-boiled and sliced
½ #10 can asparagus
2 lb. green olives stuffed with pimentos
1 lb. farmer's cheese, cubed
1 lb. Cheddar cheese, shredded

1. Blanch green beans, carrots, and cauliflower for 3 minutes. Drain well.
2. Add peas, radishes, beets, and the cabbage, and toss.
3. Marinate beef in orange and lemon juice overnight in the refrigerator. Drain. Boil beef in water until tender, about 20 minutes.
4. Purée chicken stock, vinegar, sugar, scallions, parsley, capers, pimentos, ginger, garlic, and olive oil. Adjust seasonings so that sauce is sweet and sour. Pour over vegetables and toss.
5. To assemble salad, line serving platters with lettuce. Top with vegetable mixture followed by chicken, pork, beef, and sausage. Toss well. Garnish with radishes, salami, ham, eggs, asparagus, and olives. Sprinkle salad with cheeses.

CALORIES: 484
CHOLESTEROL: 150 mg
VITAMIN A: 4674 IU

CARBOHYDRATE: 28 g
CALCIUM: 429 mg
VITAMIN C: 50 mg

PROTEIN: 36 g
SODIUM: 931 mg

FAT: 40 g
IRON: 4 mg

◆ *3* ◆ C O O K I N G   F R O M
◆ *China* ◆

Stir-fried Chinese vegetables featuring bamboo shoots, mushrooms, snow peas, and water chestnuts.

*C*hinese cooking is often ranked with French cooking as one of the world's great cuisines. The Chinese eat a tremendous variety of foods, partly because they have been daring and relentless in their search for new gastronomic sensations, and partly because for thousands of years Chinese culture has encouraged the cultivation of culinary secrets and recipes. Although many of the most popular foods are native to Asia — rice, soybeans, and tea — other important ingredients came to China through trade, and include ingredients such as pork and wheat from the Middle East, and potatoes, tomatoes, corn, and chili peppers from the New World.

In a country as large as China, each region has its own distinctive cuisine. Cantonese cooking — from the province of Canton in the south of China — is considered one of the finest regional cuisines in the country. The warm climate supports the growth of a wide variety of vegetables, the long seacoast provides many types of seafood, and numerous ports give the Cantonese access to foreign ingredients. Since the Cantonese were among the first Chinese people to emigrate to other parts of the world, most Chinese restaurants that sprang up in foreign countries prepared food from this region and this is still the style with which Westerners are most familiar. The primary Cantonese method of cooking is stir-frying; this leaves vegetables crisp and meat tender. Cantonese food is also known for its delicately seasoned, thick sauces.

Fukien province, along the east coast of China, includes a great deal of seafood in its cuisine as well, and a wide variety of ingredients is available. Fukien province is famous for its production and use of the finest soy sauce. Dishes are subtly seasoned so that the natural flavor of the ingredients comes through. Fukien cuisine is known for its light, clear soups and its reliance on soups in general. Several soups may appear at the same meal. Paper-wrapped foods and egg rolls originated here. In Shanghai province, the emphasis is on creating new combinations of ingredients, decorating food lavishly, and providing small tidbits of expertly prepared food.

The inland provinces of Szechuan, Hunan, and Yunnan are known for their highly spiced food. Szechuan in the west is surrounded by mountain ranges, which keeps the area somewhat isolated and its cuisine well defined. The temperate climate and rich soil have made it a prosperous region; rice and grains can be grown almost year round. The ingredients used in Szechuan cooking are less exotic than those of the Canton region. Though Szechuan cuisine is known for its use of chili peppers, fresh ginger, garlic, and the hot Szechuan pepper, not all Szechuan food is spicy.

Hunan province in south central China resembles Szechuan province in that it has richly cultivated farm land. As in Szechuan, chili peppers are used frequently, and garlic and ginger are important spices. Sesame oil, fermented black beans, black pepper, and scallions are prominent in Hunan cooking as well. Hunan is also known for dishes made with freshwater fish, which are abundant in the province's lakes, and for its sweet and sour dishes.

In the southwestern province of Yunnan, dairy products such as yogurt and fresh cheese have been incorporated into some dishes. Like Szechuan and Hunan, this region is known for its spicy, hot foods.

In the north, wheat is used more than rice as the staple grain. Noodle dishes, dumplings, buns, and breads abound. Scallions, chives, leeks, and garlic are used extensively, but the food is mildly seasoned and light. Because Beijing, which is located in this area, has been the center of government for many centuries, the country's best chefs have been attracted to this region, and many delicacies designed to delight dignitaries were developed here. Spring rolls, the forerunner of egg rolls, were created in this region.

In the far north live the Mongolians. They are known for their use of lamb, mutton, and winter vegetables such as onions and cabbage, that grow in the region. Although Mongolians ruled China during the 13th and 14th centuries, their diet and cooking style seem to have influenced Chinese cuisine very little. As in other provinces, wontons are made, but Mongolians use bean paste to make the dough and then fill them with minced lamb and dried tangerine peel. Grilling and barbecuing are typical cooking techniques.

Ingredients

MILK AND MILK PRODUCTS

Although cows and goats are kept, milk and milk products are not used extensively in China. Custard is occasionally served for dessert, and yogurt is added to some regional foods.

MEAT AND MEAT ALTERNATIVES

There are few protein foods that are *not* eaten in China. Fish, seafood, and chicken are the preferred flesh foods. Pork is commonly consumed, while beef is much less popular. Freshwater and saltwater fish and seafood of many varieties are acceptable. Goat, horsemeat, duck, and game birds are also eaten. In Canton, especially, exotic ingredients are sought out, including snakes, lizards, jellyfish, sea cucumbers, monkey brains, pig testicles, tree beetles, and rice worms.

Legumes are also important. Soybeans are used in a variety of preparations such as bean curd or tofu, soy sauce, bean sauce, hoisin sauce, and fermented black beans, which are made from black soybeans, rather than from the common yellow variety. Soybean sprouts are also used, although the most common bean for sprouting is the mung bean. This small, green-coated bean is also used to make bean threads, or cellophane noodles. Other beans such as black-eyed peas, fava beans, and red beans are also used.

FRUITS AND VEGETABLES

Many fruits familiar to Westerners are grown in China, as well as some less familiar ones, such as *cherimoya* or custard apple, Chinese dates (which may be black, red, or white), kumquats, loquats, litchis, persimmons, and pomegranates. Fruit, usually fresh, may be served as a between-meal snack or occasionally after a meal. Fruits are sometimes preserved with sugar or honey and spices. However, fruit is not extensively used in cooking, with the notable exception of orange and tangerine peels.

On the other hand, vegetables are used in great variety, depending on the season and on what is locally available. Many vegetables are those used in other parts of the world: asparagus, broccoli, cauliflower, cucumber, eggplant, onions, peas, potatoes, spinach, squash, tomatoes, and so forth. Chinese varieties of some of these vegetables differ from those grown in other countries; for instance, the Chinese use daikon, a long, white, mild radish; bok choy and napa varieties of cabbage; winter melon, which is a pale green squash; long beans; and several types of mushroom quite different from those grown commercially in the United States. Other vegetables, such as lily buds, snow peas, bamboo shoots, bean sprouts, water chestnuts, bitter melon, and lotus root, are distinctly Chinese.

BREADS AND CEREALS

Chinese cuisine is based on grains. In the south, no meal is complete without long-grain rice, though wheat is used to make wrappers for dumplings, egg rolls, and wontons (thin squares of dough folded around a meat, seafood, or vegetable filling, and then served in soups or fried). Rice is also used to make *congee*, a porridge that can be eaten for breakfast or as a snack, and rice flour is used to make noodles known as rice sticks, which are boiled or fried. In the north, wheat predominates, served in the form of noodles, pancakes, and dumplings. Other grains, such as corn, buckwheat, or millet, are featured in some dishes. Cornstarch is used to thicken many sauces and is also used to coat ingredients before frying.

OTHER INGREDIENTS

Peanut oil is the favored oil for frying and deep-frying, but soybean, sesame, and corn oils are also used. Lard is used mainly for stir-frying and in pastries. It is preferred over butter for cooking because it imparts a rich flavor and a clear color. Dark sesame oil, pressed from toasted sesame seeds, is used as a flavoring. Flavored oils — for example, sesame oil flavored with hot peppers, or peanut oil in which ginger and leeks have been cooked — are sometimes used for cooking.

Nuts and seeds, including almonds, cashews, peanuts, walnuts, chestnuts, sesame seeds, lotus seeds, and ginkgo nuts are used in cooking and as snacks. Watermelon seeds are a favorite snack.

Tea is consumed frequently throughout China. Tea is considered a mealtime beverage in the south; however, in the northern regions, tea traditionally follows a meal or is served between meals. Soup is the preferred mealtime beverage in the north. On special occasions rice wine may accompany the meal. Brewing and drinking tea is considered an art, and milk, cream, lemon, and sugar are never added. Several types of tea are available, depending on the method of processing. Green tea is picked and dried, while black (or red) tea is allowed to ferment. Oolong is a semifermented tea. Flower petals are sometimes added to tea to impart a delicate fragrance, and sweet teas are made from pounded almonds or other nuts. Wine, beer, and some distilled beverages are made from grains such as barley, corn, and rice and occasionally from ginger, pears, oranges, rose petals, bamboo leaves, bananas, and other unusual ingredients.

Seasonings

Herbs and spices used in Chinese cooking include star anise, a star-shaped seed cluster with a licorice-like flavor; Chinese parsley (fresh coriander leaves, also called cilantro); and Szechuan pepper, as well as the more familiar garlic, ginger root, chili peppers, and scallions. Spice mixtures such as five-spice powder (anise or fennel, clove, cinnamon or cassia, star anise, and Szechuan pepper) and curry powder, pastes (made from seasoned beans, sesame seeds, or shrimp), and sauces (including soy, hoisin, and oyster) also flavor many dishes. Rice wine, rice wine vinegar, and dark sesame oil are essential seasonings.

Preparation

Steaming, one of the oldest Chinese cooking methods, involves placing a dish containing the food on a rack above boiling water in a closed pan. Rice and fish are often cooked in this manner. Stir-frying is done in a large, round-bottomed pan called a *wok* over a hot fire or burner. The foods are cut into uniform, bite-sized pieces and then cooked quickly in a small amount of fat. Deep-frying is also used. A popular cooking method in northern China is soft-frying,

Dim sum selection of barbecued spare-ribs, chicken wings, steamed shrimp balls, and tea eggs.

in which the ingredients are coated with cornstarch and seasonings, passed through deep fat, and then cooked in a simmering sauce.

Slow-cooking, or stewing, is done in a heavy pan such as a Dutch oven. Hunan province is known for red-stewing, which is used for large cuts of pork, beef, or lamb and is done with soy sauce, which produces a rich gravy that can be served with the stewed meat or over noodles or rice. White-stewing, in which no soy sauce is used, is a technique for cooking fish and chicken; it produces a clear broth that is usually served separately as a soup.

Often, ingredients are preserved by drying, salting, or pickling, in which case they are usually soaked before use.

Meal Patterns

The Chinese usually eat three meals a day, plus snacks. Grains, called *fan*, are considered mainstays of the diet, with meat, fish, and vegetables (*ts'ai*) the accompaniments. In the southern regions, breakfast often includes the porridge congee with meat or fish. In northern areas, steamed bread, dumplings, or noodles are typical breakfast foods. Lunch and dinner include soup, rice, and/or a wheat-based food, and dishes containing meat, poultry, or fish and vegetables. The number of dishes served depends on the number of people at the table. When it is served at all, dessert is usually fresh or preserved fruit.

Soup is served first. Fan foods are then served to each individual, and the ts'ai foods are placed in the middle of the table to be shared. Chopsticks are the traditional utensils. Soup may be drunk directly from the bowl or with a porcelain spoon. Knives are considered too barbaric for the dinner table, so foods must either be cut into bite-size pieces by the cook, or be tender enough to pull apart with chopsticks.

Much attention is paid to the composition of each dish and of the meal as a whole. Contrasting textures, colors, and flavors are combined. Hot dishes complement cold ones, highly seasoned dishes accompany bland ones, and sweet flavors offset salty ones. Each meal must include the proper amounts of yin foods (those that are bland or cool, including many vegetables) and yang foods (hot, rich, or spicy). Yin foods should predominate in the summer, yang foods in the winter. Different balances of yin and yang foods are also prescribed for certain health conditions. Foods classified as yin or yang vary from region to region.

The Chinese enjoy between-meal snacks whenever they are hungry. Fruits (fresh, preserved, or dried), nuts, or small cakes or savories are preferred. Especially popular are dim sum, the selection of snacks from a huge variety of steamed and deep-fried dumplings, chicken wings, savory dishes, pastries, and cakes. These can be eaten for breakfast or lunch, as well as for snacks.

M E N U

Chinese Dinner

Egg Flower and Beef Soup
Whole Steamed Fish
Chinese Meatballs
Stir-fried Mixed Vegetables

Serving suggestions: Add steamed long-grain rice, green tea, or beer. Offer Mandarin oranges and/or litchis for dessert.

♦ *Egg Flower and Beef Soup*

YIELD: 50 portions
PORTION: 1 c.

½ c. soy sauce
6 T. sherry
5 tsp. sugar
5 oz. toasted sesame seed oil
6 T. flour
10 egg whites
1 tsp. pepper
2½ lb. beef ground, lean

1 c. vegetable oil
24 eggs
10 egg yolks
3 gal. chicken stock
2 c. cornstarch
2 c. water
1 lb. scallion tops, julienned

1. Combine soy sauce, sherry, sugar, sesame seed oil, flour, egg whites, and pepper. Add beef and stir until the beef holds together.
2. Add the oil to the beef mixture. Let it stand at room temperature for 15 minutes.
3. Whisk whole eggs and yolks together. Set aside.
4. Combine cornstarch and water. Add this to the chicken stock. Bring to a boil while stirring constantly to prevent lumps from forming.
5. Add beef mixture and beat with a whisk to separate the meat. Return to a boil then turn the stove off. Gently stir soup while pouring beaten eggs through the prongs of a fork.
6. Adjust seasoning. Garnish with scallions.

CALORIES: 203
CHOLESTEROL: 199 mg
VITAMIN A: 555 IU

CARBOHYDRATE: 9 g
CALCIUM: 43 mg
VITAMIN C: 5 mg

PROTEIN: 12 g
SODIUM: 992 mg

FAT: 22 g
IRON: 2 mg

◆ *Whole Steamed Fish*

STEAM: 10 minutes
YIELD: 50 portions
PORTION: 3–4 oz.

35 lb. whole firm white fish, cleaned and scaled
2 lb. scallions
3 c. vegetable oil
10 T. toasted sesame seed oil
3 c. soy sauce

1 T. salt
2½ tsp. pepper
¼ lb. ginger root, julienned
1½ lb. scallions, julienned
3 oz. fresh coriander

1. Place whole scallions in a 12″ × 20″ × 2″ pan and lay the fish on top. Steam in a steamer (see note) for approximately 10 minutes, or until the fish flakes easily with a fork.
2. Heat the oils in a pan. Then remove from heat and add soy sauce. Set aside. Season fish with salt and pepper; sprinkle with ginger and scallions. Pour hot oil/soy sauce mixture over the fish. Garnish with fresh coriander.

Note: Steaming may also be accomplished either on top of the stove or in the oven. To steam fish on top of the stove, place fish on a rack in a shallow pot and fill water to just below the rack. Cover pot tightly and bring to a boil. Cook for approximately 10 minutes. To steam fish in the oven, set fish on a rack in a baking pan and add water to about ¼ inch. Cover pan with foil and puncture holes for steam to escape. Bake 15 minutes at 325°F for each pound per fish.

CALORIES: 280
CHOLESTEROL: 65 mg
VITAMIN A: 679 IU

CARBOHYDRATE: 4 g
CALCIUM: 49 mg
VITAMIN C: 10 mg

PROTEIN: 28 g
SODIUM: 1318 mg

FAT: 31 g
IRON: 2 mg

◆ *Chinese Meatballs*

STEAM: 25 minutes
YIELD: 50 portions
PORTION: 2 balls

2¾ lb. glutinous rice
3 lb. canned bamboo shoots, rinsed and drained
6 lb. ground pork
1 T. salt
¾ c. soy sauce
6 eggs
6 T. sherry

2 T. sugar
3 T. ginger root, grated
6 T. toasted sesame seed oil
6 T. flour
1 lb. scallions, chopped
½ tsp. pepper
1½ c. rice vinegar
¼ c. ginger root, finely shredded

1. Rinse the rice and soak it in cold water for 1 hour. Drain and spread thinly on paper towels.
2. Grate bamboo shoots. Wrap in a towel and squeeze out moisture.
3. Combine pork, salt, soy sauce, eggs, sherry, sugar, ginger, flour, bamboo shoots, scallions, and pepper. Mix well and refrigerate for at least 2 hours. Roll meat mixture into 1-inch balls, and then coat them with rice. Place on a greased 12″ × 20″ × 2″ baking pan. Place in a steamer and steam for 25 minutes or until rice is cooked.
4. Combine vinegar and ginger and serve over warm rice balls.

CALORIES: 254
CHOLESTEROL: 61 mg
VITAMIN A: 37 IU

CARBOHYDRATE: 24 g
CALCIUM: 37 mg
VITAMIN C: 2 mg

PROTEIN: 11 g
SODIUM: 858 mg

FAT: 19 g
IRON: 2 mg

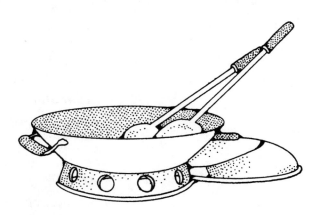

◆ *Stir-fried Mixed Vegetables*

YIELD: 50 portions
PORTION: ½ c.

1½ lb. black mushrooms, dried
2 qt. water
1½ lb. celery, cut diagonally
3 lb. canned bamboo shoots, sliced
4 lb. snow peas, tips removed
1 lb. canned water chestnuts, sliced
2 lb. carrots, peeled, sliced
  diagonally

2 c. peanut oil
2 oz. ginger root, sliced
3 T. sugar
4 T. cornstarch
½ c. cold water
1 T. salt
1½ T. dehydrated chicken boullion

1. Soak mushrooms in water until soft. Remove fibrous stems and quarter the caps. Reserve 2 cups of the soaking liquid.
2. Heat wok (see note) until very hot. Add 1½ cups oil and then the ginger. When ginger turns brown, discard. Add mushrooms and carrots. Toss well to coat with oil. Add reserved mushroom liquid and cook until evaporated. Add remaining vegetables except snow peas. Toss well to coat with oil. Stir in sugar.
3. Combine cornstarch and water. Push vegetables to the side of the wok. Add remaining oil; stir in snow peas. Season with salt and boullion, then add the cornstarch. Bring sauce to a boil and mix all ingredients together.

Note: When using a noncommercial size wok, smaller batches of the recipe may be prepared, or two or three vegetables at a time can be cooked in the wok and later combined in a serving pan. If no wok is available, a grill or large shallow soup pot over high heat may be used for stir-frying.

CALORIES: 115	CARBOHYDRATE: 8 g	PROTEIN: 2 g	FAT: 16 g
CHOLESTEROL: <1 mg	CALCIUM: 37 mg	SODIUM: 206 mg	IRON: <1 mg
VITAMIN A: 2178 IU	VITAMIN C: 9 mg		

```
◆ _____ ◆

M E N U
Dim Sum

Steamed Shrimp Balls
Tea Eggs
Barbecued Spareribs
Chicken Wings
Custard Tartlets


Serving suggestions: Other possi-
ble dim sum dishes that can be
offered include fried wontons,
spring rolls, and steamed pork
buns. Serve with jasmine or
chrysanthemum tea.

◆ _____ ◆
```

◆ Steamed Shrimp Balls

STEAM: 10 minutes
YIELD: 50 portions
PORTION: 3 balls

5 lb. small shrimp, shelled and deveined
8 oz. water chestnuts, finely chopped
½ lb. scallions, white part, finely chopped
5 oz. pork fat, finely chopped
6 T. dry sherry

1 tsp. ginger root, minced
¼ tsp. pepper
2½ tsp. salt
3 T. toasted sesame seed oil
2½ tsp. sugar
1 c. water
1 c. cornstarch
5 egg whites, beaten until foamy

1. Using a food processor, mince shrimp into a paste. Add water chestnuts, scallions, and pork fat. Mix well but do not overprocess.
2. Combine remaining ingredients. To prepare shrimp, moisten hands with ice water and roll paste into 1-inch balls. Place on a lightly oiled steam tray. Steam shrimp balls for approximately 10 minutes or until done. The shrimp balls may also be deep-fat fried in oil heated to 350°F.

CALORIES: 64   CARBOHYDRATE: 4 g   PROTEIN: 9 g   FAT: 2 g
CHOLESTEROL: 68 mg   CALCIUM: 34 mg   SODIUM: 189 mg   IRON: 1 mg
VITAMIN A: 95 IU   VITAMIN C: 2 mg

◆ Tea Eggs

YIELD: 50 portions
PORTION: 1 egg

50 eggs, small
½ c. black tea, loose
4 star anise, whole
4 cinnamon sticks

1 c. soy sauce
3 T. salt
1½ T. sugar

1. Place eggs in cold water to cover. Simmer for 15 minutes, cool, and drain.
2. Tap each egg gently with a spoon until the shell is covered with small cracks. Place in saucepan and cover with water. Add remaining ingredients and bring to a boil. Simmer for 1½ to 2 hours. Drain and cool. Remove shells before serving and cut into wedges.

CALORIES: 71   CARBOHYDRATE: 3 g   PROTEIN: 5 g   FAT: 7 g
CHOLESTEROL: 200 mg   CALCIUM: 32 mg   SODIUM: 818 mg   IRON: 1 mg
VITAMIN A: 198 IU   VITAMIN C: 0 mg

◆ Barbecued Spareribs

YIELD: 50 portions
PORTION: 2 ribs

15 lb. pork spareribs, small
2 c. hoisin sauce
1½ c. soy sauce
1 c. ketchup
1 c. dry sherry
1 c. sugar

2 T. five-spice powder
1 T. garlic, finely chopped
1 T. ginger root, grated
1 c. honey
½ c. toasted sesame seed oil
½ c. soy sauce

1. Cut between, but do not separate, each sparerib. Place in a baking pan.
2. Combine hoisin and soy sauces, ketchup, sherry, sugar, five-spice powder, garlic, and ginger and pour over ribs. Rub well. Refrigerate for 4 to 6 hours, basting and turning every hour.
3. Place ribs on a metal rack over a roasting pan containing 1 inch of water. Reserve excess marinade. Roast for 45 minutes at 375°F, turning and basting ribs with reserved marinade every 15 minutes. Increase heat to 450°F for the last 10 minutes of cooking.
4. Combine honey, sesame seed oil, and soy sauce. Brush over ribs and return to oven for 2 minutes until glazed.

CALORIES: 284
CHOLESTEROL: 60 mg
VITAMIN A: 30 IU

CARBOHYDRATE: 8 g
CALCIUM: 10 mg
VITAMIN C: <1 mg

PROTEIN: 6 g
SODIUM: 496 mg

FAT: 38 g
IRON: 1 mg

◆ Chicken Wings

FRY: 3–4 minutes
DEEP-FAT FRYER:
  350°F
YIELD: 48 portions
PORTION: 1 wing

8 lb. large chicken wings
½ c. light soy sauce
½ c. dark soy sauce
⅓ c. sugar
¼ c. pale, dry sherry
¼ c. toasted sesame seed oil

½ c. cornstarch
¼ c. flour
1 tsp. salt
4 eggs, beaten
¼ c. water

1. Remove wing tip and separate wing at first joint. Use upper part of the wing only. Cut around the tip of the narrow end and scrape the meat to the thick end, pulling meat over the bone to form a small drumstick. Repeat for each wing.
2. Combine soy sauces, sugar, sherry, and sesame seed oil. Pour over chicken. Refrigerate for at least 2 hours or overnight.
3. Combine cornstarch, flour, salt, eggs, and water. Set aside for 10 minutes. Dip wings into the batter and fry until the meat is cooked.

CALORIES: 157
CHOLESTEROL: 49 mg
VITAMIN A: 73 IU

CARBOHYDRATE: 2 g
CALCIUM: 9 mg
VITAMIN C: 0 mg

PROTEIN: 10 g
SODIUM: 200 mg

FAT: 20 g
IRON: <1 mg

◆ *Custard Tartlets*

BAKE: 35 minutes
OVEN: 350°F
YIELD: 48 portions
PORTION: 1 tartlet

12 egg yolks
8 eggs, whole
1½ lb. sugar
1 qt. half & half

2 c. whole milk
4 tsp. vanilla extract
48 tartlet shells, unbaked
 (tart pastry, page 87)

1. Beat egg yolks and eggs together. Add remaining ingredients and beat lightly until combined. Do not overbeat.
2. Fill each tart ⅔ full with egg mixture. Bake in the lower third of the oven for 30–40 minutes. The custard will set but should not turn brown or crack. Cool for 15 minutes before unmolding.

CALORIES: 294
CHOLESTEROL: 141 mg
VITAMIN A: 511 IU

CARBOHYDRATE: 30 g
CALCIUM: 51 mg
VITAMIN C: <1 mg

PROTEIN: 5 g
SODIUM: 241 mg

FAT: 25 g
IRON: 1 mg

♦4♦ COOKING FROM
♦Eastern Europe and the USSR♦

Russian menu of pirozhki (mushroom-filled turnovers), kotlety pozharsky (chicken cutlets), kasha, and vegetables in a sour cream dressing.

*H*ospitality is emphasized throughout Eastern Europe and the Soviet Union, and great quantities of food and drink are often offered to guests. The ability to eat and drink much is admired. Classic foods from this part of the world are often rich and tangy-flavored. Grains are grown throughout the area, and bread, especially dark bread, is a staple. Dairy products are also prominent in the diets of this region. Because the climate is cold for the greater part of the year, many foods from this region must be preserved. This is accomplished mainly by salting, fermenting, pickling, and smoking. As a result, many sour and salty foods are eaten.

In addition to influences from neighboring European countries, expansion of the Russian empire as far south as the Black Sea, and as far east as India and China, brought Middle Eastern, Asian, and Asian Indian ingredients and cooking techniques to Russia. During the 19th century, these influences were melded into a unified cuisine among the ruling classes of central Russia. Elaborate meals were eaten by the nobility, and *zakuski* (literally, "small bites"), including hot and cold hors d'oeuvres and open-faced sandwiches, were elevated to an art form. Meanwhile, peasants existed on a diet of bread, soup, *kasha* (cooked buckwheat), and *kvas*, a thin beer made from grain or leftover bread.

Diets in different parts of the Soviet Union varied greatly historically and still do today. In the Baltic region, fish are abundant, and butter, cream, and eggs are used extensively. Farther south, in the Ukraine, grains, sunflower seeds, and a variety of fruits, nuts, and vegetables are grown. A Middle Eastern influence is apparent in Georgia and Armenia in ingredients such as grape leaves, sesame seeds, and chickpeas. Most of the steppes of central Asia are bleak and arid, with extremes in temperature. Dairy products such as fermented mare's milk (*kumiss*) are a specialty there.

39

In Poland, soups are an important part of the cuisine. Fish are plentiful, and dairy foods are popular. Winter vegetables such as cabbage, potatoes, onions, and beets are commonly cultivated; wild mushrooms and berries are gathered; and game is hunted. Juniper wood is used to smoke meats and sausage, imparting a distinctive flavor.

In Czechoslovakia, freshwater fish are favored, and pork and goose are the most popular meats. Dumplings are a specialty and are served in soup, with meat and poultry, and in desserts. Czechoslovakian cuisine has been influenced by Austria, and is known for its cakes and puddings. Beer is the national beverage and the Pilsner beer produced here is considered to be among the world's finest.

Austrian, French, and Turkish influences can be found in Hungarian cooking. Pork and veal are the favored meats, and freshwater fish are eaten. Paprika, introduced from the New World, has become an integral part of the cuisine, and sour cream is used often. Salads are commonly eaten, and tomatoes and green peppers are popular.

Romania has experienced rule by Hungarians, Turks, and Russians, all of whom have left their mark on its cuisine. Meats are eaten more commonly than fish, since few types of fish are available. Romanians have a love of corn, which has become an important part of the diet, though it was introduced only a few hundred years ago. Middle Eastern contributions emphasize garlic, olive oil, and eggplant.

Ingredients

MILK AND MILK PRODUCTS

Foods made from cow's milk are widely eaten in the Soviet Union and Eastern Europe. Sheep, goats, and mares are also milked in some regions. Buttermilk, sour milk, and sour cream are especially popular. Cream and yogurt are used in some dishes. People drink fresh milk as well as fermented milk beverages such as *kefir* (somewhat like buttermilk). Fresh cheeses, such as cottage cheese and pot cheese, are favored.

MEAT AND MEAT ALTERNATIVES

Pork, especially as bacon, ham, and sausages, is the most commonly consumed meat. Mutton is also well liked. In many areas, veal is eaten more than beef because the offspring of milking cows cannot be kept through the winter. Often, only the poorest cuts of beef are available. But game meats, such as boar, hare, and venison, are popular in most regions. Chicken, readily available in some areas, scarce in others, is well liked, especially in the Soviet Union, as are wild birds such as grouse, partridge, pheasant, squab, quail, and woodcock. Roast duck or goose is served on holidays. Eggs are commonly used.

Both freshwater and saltwater varieties of fish are eaten often. Carp, cod, eel, herring, perch, pike, sturgeon, and trout are just a few that are available. Caviar, or fish eggs, especially from sturgeon, are a specialty throughout the area.

FRUITS AND VEGETABLES

Apples, grapes, and pears are fruits that grow well in most of Eastern Europe and Russia. Rhubarb is raised in some areas, and peaches, plums, cherries, and melons are grown in the southern regions. In most areas, numerous kinds of wild berries are collected in addition to the familiar strawberries, blueberries, and raspberries. Dried fruits such as raisins and prunes are used.

Root vegetables and other vegetables that store well over the long winter are the most popular in northern regions. Cabbage, onions, carrots, potatoes, beets, celeriac (celery root), and rutabaga are some of the most commonly used. In the Soviet Union and in all of Eastern Europe, wild mushrooms are hunted. The many different kinds are used in meatless dishes or when meat is scarce to add a hearty flavor.

BREADS AND CEREALS

Grains, especially rye, barley, and buckwheat, are the mainstays of the diet. Rye bread (including black bread and pumpernickel) or wheat bread is eaten daily. In much of the area, a great deal of attention is given to bread making, and dozens of different kinds are available. In Hungary bread is often fried and served with butter or rubbed with garlic. Porridge from oats or barley is common, as is kasha. Millet and rice are used in some areas, and corn is grown in the south. Dumplings are added to soups and stews, particularly in the Ukraine and Czechoslovakia. Egg noodles are a common side dish. Buckwheat is also used to make thin pancakes called *blini*, which are served with different toppings such as butter, jam, sour cream, smoked salmon, or caviar. Wheat flour serves as the base for most desserts.

OTHER INGREDIENTS

Butter and lard are the most commonly used fats. Chicken fat, goose fat, salt pork, and suet are used in some dishes. Vegetable oils are used in Poland. Almonds, chestnuts, filberts (hazelnuts), and walnuts are the most commonly eaten nuts. Sunflower seeds are frequently eaten as a snack.

Tea is the preferred hot beverage in the Soviet Union, while coffee is consumed throughout the rest of Eastern Europe. Vodka is consumed at every opportunity in Russia, and is popular in neighboring countries as well. Many flavors of vodka are created by steeping herbs or fruit in the liquor. Champagne, juice, kvas, cognac, and mineral water are also popular beverages, and liqueurs are often served with dessert. In areas that produce wine, such as Soviet Georgia and Hungary, that is the preferred alcoholic beverage.

Seasonings

Chives, cinnamon, coriander, dill, lemon juice, nutmeg, parsley, pepper, and vinegar are common seasonings. Horseradish, caraway seeds, and poppy seeds appear in many dishes; mustard and mayonnaise are common condiments. Paprika, used especially in Hungarian cooking, is available in several degrees of piquancy, varying from mild to medium-hot. Garlic is used in southern regions such as Hungary and Romania. Honey is the traditional sweetener.

Preparation

Early Russian stoves were made of clay or brick and occupied as much as one third of the living space. Everything was cooked in the oven, since the stoves had no burners. Baking, braising, and stewing were, and still are, popular cooking methods.

Soups and stews are essential to Russian and Eastern European cuisines. The most commonly eaten in the Soviet Union are beet soup (*borshch*), cabbage soup (*shchi*), and fish soup (*ukha*). Wild mushrooms flavor many soups, such as Czech mushroom and barley soup and Polish beet and mushroom soup. Dumplings are often added to these. In Hungary, cooking in a cauldron is traditional, and many dishes, such as the well-known *gulyás* or goulash, a paprika-spiced stew of beef and potatoes, call for meat to be stewed slowly.

Chicken is a favorite entrée, often served simply roasted or as breaded cutlets. In Russia, chicken Kiev is made from chicken breasts that are rolled around a core of herbed butter, then breaded and fried. Roast duck or goose is served on holidays. Fresh fish are occasionally eaten, but smoked or salt-cured varieties are more common. Smoked eel, salmon, and sturgeon are considered delicacies. Both boiled and stuffed eggs are also popular.

Ground meats are also everyday fare. Stuffings and fillings are popular and are an effective way to make scarce ingredients go further. Pastries are stuffed with meat mixtures, such as in the Russian *pirozhki*. In Poland, meat, cheese, potato, sauerkraut, or even fruit may fill *pierogi*. Stuffed cabbage leaves are popular in the north, while stuffed grape leaves are eaten in the south. Dumplings may be made with meat or fruit fillings.

Preserving foods to last through the winter is important for survival in northern climates. Thus, ground meat is preserved with salt and spices and made into sausages. The spicy Polish *kielbasa* (garlic-flavored pork) and Czechoslovakian *jaternice* (pork) are good examples. Salting and pickling keep cabbage (as sauerkraut), mushrooms, cucumbers, beets, and other vegetables, as well as fish like herring, usable through the winter. Meats and mushrooms are often dried for later use. Fruits are made into jams and preserves.

An Eastern European meal: varzá cu porc (sauerkraut with pork garnished with sour cream and dill), paprikasaláta (roasted sweet pepper salad), and egg noodles.

Breads include simple loaves for everyday consumption, as well as hundreds of fancy types of buns and decorated breads. Many desserts are made with yeasted doughs. Desserts are taken very seriously, and a vast array of pastries, tortes, cream puffs, filled doughnuts, cheesecake, *mazurkas* (cookies with toppings), ice cream, gelatin desserts, and cakes are consumed.

Meal Patterns

Four to five meals a day are customary, including coffee breaks (drunk with small sandwiches made with rolls or pastries). Breakfast consists of tea or coffee and oatmeal or a porridge of barley, rye, or rice. Sometimes toast with butter and jam is eaten, and eggs, sausage, ham, and cheese may be included. For people working away from home, lunch may be a sandwich or a meat pastry. At home, lunch is often soup and sausages with potatoes. Supper may include soup or stew, a meat or fish entrée and dumplings, potatoes, noodles, or stuffed cabbage served with pickled vegetables, followed by dessert. Dark rye breads or rolls are eaten with most meals. A more elaborate meal for guests would include appetizers, or *zakuski*, including salads of vegetables in sour cream, sausages, bread, pickled fish and vegetables, smoked fish, and small open-faced sandwiches of fish, ham, or tongue. Caviar is the most popular zakuska, usually garnished with minced onions or sour cream. Evening tea is often served with sandwiches and dessert foods. The Russian tradition of serving one course at a time, rather than putting all the food out at once, was not adopted in Europe until the mid-19th century.

M E N U
Eastern European Supper

Mushroom Soup
Varzá cu Porc
(sauerkraut with pork)
Paprikasaláta
(sweet pepper salad)
Fruit Dumplings

Serving suggestions: Offer egg noodles and pumpernickel bread with the entrée; serve with beer or fruit juice, and coffee with dessert.

M E N U
Formal Russian Dinner

Pirozhki
(mushroom-filled turnovers)
Shchi
(cabbage soup)
Kotlety Pozharsky
(chicken cutlets)
Mixed Vegetables in
Sour Cream Dressing
Kasha
(buckwheat groats)

Serving suggestions: Offer smoked salmon, caviar-stuffed hard-boiled eggs, and dark rye bread with the pirozhki as appetizers, plus beer or fruit juice. Serve a fruit compote for dessert.

Eastern European Supper

◆ *Mushroom Soup*

YIELD: 50 portions
PORTION: 8 oz.

½ lb. butter
4 lb. mushrooms, sliced
1 lb. onions, chopped
4 oz. leeks, cleaned and chopped
2 oz. lemon juice
2 T. paprika

2½ oz. flour
2½ gal. chicken stock
10 egg yolks, beaten
4 lb. sour cream
½ c. fresh dill, minced

1. Sauté onions and leeks in butter. Add mushrooms and lemon juice.
2. Stir in paprika and flour. Add chicken stock slowly. Simmer covered for 30 minutes.
3. Blend egg yolks, sour cream, and dill. Slowly add 1 quart of stock mixture to the cream. Combine the two mixtures. Stir over low heat until thickened (1–2 minutes).

CALORIES: 107   CARBOHYDRATE: 12 g   PROTEIN: 5 g   FAT: 8 g
CHOLESTEROL: 31 mg   CALCIUM: 89 mg   SODIUM: 713 mg   IRON: 2 mg
VITAMIN A: 2921 IU   VITAMIN C: 45 mg

◆ *Varzá cu Porc (Sauerkraut with Pork)*

BAKE: 1 hour
OVEN: 250°F
YIELD: 50 portions
PORTION: 4 oz.

3 lb. onions, sliced
6 lb. leeks, sliced (white portion only)
1 lb. bacon fat
1 #10 can sauerkraut, drained
4 oz. flour
2½ c. tomato paste

1¼ gal. beef stock
2 oz. sugar
½ c. lemon juice
1 oz. fresh dill, minced
10 lb. smoked pork or ham, cut into 2" pieces
1 qt. sour cream

1. Sauté onions and leeks until tender. Remove them with a slotted spoon and combine with sauerkraut.
2. Blend flour with bacon fat. Add tomato paste, stock, sugar, lemon juice, and dill. Cook over medium heat for 15 minutes.
3. Layer meat and sauerkraut in two 12" × 20" × 2" baking pans. Cover with tomato sauce and bake.
4. Serve with sour cream.

CALORIES: 399   CARBOHYDRATE: 14 g   PROTEIN: 24 g   FAT: 42 g
CHOLESTEROL: 120 mg   CALCIUM: 86 mg   SODIUM: 1869 mg   IRON: 3 mg
VITAMIN A: 612 IU   VITAMIN C: 21 mg

♦ *Paprikasaláta (Sweet Pepper Salad)*

BAKE: 10–15
  minutes
OVEN: 450°F
YIELD: 50 portions
PORTION: 4 oz.

16 lb. sweet peppers, large
3 c. white vinegar
7 T. sugar

6 T. salt
2 tsp. pepper
3 lb. mayonnaise

1. Place whole peppers in the oven for 10–15 minutes until the skin blisters. Remove and place in a brown paper bag for 10 minutes. Peel off skin; remove seeds and stems. Cut into julienne slices.
2. Combine vinegar, sugar, salt, and pepper. Toss with roasted peppers. Chill well.
3. Drain and toss with mayonnaise.

CALORIES: 221
CHOLESTEROL: 19 mg
VITAMIN A: 411 IU

CARBOHYDRATE: 6 g
CALCIUM: 21 mg
VITAMIN C: 77 mg

PROTEIN: 1 g
SODIUM: 955 mg

FAT: 41 g
IRON: < 1 mg

♦ *Fruit Dumplings*

YIELD: 50 portions
PORTION:
  1 dumpling

5 lb. flour, sifted
2 T. salt
1½ oz. baking powder
20 eggs
1½ c. milk

12 oz. flour
8 oz. sugar
1 #10 can cherries or plums, pitted
  and drained
8 oz. butter, melted

1. Sift flour, salt, and baking powder. Add unbeaten eggs; stir well. Add enough milk to make a stiff dough. Lightly knead. Pinch off small balls of dough and roll out into 3-inch circles, ¼ inch thick. Do not make them too thin.
2. Place ½ teaspoon flour and 1 teaspoon sugar in each round. Place fruit over flour. Moisten edges with water and bring edges together. Seal well. Drop into boiling water and boil for approximately 10 minutes. Drain. Serve warm, drizzled with melted butter.

CALORIES: 305
CHOLESTEROL: 116 mg
VITAMIN A: 341 IU

CARBOHYDRATE: 54 g
CALCIUM: 65 mg
VITAMIN C: 2 mg

PROTEIN: 8 g
SODIUM: 388 mg

FAT: 9 g
IRON: 3 mg

◆ *Pirozhki (Mushroom-filled Turnovers)*

BAKE: 20 minutes
OVEN : 400°F
YIELD: 50 portions
PORTION:
  1 turnover

1 T. (envelope) active dry yeast
¼ c. lukewarm water
4 oz. butter, melted
1 c. lukewarm milk
1 tsp. salt
2 tsp. sugar

1¼ lb. flour
3 eggs
1 egg yolk
2 T. water
mushroom filling (recipe below)

1. Dissolve yeast in water.
2. Combine butter, milk, salt, and sugar. Add to yeast.
3. Add flour 1 cup at a time to the yeast mixture, alternating with the eggs. Beat well after each addition. Add enough flour to make a soft dough. Knead till smooth and elastic. Place in an oiled bowl, turning once. Cover with a damp towel and let rise in a warm place until doubled in volume (about 1½ hours).
4. Pinch off small pieces of dough and pat into circles 2½ inches in diameter.
5. Place 2 teaspoons of mushroom filling in the center of each circle. Fold into a semicircle and seal edges. Place on greased cookie sheet, cover, and let rise 20 minutes.
6. Mix yolk and water and brush tops. Bake until golden.

Mushroom Filling

¾ lb. mushrooms, chopped
¾ c. (2 bunches) scallions, chopped
4 T. butter
salt to taste

4 T. fresh dill or parsley,
  chopped finely
3 oz. sour cream, room temperature

1. Sauté mushrooms and scallions in butter. Add salt to taste. Cool.
2. Add dill or parsley and sour cream.

CALORIES: 80	CARBOHYDRATE: 9 g	PROTEIN: 2 g	FAT: 4 g
CHOLESTEROL: 24 mg	CALCIUM: 13 mg	SODIUM: 77 mg	IRON: <1 mg
VITAMIN A: 165 IU	VITAMIN C: <1 mg		

◆ Shchi (Cabbage Soup)

YIELD: 50 portions
PORTION: 8 oz.

1½ lb. onions, sliced
2 lb. leeks, sliced
2 lb. carrots, sliced
½ lb. celery, sliced
2 lb. turnips, diced

½ lb. bacon fat
2½ gal. beef stock
7 lb. cabbage, shredded
3¾ c. tomato paste
1 oz. fresh dill or parsley, chopped

1. Sauté onions, leeks, carrots, celery, and turnips in bacon fat.
2. Add beef stock and bring to a boil. Add cabbage and tomato paste. Reduce heat and simmer for 1 hour. Sprinkle with chopped dill or parsley.

CALORIES: 107
CHOLESTEROL: 31 mg
VITAMIN A: 2921 IU

CARBOHYDRATE: 12 g
CALCIUM: 89 mg
VITAMIN C: 45 mg

PROTEIN: 5 g
SODIUM: 713 mg

FAT: 8 g
IRON: 2 mg

◆ Kotlety Pozharsky (Chicken Cutlets)

FRY: 8–10 minutes
DEEP-FAT FRY:
  325°F
YIELD: 40 portions
PORTION: 4 oz.

3½ c. milk
40 slices white bread, stale
10 lb. ground chicken or turkey
8 oz. butter, softened

1 T. salt
1 tsp. pepper
1 lb. bread crumbs

1. Soak bread in milk. Squeeze dry and mix with chicken.
2. Add butter, salt, and pepper.
3. Shape into 4-ounce oval patties. Cover with bread crumbs and deep-fry.

CALORIES: 436
CHOLESTEROL: 115 mg
VITAMIN A: 201 IU

CARBOHYDRATE: 20 g
CALCIUM: 91 mg
VITAMIN C: <1 mg

PROTEIN: 32 g
SODIUM: 534 mg

FAT: 40 g
IRON: 3 mg

◆ Mixed Vegetables in Sour Cream Dressing

YIELD: 50 portions
PORTION: ¾ c.

3 lb. carrots, sliced and steamed
1 #10 can beets, diced and drained
4 lb. potatoes, boiled and sliced
2½ lb. frozen peas, thawed

6 oz. dill pickles, finely chopped
3 lb. sour cream
1 tsp. salt or to taste
1 tsp. pepper or to taste

Combine all ingredients and chill.

CALORIES: 118
CHOLESTEROL: 15 mg
VITAMIN A: 3354 IU

CARBOHYDRATE: 14 g
CALCIUM: 56 mg
VITAMIN C: 12 mg

PROTEIN: 3 g
SODIUM: 227 mg

FAT: 8 g
IRON: 1 mg

◆ *Kasha (Buckwheat Groats)*

YIELD: 50 portions
PORTION: ½ c.

4½ lb. kasha
10 eggs, lightly beaten
2 tsp. salt

1 gal. boiling water* or stock
8 oz. butter

1. Combine kasha and eggs. Put this into an ungreased skillet and cook, stirring constantly, until grains are toasted and separated.
2. Add salt and boiling water. Cover and cook slowly for about 30 minutes, or until liquid is absorbed. Stir in butter. Fluff with a fork and serve.

CALORIES: 228	CARBOHYDRATE: 36 g	PROTEIN: 7 g	FAT: 6 g
CHOLESTEROL: 65 mg	CALCIUM: 60 mg	SODIUM: 137 mg	IRON: 2 mg
VITAMIN A: 190 IU	VITAMIN C: 0		

*Nutrient analysis was calculated using water.

◆ *5* ◆ COOKING FROM
◆ *France* ◆

A French menu featuring pork and veal terrine, poulet à la Normande (chicken with cream and cider sauce), green salad with Roquefort, and tarte au chocolat.

*F*rench cuisine is considered one of the greatest in the world. France's fertile soil, varied climate, and sizable seacoast make a wide selection of ingredients available. The cuisine is characterized by the use of very fresh, regional ingredients often served with delicate sauces. Texture, flavor, and color are carefully balanced. The various courses in a single meal are carefully planned to complement one another.

French cooking has been traditionally divided into classic cuisine (called *haute* or *grande* cuisine), which features elegant fare, and provincial or home cooking, which uses local ingredients in less complex dishes. Haute cuisine was developed for royalty during the 17th and 18th centuries. After the French Revolution ended in 1789, the chefs who had cooked for royalty were dispersed. They later resurfaced on the staffs of many hotels and restaurants, which were open to the public. These were considered to be the first public eating establishments where a meal in the tradition of royalty could be eaten. Before that time, inns and taverns did not have sophisticated kitchens and offered only the simplest food to guests.

Perfection is aspired to in haute cuisine. Vegetables and fruit must be picked at the peak of flavor and meats, poultry, and fish must be absolutely fresh. Foods must be cooked for precisely the right amount of time and they must be served at precisely the right temperature. Every ingredient is carefully considered and exactly prepared. Sauces, a distinctive feature in haute cuisine, are subtly seasoned so as not to overpower the food.

Provincial, or regional, cooking provides simpler, more affordable dishes, while still adhering to many of the principles of haute cuisine, including the use of fresh ingredients, sauces, and a carefully balanced menu.

In the northwestern regions of Brittany and Normandy, which have an extensive coastline, seafood is plentiful. Delicate Belon oysters come from this area. Excellent lamb and mutton are produced, as well as the richest dairy products in the country. Cheese is a specialty. Apples are widely grown and made into cider and calvados, an apple brandy. Crêpes originated in this region.

In the west-central part of the country is the Touraine region, known as the garden of France because of its fertile river valley. A variety of fruits and vegetables grows here, especially table grapes and prunes. In the center of northern France is the Ile-de-France area, which surrounds Paris, and is home to haute cuisine. Ingredients from throughout the country are available, although beef, pork, and veal are specialties. Just to the east is Champagne, known for its sparkling wine of the same name. In the northeast, Alsace and Lorraine are influenced by their proximity to Germany. Sausages such as *andouille* made from heavily spiced pork or lamb's stomach, and sauerkraut are featured in the hearty cuisine. Beer and Alsatian white wines are made. *Charcuterie*, the art of preparing pork and pork products such as sausages, hams, *pâtés* (finely ground and seasoned spreads of meat or liver), and *terrines* (coarsely ground or chopped leftover meats baked with spices in a pan), originated in this region.

The mountainous Franche-Comté region bordering Switzerland is known for the Bresse chicken, which has a very delicate flavor. Just to the west of this area is Burgundy, known for its wines. The hearty dishes of the region are often seasoned with mustard and wine as well as garlic. The principal city of Dijon is famed for its mustard. In the southwest is Bordeaux, also known for its wine, which has long lent its flavor and its name to haute cuisine's *Bordelaise* sauce. Brandy from Cognac is a specialty.

The south central portion of France is the Languedoc region, which specializes in *cassoulet*, a dish containing duck or goose, pork or mutton, sausage, and white beans, among other ingredients. Finally, Provence, in the southeast corner of the country, has a unique style of cooking that is influenced by its Mediterranean location. Olives and olive oil, garlic, tomatoes, eggplant, zucchini, and seafood are predominant. *Bouillabaisse*, a fish stew with tomatoes, garlic, saffron, and olive oil, originated here. Pasta is also popular in this region.

Recently, some French chefs have created a healthier variation of haute cuisine called *nouvelle* cuisine or cuisine *minceur*. The basic values of haute cuisine are retained, but much of the excess fat, sugar, and salt has been removed. The goal is to allow people to indulge in the finest dishes French cuisine has to offer, without consuming excessive amounts of fat and cholesterol.

Ingredients

MILK AND MILK PRODUCTS

Milk is used in some French dishes, although it is not considered to be a beverage by many adults. Fresh cream, called *fleurette*, is used more often, and is added to sauces or whipped for desserts. Also popular is *crème fraîche*, a slightly fermented, thick, tangy cream. Yogurt is occasionally consumed. Cheese is eaten at many meals and is considered part of dessert. Many regional specialties are produced, including the semisoft Brie and Camembert, the salty and tangy Roquefort, the semihard Pont l'Évêque, the buttery Port-Salut, and goat cheeses such as Montrachet.

MEAT AND MEAT ALTERNATIVES

Beef, including organ meats, lamb, pork, horsemeat, and veal, are commonly eaten. Game meat, especially hare, is popular. Chicken (hens, roosters, and capons, which are neutered roosters), duck, goose, and small birds such as squab and quail are frequently eaten. Eggs are used extensively.

Fish are often consumed, especially in coastal areas; some of the most popular are sole, salmon, herring, anchovies, and trout. Shellfish is especially well liked, as are lobsters, oysters, and mussels. Snails, called *escargots*, are a specialty. Beans, particularly the small white (also called navy) variety are used.

FRUITS AND VEGETABLES

Berries, such as black currants, raspberries, and strawberries, including the small wild type, are especially favored. Grapes and other temperate fruits such as apples, melons, peaches, and pears are also frequently eaten. Among the most popular vegetables are artichokes, asparagus, carrots, celery (including the root celeriac), eggplant, fennel, green beans, zucchini, lettuce, leeks, mushrooms (including *cèpes*, *chanterelles*, and *morels*), onions, sorrel, spinach, and tomatoes. Potatoes are a favorite vegetable. Truffles, a type of fungus, are a regional specialty.

BREADS AND CEREALS

Wheat flour (white) breads are served at every meal, and remain on the table from appetizers through dessert. Refined wheat flour is also used to make pastries, tarts, cakes, and other desserts and to thicken sauces.

OTHER INGREDIENTS

Unsalted butter is used in cooking throughout France. In some regions other fats and oils are also used, such as olive oil in Provence, and goose fat in Alsace and Lorraine. Nuts are often used in desserts. Almonds, chestnuts, filberts (hazelnuts), pecans, and walnuts are most common.

Coffee is the most popular nonalcoholic beverage, often consumed with steamed milk (*café au lait*) at breakfast and strong and black after, but not with, dessert. Hot chocolate, cider, and other fruit juices are also commonly consumed. French wines are renowned, and strict rules of etiquette exist for serving them. Dry white wine should be served with hors d'oeuvres and fish and should be chilled. Dry red wine, which should be served at room temperature, goes with meat and cheese. With dessert, a sweeter white wine or a sparkling wine can be served. The dry white wine should always be served before the red wine. If two wines of the same color are to be served, the lighter and drier should come first, the younger should be served before the older, and the less important wine before the more prestigious. Children are served wine diluted with water. Drinking water is enjoyed almost as much as wine, and bottled water is used if local water is unacceptable. Wine-based apéritifs are traditionally served and distilled liquors, such as brandy (including Cognac) and fruit liqueurs, are common after the meal.

Seasonings

The most commonly used herbs in French cuisine are basil, bay leaves, chervil, chives, fennel, marjoram, parsley, rosemary, sage, savory, tarragon, and thyme. The fresh forms are preferred and many people grow herbs in a kitchen garden or window box. A combination of fresh parsley, chives, tarragon, and chervil is known as *fines herbes* and is used in many dishes. *Bouquet garni*, a mixture of dried parsley, thyme, and bay leaves, is another useful combination. Other seasonings, including capers, cinnamon, cloves, fennel seeds, garlic, mustard, and shallots are popular. Pepper (including black, white, green, or pink peppercorns) is also common. Wine is often added to foods for flavor, as are Cognac, coffee, and chocolate.

Preparation

Meat, poultry, or fish is the centerpiece of a French meal. Roasting, baking, and simmering are the most common cooking methods. In provincial cooking, meat juices are often used to make a simple sauce. The cooking of vegetables is no less important; these are steamed in a small amount of water or stock; sugar may be added to create a glaze, or they may be "refreshed" (boiled, plunged immediately into cold water, and then reheated with butter just before serving). Aside from salads, few foods are served raw.

Stocks and sauces are the basis of haute cuisine. Most are variations of five basic sauces: *béchamel*, made from milk seasoned with onions, thyme, nutmeg, and pepper and thickened with *roux* (flour cooked in butter or other fat); *espagnole*, made from brown meat stock and *mirepoix* (minced carrots, onions, and celery seasoned with bay leaves and thyme) thickened with roux; tomato sauce, made with white stock, tomatoes, onions, carrots, garlic, butter, and flour; *hollandaise*, made with butter and lemon juice thickened with egg yolk; and *velouté*, made from white stock thickened with roux. Classic cold sauces include mayonnaise and vinaigrette, an oil and vinegar dressing.

Baking is a specialty. The simple, crusty bread known as French bread (often shaped in a long, thin loaf called a *baguette*) is eaten daily. Other types of popular breads include rich, buttery *brioche* and flaky *croissants*. French pastries are famous. Savory and sweet tarts are common, including custard-filled, herb-seasoned tarts known as quiches, and dessert tarts with fresh fruit, nuts, or chocolate. Cakes often feature light sponge layers (called *genoise*) and fillings. Pastries made from the expansive dough called *pâte à choux*, including cream puffs, and from the multilayered puff pastry, such as napoleons, are enjoyed on special occasions.

Meal Patterns

Three meals a day are usually eaten in France. Breakfast is small, often just a croissant and café au lait. Traditionally, dinner is eaten at noon. It is the largest meal of the day and begins with an appetizer, such as pâté or, perhaps, creatively used leftovers. For a special occasion, a fish course would precede the main course of meat or poultry, but usually the main dish would follow the appetizer and might be meat, fish, or poultry. A vegetable may be served with or after the main dish, or may be omitted if the appetizer or main dish contains vegetables. Salad is served after the main course and usually consists of tossed greens with a light dressing. Dessert is usually cheese and fruit, though on special occasions cakes, pastries, custards, or ice cream may be eaten.

Wine accompanies the meal. For an elaborate dinner, a different wine would be served with each course, but for a family meal, one or two wines suffice. Bread is available throughout the meal and is eaten with every course, including the dessert cheese.

Supper is a light meal, often consisting of soup or a casserole with bread and wine. This pattern is retained in some rural regions, with schools and offices closing for two hours at lunch, but increasingly, the noon meal is light (fast food is popular) and the evening meal is larger.

Creole and Cajun Cuisine

The French who came to America adapted their traditional cooking methods to ingredients available in their new environment, guided by Native American knowledge of plants and animals. Spanish and African influences were added as more immigrants arrived, especially in the South. In the New Orleans area, this international blend resulted in Creole cuisine. Later, when the French Acadians from Canada settled in rural Louisiana, they developed a country-style version of Creole cooking called Cajun. Creole cooking is more subtle and more closely related to classic French cuisine than the highly spiced Cajun dishes, but the two are closely allied.

Seafood, including crab, shrimp, oysters, and crayfish (for which the region is famous) is prominent in the cuisine. Game, pork, rice, corn products, tomatoes, chayote squash (called *mirlitons*), eggplant, chili peppers, and hot sauce are other typical ingredients in Creole and Cajun cooking. Soups and stews are popular. Gumbo is a stew of seafood, meat, and/or poultry and okra and other vegetables thickened almost always with a roux and sometimes also with *filé* (powdered sassafras leaves mixed with thyme). Gumbo is served over rice. Jambalaya is a rice dish originally made with ham, now prepared with a variety of meats and seafoods. Nearly all dishes, from fresh shucked oysters to gumbo and jambalaya, are served with hot sauce on the side. French-style sausages, including spicy pork Cajun sausage and the mild veal *boudin blanc* are served at many meals. They are especially popular with red beans and rice. Examples of modified French dishes still prepared in Louisiana include bouillabaisse made with local fish and seafood, *beignets*, a French-style dough-nut, and *pain perdu*, or French toast. The roux used in Louisiana is usually made with fat or vegetable oil instead of butter. Chicory is commonly added to coffee, which is drunk *noire* (black) or *au lait* (with hot milk).

◆ ━━━━━━ ◆

M E N U
French Dinner

Pork and Veal Terrine
Poulet à la Normande
(chicken with cream and cider sauce)
Green Salad with Roquefort Cheese
Tarte au Chocolat
(chocolate tart)

*Serving suggestions: Offer sliced
French bread with the terrine;
steamed rice and seasonal vegetable (such as fresh peas or braised
carrots), and white wine or apple
juice with the chicken. Serve
coffee with dessert.*

◆ ━━━━━━ ◆

◆ ━━━━━━ ◆

M E N U
Cajun Dinner

*Shrimp and Okra Bisque with
Herbed Hush Puppies*
Blackened Redfish
Cajun Corn
Bread Pudding with Hard Sauce

*Serving suggestions: Provide hot
sauce with the meal; offer
steamed rice with the fish;
and serve coffee (with chicory),
iced tea, or beer.*

◆ ━━━━━━ ◆

◆ *Pork and Veal Terrine*

BAKE: 1½ hours
OVEN: 350°F
YIELD: 50 portions
PORTION: 1 slice

1 lb. onions, finely chopped
¼ lb. butter
2¼ c. brandy (beef stock may be substituted)
4 lb. pork, finely ground
4 lb. veal, finely ground
2 lb. pork fat, ground
8 eggs, lightly beaten

2 tsp. salt
½ tsp. pepper
2 tsp. thyme
⅛ tsp. allspice
2 lb. bacon, sliced, blanched
2 lb. boiled ham, cut into strips ¼″ wide
4 bay leaves

1. Sauté onions in butter until soft.
2. Boil brandy until volume is reduced by half. Combine brandy and onions in a mixer.
3. Add ground meats, fat, eggs, and seasonings to the onion mixture. Beat thoroughly until mixture is light and fluffy.
4. Line bottom and sides of four 2-quart loaf pans with bacon. (Reserve extra bacon strips for top.)
5. Spread one-eighth of terrine mixture in each dish. Layer with ham strips. Add remaining terrine mixture.
6. Place a bay leaf on top of each pan. Cover with bacon. Seal tightly with aluminum foil and a lid.
7. Set baking dishes in water and bake until terrine has separated from sides of pan.
8. Remove from oven. Remove lid and place a heavy weight on foil to pack down the terrine. Cool at room temperature, refrigerate overnight (6–8 hours). Remove weights. Cut into ¾-inch slices.

CALORIES: 512   CARBOHYDRATE: 15 g   PROTEIN: 24 g   FAT: 65 g
CHOLESTEROL: 135 mg   CALCIUM: 23 mg   SODIUM: 1017 mg   IRON: 2 mg
VITAMIN A: 115 IU   VITAMIN C: 8 mg

Poulet à la Normande
(Chicken with Cream and Cider Sauce)

BAKE: 1½ hours
OVEN: 400°F
YIELD: 48 portions
PORTION: 1 piece

16 lb. tart cooking apples, peeled, cored, and quartered
1 c. lemon juice
1 c. oil
4½ lb. butter
48 chicken quarters
4 oz. scallions, finely chopped
1 tsp. thyme

10 cloves
¼ c. sugar
1 gal. hard apple cider (nonalcoholic cider may be substituted)
2 T. cornstarch
3 qt. heavy cream
1 T. salt or to taste
½ tsp. pepper or to taste

1. Sprinkle apples with lemon juice to prevent browning.
2. Sauté apples in oil and ½ pound butter over moderate heat until lightly browned or half-cooked (5–6 minutes). Drain and reserve liquid. Spread apples evenly in two 12″ × 20″ × 2″ greased pans.
3. Brown chicken using 3½ pounds of butter. Place chicken on top of apples. Strain juices over chicken and apples.
4. Melt remaining ½ pound butter and stir in scallions, thyme, cloves, and sugar. Cook gently for 6–7 minutes. Add reserved apple liquids. Turn up heat and add hard cider, ½ cup at a time. Pour mixture over chickens, cover tightly, return to oven and cook until tender (45–55 minutes). Remove chicken. Strain cooking juices and reserve.
5. Dissolve cornstarch in 1 cup of cream. Blend with remaining cream. Mix with cooking juices. Cook over low heat until sauce thickens, stirring constantly.
6. Season to taste. Serve chicken with cooked apples and sauce.

CALORIES: 725   CARBOHYDRATE: 32 g   PROTEIN: 23 g   FAT: 82 g
CHOLESTEROL: 201 mg   CALCIUM: 51 mg   SODIUM: 546 mg   IRON: 2 mg
VITAMIN A: 1868 IU   VITAMIN C: 9 mg

◆ Green Salad with Roquefort Cheese

YIELD: 50 portions
PORTION: 1 c.

9 lb. lettuce, torn (romaine, red leaf, Bibb, curly endive)
1 lb. bacon, cooked and crumbled
1 lb. croutons
½ lb. Roquefort cheese, crumbled
⅓ oz. parsley, chopped finely

Toss lettuce with vinaigrette. Mix in bacon, croutons, and Roquefort cheese. Garnish with parsley.

Vinaigrette

¾ c. lemon juice
¾ c. tarragon wine vinegar
1 T. garlic, minced
1 T. prepared mustard, Dijon-style
1 T. salt
2 tsp. pepper
1½ c. olive oil
1½ c. vegetable oil

1. Combine lemon juice, vinegar, garlic, mustard, salt, and pepper and mix thoroughly.
2. Whisk in oils in a thin stream until combined.

CALORIES: 200
CHOLESTEROL: 7 mg
VITAMIN A: 1642 IU
CARBOHYDRATE: 10 g
CALCIUM: 99 mg
VITAMIN C: 18 mg
PROTEIN: 4 g
SODIUM: 397 mg
FAT: 29 g
IRON: 1 mg

◆ Tarte au Chocolat (Chocolate Tart)

BAKE: 60–75 minutes
OVEN: 325°F
YIELD: 48 portions
PORTION: 1 slice

2 lb. semisweet chocolate
2¼ lb. unsalted butter
30 eggs
4 lb. sugar
1 lb. flour
3 tsp. vanilla flavoring
6 9½" pie crusts, unbaked
(tart pastry, page 87)

1. Melt butter over low heat. Add chocolate. Stir until melted and well-blended. Cool.
2. Beat eggs, sugar, flour, and vanilla together until light. Blend in chocolate mixture.
3. Fill pie crusts with above mixture. Bake until pastry is very light brown. Do not overcook.

CALORIES: 657
CHOLESTEROL: 234 mg
VITAMIN A: 1112 IU
CARBOHYDRATE: 70 g
CALCIUM: 36 mg
VITAMIN C: 0 mg
PROTEIN: 8 g
SODIUM: 432 mg
FAT: 55 g
IRON: 2 mg

Cajun Dinner

◆ *Shrimp and Okra Bisque*

YIELD: 50 portions
PORTION: 1 c.

6 bay leaves
2 T. salt
3 T. dry mustard
2 T. cayenne or to taste
2 T. thyme
1½ T. pepper
1 T. basil, dried and crumbled
1½ c. oil
5 lb. okra, sliced
2 lb. onions, finely chopped
¾ lb. celery, finely chopped

1½ lb. green pepper, finely chopped
¾ lb. butter or margarine
4 T. garlic, minced
1½ c. flour
¼ c. oil
2½ gal. seafood stock
2½ lb. okra, sliced
1 lb. scallions, finely chopped
4½ lb. medium shrimp, peeled
  and deveined

1. Combine bay leaves, salt, dry mustard, cayenne, thyme, pepper, and basil.
2. Sauté okra in oil until brown.
3. Add onions, green peppers, and celery to okra and cook 1 minute.
4. Add butter; cook until melted.
5. Add garlic and seasoning mixture. Sauté for about 5 minutes.
6. Add flour and oil. Cook until mixture thickens, stirring constantly.
7. Add ½ gallon stock, stirring until flour is dissolved. Add remaining stock, bring to a boil and cook, stirring, until soup becomes slightly thickened. Simmer 5 minutes, stirring occasionally.
8. Stir in okra and scallions. Simmer for 10 minutes.
9. Add shrimp and cook until they turn pink.

CALORIES: 249
CHOLESTEROL: 77 mg
VITAMIN A: 838 IU

CARBOHYDRATE: 11 g
CALCIUM: 109 mg
VITAMIN C: 35 mg

PROTEIN: 14 g
SODIUM: 1022 mg

FAT: 28 g
IRON: 2 mg

Herbed Hush Puppies

BAKE: 3–4 minutes
OVEN: 350°F
YIELD: 50 portions
PORTION: 2

1¾ lb. cornmeal
1 lb., 2 oz. all-purpose flour
3 T. baking powder
2 tsp. salt
1 tsp. pepper
1 tsp. thyme
¼ tsp. oregano, crumbled

½ lb. scallion tops, minced
1½ T. garlic, minced
8 eggs, beaten
1 qt. milk
6 oz. vegetable shortening or lard, melted

1. Combine the cornmeal, flour, baking powder, salt, pepper, thyme, and oregano.
2. Stir in scallions and garlic.
3. Combine eggs, milk, and shortening. Add to cornmeal mixture. Mix well. Chill dough at least one hour.
4. Using a no. 30 scoop, deep-fry the hush puppies until very golden brown. Drain. Serve warm.

CALORIES: 227
CHOLESTEROL: 81 mg
VITAMIN A: 926 IU

CARBOHYDRATE: 21 g
CALCIUM: 13 mg
VITAMIN C: 27 mg

PROTEIN: 4 g
SODIUM: 591 mg

FAT: 23 g
IRON: 1 mg

Blackened Redfish

YIELD: 50 portions
PORTION: 3 oz.

16 lb. redfish or red snapper fillets, skinned
3 lb. butter
¾ c. lemon juice
1 T. thyme

1 tsp. oregano, dried
2 T. pepper
1½ T. cayenne
1 T. salt

1. Keep fish in refrigerator until ready to use. The fish should be well-chilled.
2. Melt butter over low heat. Stir in lemon juice, thyme, oregano, pepper, cayenne, and salt. Cook 10 minutes; cool.
3. Pat fish dry. Dip each fillet into butter mixture and place in very hot skillet. Fish should blacken quickly. (It will look burned.) Turn and cook other side. Brown remaining butter mixture in skillet; serve over fish.

CALORIES: 332
CHOLESTEROL: 134 mg
VITAMIN A: 1019 IU

CARBOHYDRATE: 1 g
CALCIUM: 93 mg
VITAMIN C: 2 mg

PROTEIN: 29 g
SODIUM: 433 mg

FAT: 23 g
IRON: <1 mg

♦ Cajun Corn

YIELD: 50 portions
PORTION: ½ c.

1 lb. bacon fat
2 lb. sweet peppers, finely chopped
1½ lb. onions, chopped
1 T. garlic, minced
10 lb. frozen corn kernels
1 #10 can tomatoes, peeled, seeded, and chopped

1 T. thyme
2 T. salt or to taste
1 T. pepper
1 qt. chicken stock

1. Sauté sweet peppers, onions, and garlic in bacon fat for 5 minutes.
2. Add corn, tomatoes, thyme, salt, and pepper. Continue cooking for 5 minutes.
3. Stir in stock. Simmer for about 45 minutes or until most of the stock has cooked off.

CALORIES: 215
CHOLESTEROL: 80 mg
VITAMIN A: 925 IU

CARBOHYDRATE: 21 g
CALCIUM: 13 mg
VITAMIN C: 27 mg

PROTEIN: 4 g
SODIUM: 590 mg

FAT: 23 g
IRON: 1 mg

♦ Bread Pudding with Hard Sauce

BAKE: 45 minutes
OVEN: 325°F
YIELD: 50 portions
PORTION: ½ c.

2 dozen egg yolks
3½ lb. sugar
½ c. vanilla (if not using hard sauce, use ¼ c. vanilla and ⅓–½ c. rum or whiskey)
1 lb. butter or margarine, melted

2 lb. French bread, cubed, soaked in milk (do not remove crusts)
1 qt. milk
1 qt. hard sauce (recipe below)

1. Combine eggs, sugar, vanilla, and butter.
2. Pour egg mixture over soaked bread. Add additional milk and bake.
3. Bread pudding can be served warm with hard sauce or chilled without sauce.

Hard Sauce

12 oz. butter, unsalted
1 lb., 4 oz. brown sugar

¾ c. rum or whiskey

Cream butter and sugar until smooth and fluffy. Blend in rum or whiskey a little at a time. Chill before serving.

CALORIES: 360
CHOLESTEROL: 165 mg
VITAMIN A: 615 IU

CARBOHYDRATE: 50 g
CALCIUM: 50 mg
VITAMIN C: <1 mg

PROTEIN: 3 g
SODIUM: 200 mg

FAT: 20 g
IRON: 1 mg

*Cajun shrimp and
okra bisque served
with herbed hush
puppies.*

·6· COOKING FROM
·*Germany*·

A typical German dessert, mandeltorte (almond cake with chocolate frosting).

German food is fortifying. It features meaty entrées, plenty of dairy foods, and abundant desserts. For much of its history, Germany has been a collection of separately ruled states, and its boundaries have changed many times. Therefore, there are distinct regional differences in its cuisine, and there is considerable overlap between the cooking styles of Germany and its neighbors, including Austria, Belgium, the Netherlands, Switzerland, France, Poland, and Czechoslovakia.

The core of German cuisine is meat, poultry, fish, and milk products. The cold climate limits the cultivation of fresh fruits and vegetables, and in earlier times many foods were preserved. Cheese, pickles, sausages, sauerkraut, and sour cream are a few of these traditional items still commonly used today.

The northern coast of Germany provides the country's only contact with the sea. Fish and shellfish hold a prominent place in the cuisine. Poultry is eaten more often in this region than in others; some areas are famous for their goose dishes, others for duck and chicken. Potatoes, wheat, and barley are grown. Hearty soups made of cabbage and bacon are eaten.

Central Germany is hilly, and supports vineyards, orchards, and sheep, as well as potatoes. The Westphalia area is famous for its hams, its pumpernickel bread, and its beer. The casseroles of Westphalia feature pork, often accompanied by potatoes and vegetables. The Rhine valley is known for its white wines. Many kinds of sausages are made in the central region, including *Frankfurter würstchen*, the forerunner of the American hot dog. Saxony is known for its pastries and yeasted cakes. Potato dumplings are an important part of the cuisine; the art of making them is traditionally passed on from mother to daughter.

Southern Germany is mountainous. Grapes grow well, and wines are produced. Beer is also very popular. Pork is prominent in this region, and there is a long history of sausage making. *Spätzle*, a type of tiny noodle, is frequently eaten. Bavaria is influenced by its proximity to Austria, and strudel is made here not only with sweet fillings, but occasionally with savory fillings as well. The area known as Baden has more in common with France; snails and other typically French foods are eaten.

Ingredients

MILK AND MILK PRODUCTS

Dairy foods are popular in Germany. Whipped cream is especially favored, although fresh milk, buttermilk, sour cream, and yogurt are also common. Cheese is served almost daily. *Blaukäse* (blue cheese), flavorful Limburger (a semihard, fermented cheese), and mildly sharp Tilsiter are a few common types. Dutch and Swiss cheeses are also popular, such as robust Edam, Gouda, and Emmenthal ("Swiss" cheese).

MEAT AND MEAT ALTERNATIVES

Pork is the favorite meat. German cured pork products are known worldwide, from various hams (such as Black Forest and Westphalian) to over one thousand different types of sausages (or *wurst*). Four basic types are made: *rohwurst*, cured and smoked sausages that are eaten without cooking; *bruhwurst*, smoked and precooked sausages that are usually simmered before consumption; *kochwurst*, sausages similar to cold cuts that are eaten without cooking; and *bratwurst*, fresh sausages prepared by pan frying. *Mettwurst* (spreadable, finely ground veal mixed with pork), *leberwurst* (liverwurst), *weinerwurst* (made from beef and pork), and *blutwurst* (blood sausage) are just a few examples of the tremendous variety available.

Organ meats and blood are often used. Beef and veal are eaten. Game animals of all types are favored, especially hare, venison, and wild boar. Poultry is sometimes served, most notably goose and chicken. Eggs are eaten at breakfast and are also used in many dishes. Both freshwater and saltwater fish are popular, including carp, eel, herring, halibut, flounder, and trout. Shellfish, including lobster, mussels, and oysters, are eaten. Legumes are occasionally used, including lentils and white beans.

FRUITS AND VEGETABLES

Apples predominate, although cherries, pears, berries (such as lingonberries, gooseberries, and strawberries), grapes, plums, peaches, and rhubarb are also common. Dried fruits are eaten, particularly prunes, raisins, currants, pears, apricots, and apples.

Cabbage (both red and green) and potatoes are eaten almost daily. Other members of the cabbage family are popular, including kale, Brussels sprouts, and cauliflower. Carrots, beets, and turnips are commonly eaten root vegetables.

Asparagus, sweet peppers, onions, tomatoes, green beans, celery, leeks, mushrooms, kohlrabi, peas, and cucumbers are also used.

BREADS AND CEREALS
Rye and wheat are the most common grains, but oats, barley, and rice are also used. Breads of all types are popular, as are dumplings and pastries.

OTHER INGREDIENTS
Butter is the favored fat, although rendered fats such as lard, chicken fat, and goose fat are used in some dishes. Vegetable oils are used only occasionally. Nuts are added to many baked goods. Almonds, filberts (hazelnuts), and walnuts are the most common.

Coffee is the most popular hot beverage, though tea and hot chocolate are also consumed. Beer is the alcoholic beverage of choice, and nearly every town has its own brewery. Beer comes in many types: dark or light, sweet or bitter, weak or strong. All are typically bottom-fermented Pilsner-style, common in U.S. beers. Germany produces many fine white wines, as well as a few red wines. Distilled fruit liqueurs such as kirsch and schnapps are also consumed.

Seasonings
Caraway seeds flavor many breads, cabbage dishes, and cheeses. Poppy seeds are added to some sweet breads and desserts. Cinnamon, allspice, cardamom, ginger, and cloves are some of the most common spices. Garlic, bay leaves, black pepper, mustard, horseradish, and juniper berries are also popular seasonings. Some of the favored herbs are chives, parsley, chervil, dill, borage, tarragon, savory, sorrel, and watercress, all of which are combined to make *grüne sosse*, or green sauce, served with fish, meats, and hard-cooked eggs.

Preparation
Meats and poultry are usually fried, roasted, or stewed. *Sauerbraten*, beef marinated in wine, vinegar, and pickling spices, then slowly roasted, is a national specialty. *Schnitzel*, a veal or pork cutlet, breaded and fried, is an example of a fried dish, while the one-pot meal called *eintopf*, in which meat, vegetables, and potatoes are simmered for several hours, is a typical stewed dish. This and other stewed dishes are often topped off with *knödeln*, or dumplings. Roast goose stuffed with apples is a Christmas specialty. Finely chopped beef (and occasionally veal or pork) is sometimes served raw, seasoned with chopped onion and parsley, as steak Tartar.

Fish, especially eel, are enjoyed smoked. Herring are often pickled and may then be served as "rollmops," rolled around pieces of raw onion and pickles. Fresh fish may be poached, sautéed, baked, or broiled and served with various sauces.

Vegetables are frequently boiled. Potatoes are also served in numerous other ways, including pan-fried, French-fried, mashed, and as dumplings. Cabbage is cooked fresh or as sauerkraut (salted and fermented). Salads are served, especially cole slaw, potato salad, and meat salads. Breads and rolls (mostly whole grain, including whole wheat, pumpernickel, and rye) are eaten at most meals. Pastries of all kinds are consumed nearly daily as well. Coffee cakes, nut- or fruit-filled tarts and tortes, and cheesecake are just a few of the specialties. One of the best known sweets is *Schwarzwälder kirschtorte* (Black Forest cake), which features chocolate cake layered with cherries, whipped cream, and kirsch. Apple strudel is made from sheets of paper-thin dough rolled around apples seasoned with raisins and cinnamon. Other desserts include *mohnkuchen*, a poppyseed cake, and *stollen*, a special Christmas fruitcake.

Meal Patterns

Breakfast, or *frühstück*, includes bread or rolls with butter and jam and coffee. Boiled eggs, cheese, and ham are often added, especially in northern Germany. Between 9 and 10 A.M., most Germans snack on sandwiches, pastries, or bread and fruit with coffee or beer. Traditionally, this snack was an elegant meal, often eaten in a restaurant. Lunch, called *mittagessen*, is the main meal of the day, even when eaten away from home. It usually begins with soup and is followed by a meat course served with vegetables. Stewed fruit or pudding generally completes the meal. In well-to-do families, a fish course would be inserted after the soup, and a cheese course and a candy would follow dessert. *Kaffee*, or afternoon coffee, can be a simple cookie or pastry with a cup of coffee, or it can include lots of little sandwiches and cakes. Supper, called *abendbrot* (meaning "evening bread") is traditionally light, and includes bread and butter and a selection of sausages, cheeses, cold cuts, and perhaps a salad or an egg dish. Usually people make an open-faced sandwich, which is eaten with a knife and fork. Snacking is common. Stands selling sausages, French fries, beer, and soft drinks are found on nearly every city corner.

Pennsylvania Dutch Cooking

Many German foods are familiar to Americans. Hot dogs, hamburgers, pretzels, rye bread, cole slaw, sauerkraut, potato salad, and jelly doughnuts all have their origins in Germany. The American beer industry was dominated by German immigrants for many years.

Many Germans came to America and settled in eastern Pennsylvania, where they became known as Pennsylvania Dutch (from "Deutsch," meaning German). Their cooking is hearty and includes many German-style dishes, such as *scrapple*, or *ponhaus*, a pork and cornmeal mixture often served for breakfast (originally made from sausage broth and buckwheat in Germany and called *pannhas*). Breakfast might also include potatoes with fried ham, bacon, or

A hearty Pennsylvania Dutch breakfast featuring funnel cake, apple rings, and potato cakes served with bacon and eggs.

sausage, fritters, and cake. *Fastnachts* and funnel cakes, two types of doughnuts, are often eaten as a midmorning snack. Cinnamon rolls, similar to German *schnecken*, are also made.

As in Germany, for the Pennsylvania Dutch the noon meal is usually the largest, and consists of meat, potatoes, noodles or dumplings, several vegetables, bread, pudding, fruits, and pie. A selection of "sweets and sours" is served with lunch and supper, including crab apple jelly, apple butter, pickles, and pepper relish. A typical main dish with a German origin is *boova schenkel*, beef stew with dumplings. Supper is also a large meal that can include cold beef or ham, fried potatoes, cheese, bread, soups, corn pone, apple dumplings, steamed puddings, and shortcake as the main part of the meal, with pie and/or cake for dessert. One of the better known Pennsylvania Dutch pies is shoofly pie, a molasses and brown sugar cake developed from the German crumb cake called *streuselkuchen*.

```
┌─────────────────────────────────────┐
│ ◆                               ◆   │
│        ─────────────                │
│        M E N U                      │
│        German Dinner                │
│                                     │
│        Pickled Beet Salad           │
│      Celeriac and Apple Salad       │
│           Sauerbraten               │
│        (marinated pot roast)        │
│      Baked Kale and Potatoes*       │
│           Mandeltorte               │
│          (almond torte)             │
│                                     │
│     Serving suggestions: Salads may │
│     be served as a meal with pickled│
│       herring, sliced cold cuts, and│
│     pumpernickel bread; offer beer, │
│       Riesling wine, or fruit juice.│
│                                     │
│     *Boiled potatoes and red cabbage│
│        may be served instead.       │
│ ◆       ─────────────           ◆   │
└─────────────────────────────────────┘
```

M E N U **German Dinner**

◆ *Pickled Beet Salad*

YIELD: 50 portions
PORTION: ½ c.

1 qt. red wine	9 peppercorns
1 qt. cider vinegar	1 tsp. salt
1½ lb. onions, peeled and thinly sliced	12–14 lb. beets, cooked and sliced, or 2 #10 cans, drained
6 cloves, whole	1½ c. olive oil
¾ tsp. coriander, ground	2 T. horseradish, grated

1. Mix together wine, vinegar, onions, and spices. Bring to a boil.
2. Pour hot, spiced vinegar over beets. Chill at least 24 hours. Remove whole cloves and peppercorns.
3. Whisk oil and horseradish together and add to beets. Mix thoroughly with dressing.

CALORIES: 112 CARBOHYDRATE: 9 g PROTEIN: 2 g FAT: 13 g
CHOLESTEROL: 0 mg CALCIUM: 27 mg SODIUM: 91 mg IRON: 1 mg
VITAMIN A: 23 IU VITAMIN C: 7 mg

♦ Celeriac and Apple Salad

YIELD: 50 portions
PORTION: ½ c.

3 c. mayonnaise
1½ c. sour cream
⅓ c. fresh dill, finely chopped
⅓ c. fresh parsley, finely chopped
1 T. salt

½ tsp. pepper
3 lb. tart apples, peeled, cored, and cut into ¼" slices
9 lb. celeriac (celery root), peeled and cut into ⅛" slices

1. Combine mayonnaise, sour cream, dill, parsley, salt, and pepper.
2. Stir in apple slices; cover and set aside.
3. Drop celeriac into lightly salted boiling water to cover. Cook over medium heat for 20–25 minutes or until just tender. Do not overcook.
4. Drain and pat dry. Add celeriac to dressing and mix. Serve chilled.

CALORIES: 137	CARBOHYDRATE: 6 g	PROTEIN: 2 g	FAT: 21 g
CHOLESTEROL: 13 mg	CALCIUM: 57 mg	SODIUM: 234 mg	IRON: 1 mg
VITAMIN A: 137 IU	VITAMIN C: 5 mg		

♦ Sauerbraten (Marinated Pot Roast)

MARINATE: 5 days
BAKE: 4–5 hours
OVEN: 350°F
YIELD: 50 portions
PORTION: 4–5 oz.

20 lb. round steak
2 T. salt
1 tsp. pepper
1 lb. onions, sliced
2 lb. carrots, sliced
1½ lb. celery, chopped
6 cloves
6 peppercorns

1 gal. red wine vinegar
6 bay leaves
2 gal. water
1½ c. oil
2½ c. oil
2½ c. flour
½ c. sugar
12–15 gingersnaps, crushed

1. Season meat with salt and pepper.
2. Combine onions, carrots, celery, cloves, peppercorns, vinegar, bay leaves, and enough water to cover meat. Cover and refrigerate 5 days.
3. Drain meat and reserve marinade. Sauté in oil until browned on all sides.
4. Add marinade and bring to boil. Lower heat and simmer 3 hours.
5. Heat oil; add flour and blend. Add sugar and brown. Stir into meat mixture. Cover and cook 1 more hour or until meat is tender.
6. Remove meat. Stir gingersnaps into juices and cook until thickened. Pour gravy over meat.

CALORIES: 486	CARBOHYDRATE: 11 g	PROTEIN: 32 g	FAT: 56 g
CHOLESTEROL: 96 mg	CALCIUM: 33 mg	SODIUM: 364 mg	IRON: 4 mg
VITAMIN A: 2062 IU	VITAMIN C: 3 mg		

◆ *Baked Kale and Potatoes*

BAKE: 20 minutes
OVEN: 400°F
YIELD: 50 portions
PORTION: ½ c.

18 lb. kale
2½ lb. lean bacon, coarsely diced
2½ c. beef or chicken stock
2 T. salt or to taste
1½ tsp. ground nutmeg
15 lb. medium boiling potatoes, peeled and cut into ½" cubes

1 lb. butter, softened
2½–3 c. milk
2 T. salt or to taste
1 tsp. pepper or to taste
10 egg yolks
4 oz. butter, softened

1. Wash and trim kale. Boil for 10 minutes. Drain thoroughly and chop coarsely.
2. Cook bacon until crisp. Add kale and mix well.
3. Stir in stock, salt, and nutmeg. Simmer, uncovered, for 20 minutes, stirring occasionally.
4. Boil potatoes until tender. Do not overcook. Drain, return to pan. Shake over low heat until dry. Mash potatoes.
5. Mix butter into potatoes. Beat in milk, a cup at a time, until mixture is thick enough to hold its shape.
6. Add salt, pepper, and egg yolks, one at a time.
7. Spread kale in two greased 12" × 20" × 2" baking pans. Top with potatoes, dab with butter. Bake until golden brown.

CALORIES: 301   CARBOHYDRATE: 35 g   PROTEIN: 14 g   FAT: 23 g
CHOLESTEROL: 87 mg CALCIUM: 343 mg   SODIUM: 862 mg   IRON: 4 mg
VITAMIN A: 13981 IU VITAMIN C: 176 mg

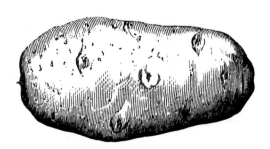

♦ *Mandeltorte (Almond Torte)*

BAKE: 1 hour
OVEN: 350°F
YIELD: 48 portions
PORTION: ⅛ cake

3 lb. sugar
36 egg yolks
1⅛ c. lemon juice
3 T. lemon peel, grated

2 T. cinnamon
2 lb. almonds, ground
12–15 oz. bread crumbs, toasted
36 egg whites

1. Beat egg yolks with sugar until double in volume.
2. Mix in lemon juice and peel, cinnamon, and almonds. Slowly stir in bread crumbs. Add enough to make a light but thick batter.
3. Beat egg whites until stiff. Fold carefully into the batter. Bake in six greased 8-inch tube pans.
4. Cool and remove from pans. Frost with chocolate frosting.

Chocolate Frosting

3 lb. unsalted butter, softened
1 c. cream
3 lb. confectioner's sugar

¾ lb. unsweetened chocolate, melted, cooled
2 tsp. vanilla or rum flavoring

1. Cream butter. Add cream and mix well.
2. Gradually add sugar and beat until creamy.
3. Mix in chocolate and vanilla, continue beating at high speed until fluffy.

CALORIES: 684	CARBOHYDRATE: 68 g	PROTEIN: 10 g	FAT: 64 g
CHOLESTEROL: 263 mg	CALCIUM: 91 mg	SODIUM: 144 mg	IRON: 2 mg
VITAMIN A: 1140 IU	VITAMIN C: 2 mg		

♦ —————— ♦

M E N U

Pennsylvania Dutch Breakfast

Scrapple
Funnel Cakes
Potato Cakes with Bacon
Apple Rings

Serving suggestions: Offer eggs, coffee, and fruit juice.

♦ —————— ♦

Pennsylvania Dutch Breakfast

◆ *Scrapple*

YIELD: 50 portions
PORTION: 2 slices

16 lb. pork shoulder
1 T. salt
1 tsp. pepper
1 T. summer savory

2 tsp. marjoram
2 tsp. thyme
2¾ lb. yellow cornmeal

1. Boil pork in water seasoned with salt and pepper. Cook until very tender. Add water as necessary.
2. Remove meat from bones; strain cooking stock and reserve 1½ gallons. Shred meat and return to liquid.
3. Add seasonings and cornmeal slowly, stirring constantly. Simmer 15 minutes, or until mixture has thickened.
4. Pour into five 4″ × 9″ loaf pans to mold. Cool.
5. Cut slices ¼ to ½ inch thick and fry on greased grill until brown and crisp on both sides.

CALORIES: 374
CHOLESTEROL: 80 mg
VITAMIN A: 111 IU

CARBOHYDRATE: 19 g
CALCIUM: 15 mg
VITAMIN C: 0 mg

PROTEIN: 20 g
SODIUM: 631 mg

FAT: 42 g
IRON: 4 mg

◆ *Funnel Cakes*

FRY: 3–4 minutes
DEEP-FAT FRYER:
  350–375°F
YIELD: 48 portions
PORTION: 1 cake

2 qt. milk
8 eggs, lightly beaten
1 tsp. baking soda, dissolved in a
  little lukewarm water

4 oz. sugar
2 lb. flour
½ tsp. salt
4 oz. confectioner's sugar

1. Combine milk, eggs, and baking soda.
2. Combine dry ingredients in another bowl.
3. Add enough of the dry ingredients to milk and egg mixture to form a waffle-like batter. Pour approximately ⅓ cup batter through a funnel into hot fat, making a free-form circular cake. Fry until golden brown.
4. Dust with confectioner's sugar when partly cooled.

CALORIES: 208
CHOLESTEROL: 50 mg
VITAMIN A: 95 IU

CARBOHYDRATE: 21 g
CALCIUM: 57 mg
VITAMIN C: <1 mg

PROTEIN: 5 g
SODIUM: 70 mg

FAT: 20 g
IRON: 1 mg

◆ *Potato Cakes with Bacon*

FRY: 3–5 minutes
DEEP-FAT FRY:
    350°F
YIELD: 50 portions
PORTION: 4 oz.

5 lb. bacon
10 lb. potatoes, peeled, boiled,
    and mashed
18 eggs, beaten
3 c. milk

2 lb. onions, finely chopped
4 oz. oil
1½ T. salt
½ tsp. pepper

1. Brown bacon until crisp. Reserve fat.
2. Add eggs and enough milk to potatoes to make a thick batter.
3. Sauté onions in oil until soft.
4. Add onions, salt, and pepper to potato mixture. Pour approximately ½ cup of batter into hot bacon fat and brown on both sides.
5. Serve with bacon.

CALORIES: 260   CARBOHYDRATE: 23 g   PROTEIN: 8 g   FAT: 28 g
CHOLESTEROL: 163 mg   CALCIUM: 41 mg   SODIUM: 525 mg   IRON: 1 mg
VITAMIN A: 121 IU   VITAMIN C: 21 mg

◆ *Apple Rings*

FRY: 4–6 minutes
DEEP-FAT FRYER:
    365°F
YIELD: 50 portions
PORTION: 2 apple
    rings

10 T. sugar
2 lb. flour
2 T. baking powder
2½ tsp. salt
5 eggs, beaten

1½ qt. milk
7–8 lb. apples, peeled, cored, and
    sliced into rings
½ lb. sugar
2 T. cinnamon

1. Combine first four dry ingredients.
2. Blend beaten eggs and milk.
3. Slowly add dry ingredients to egg and milk mixture to make a batter.
4. Coat apple rings with batter and fry. Drain and cool.
5. Combine sugar and cinnamon. Sprinkle on apple rings.

CALORIES: 281   CARBOHYDRATE: 33 g   PROTEIN: 4 g   FAT: 27 g
CHOLESTEROL: 30 mg   CALCIUM: 61 mg   SODIUM: 160 mg   IRON: 1 mg
VITAMIN A: 94 IU   VITAMIN C: 3 mg

◆ 7 ◆ COOKING FROM
◆ *Great Britain and Ireland* ◆

High tea selection of scone, toast and marmalade, and lemon curd tartlet.

*H*earty, simple fare is characteristic of Great Britain (England, Scotland, Wales, and Northern Ireland) and Ireland. Although the nobility once feasted on imported delicacies, they provided their workers with two simple meals a day, consisting mostly of bread, cheese, and ale, with a little meat or fish and *pottage*, a stew of vegetables, beans, and oats. During the Middle Ages, new spices, nuts and fruits, and cooking techniques were introduced, but 16th-century Puritans discouraged sensual pleasures, including those of the palate.

British cooking did not change much until the 1700s, when colonization of the New World and improved transportation brought better quality and a greater variety of meats, vegetables, and grains to the marketplace. Sugar and tea became cheaper. Potatoes, which had become popular in Ireland, took root in Great Britain. Cheap grains were imported from the colonies, and finer flour was made. Although the British aristocracy has long enjoyed foreign foods, particularly those from France, cookbook writers of the 17th and 18th centuries disdained the French dishes and advised the use of domestically grown foods, which were thought to be more suitable. Both the British and Irish take pride in the simplicity and naturalness of their cuisine, and in their ability to cook foods so that the flavor is enhanced rather than obscured.

Ingredients
MILK AND MILK PRODUCTS

Cows have been kept in Britain for thousands of years, and milk and milk products have long formed an important part of the British diet. Milk is consumed as a beverage, on oatmeal, and in puddings and many other dishes.

Fresh cream, sour cream, double cream (about 30 percent butterfat), and clotted cream (scalded, cooled, and separated by skimming) are used in a variety of ways. Cheeses have been made for centuries. Different regions produce various types of cheese: Caerphilly, for example, is a delicate semisoft cheese from Wales; Cheddar is a hard cheese made in numerous English and Scottish counties; and Stilton is a blue-veined cheese from East Anglia.

MEAT AND MEAT ALTERNATIVES

Beef is especially favored, including roasts and organ meats such as brains, kidneys, liver, sweetbreads, tongue, and tripe. Lamb is also common. Pork and veal are eaten, as well as game meats such as hare and venison. Poultry (such as chicken, duck, and goose) and small birds (pheasant and thrush, for example) are used in some dishes, and eggs are popular.

Fish and shellfish are also typical in the cuisine. Bass, crab, cod, eel, haddock, herring, mackerel, oysters, perch, pike, salmon, shrimp, sole, sturgeon, trout, and whiting are among those most often eaten.

FRUITS AND VEGETABLES

Berries are favorites in Great Britain, and gooseberries, raspberries, and strawberries are used in many dessert recipes. Apples, cherries, currants, grapes, pears, plums, raisins, and rhubarb are also very popular fruits.

Potatoes, which originated in Central and South America, were introduced to Ireland in the late 16th century. They grew well in the poor soil and were readily incorporated into the Irish diet. Today, potatoes are popular throughout the region.

Vegetables that grow in a cold climate and store well have always been important in the British and Irish diets. These include beets, cabbage, kale, leeks, onions, peas, and turnips. Other commonly used vegetables include Brussels sprouts, cauliflower, celery, cucumbers, green beans, and tomatoes.

BREADS AND CEREALS

In Ireland and northern Great Britain, the climate supports the cultivation of oats and barley, and these are extensively used in soups and puddings, as hot cereal or porridge, and in bread and oat cakes. In southern regions, wheat is more predominant. Rice and rye are used in some dishes.

OTHER INGREDIENTS

Butter, lard, and bacon drippings have been the traditional fats in Great Britain. Today, margarine and vegetable oil are used as well.

Nuts are featured in many dishes, particularly desserts. Almonds, both sweet and bitter types, are common. Chestnuts, filberts (hazelnuts), pecans, and walnuts (including black walnuts) are also frequently consumed.

Coffee and chocolate have long been popular hot beverages, but tea became favored in the 18th century. It is usually prepared with sugar and cream or lemon. Beer brewed from grains or honey (called mead) has been produced for centuries in Great Britain. Today beer, including ale and stout, is still among the most popular beverages. Wine is also common, and fortified wines such as port and sherry are especially favored. Whiskey, an Irish and Scotch specialty, is also consumed.

Seasonings

Standard seasonings include chives, cinnamon, cloves, ginger, horseradish, mace, marjoram, mint, mustard, nutmeg, oregano, paprika, parsley, pepper, rosemary, sage, thyme, and vanilla. Flavorful condiments such as mint jelly, Worcestershire sauce, and Indian-style chutneys often accompany meats.

Pork with apples and ale served with colcannon.

Preparation

Beef, lamb, game, and poultry were originally roasted whole on a spit over an open fire, but today they are baked or broiled in an electric or gas oven. Leftover meat is well used, eaten either cold or chopped and used as an ingredient in hash, stews, and savory puddings and pies, such as *stobhach Gaelach* (Irish stew made with lamb neck), shepherd's pie (ground meat topped with onions and potatoes), and the famous steak and kidney pie. Pork is usually eaten as ham, bacon, or sausage, commonly called *bangers.*

Fish is most popular fried. Fish and chips are available on every street corner. The fish is battered and then deep-fried; the chips are actually fried potato slices, similar to French fries, and are served with malt vinegar. Fish is also commonly dried, smoked, or salt-cured. Kippers, small dried and smoked herring, are eaten as appetizers or at breakfast.

Potted foods, which are similar to French pâté, are popular throughout the region. Beef, ham, chicken, trout, and shrimp are just some of the foods that are minced and pounded, mixed with spices such as allspice, cloves, ginger, and nutmeg, then covered with lard or butter for preservation.

Many people eat eggs daily at breakfast—boiled, poached, fried, or scrambled. Cheese is also favored. It is featured in Welsh rarebit (cheese sauce served over toast) and in the "ploughman's lunch": a wedge of Cheddar, a slice of bread, some pickled onions, and a pint of ale.

Vegetables are usually cooked or pickled. Potatoes are popular mashed (often called "mash"), as *boxty*, a type of potato pancake, and mixed with other vegetables as in Irish *colcannon*, in which mashed potatoes, cabbage or kale, and leeks are combined.

Sweet desserts often take the forms already familiar for savory dishes—pies and puddings. Plum pudding, a traditional Christmas specialty, evolved from its original form as a porridge of wheat and milk, to become the more solid mixture of dried fruits, flour, sugar, suet, and spices it is today. A trifle combines layers of pound cake, custard, fresh fruit or jam, sherry, and whipped cream.

Meal Patterns

Four meals a day are traditional in Great Britain and Ireland. Historically, a large breakfast starts the day. At the turn of the century, a breakfast of oatmeal, bacon (or ham or sausage), eggs, toast, grilled tomatoes or mushrooms, and smoked fish or deviled kidneys was served. Large breakfasts are still popular on weekends.

With the change from a rural to a fast-paced urban society came the eating pattern common today: an early, light breakfast, a small lunch eaten away from home (often obtained from street vendors or pubs), tea during the afternoon, and the main meal at the end of the day. On Sundays the midday meal may be larger than the evening meal. The main meal generally consists of a meat (the centerpiece of the meal), a vegetable, and potatoes, rice, or bread and butter, usually followed by dessert (often called "pudding"). This pattern was brought to the United States by immigrants from Ireland and Great Britain. Afternoon tea may be a simple pot of tea and a light snack, or it can be quite elaborate. High tea can include potted meats, salmon cakes, ham salad, fruit, cakes, pastries, and biscuits such as shortbread or scones. When high tea is consumed, the later evening meal may be skipped.

◆ ━━━━━━━━━━ ◆

M E N U

Irish Dinner

Mustard Soup
Pork with Apples and Ale
Colcannon or Pease Pudding
Summer Pudding

*Serving suggestions: Offer bread
and beer or fruit juice.*

◆ ━━━━━━━━━━ ◆

Irish Dinner

◆ *Mustard Soup*

YIELD: 48 portions
PORTION: 1 c.

1 lb. unsalted butter
3 lb. onions, finely chopped
1 lb. flour
1½ gal. chicken stock
1 T. Worcestershire sauce or to taste
1 tsp. pepper or to taste

3 c. prepared English-style mustard
(such as Colman's)
12 egg yolks
3 qt. light whipping cream
2 lb. iceberg lettuce, finely shredded

1. Melt butter, sauté onions until soft, and stir in flour. Gradually incorporate the stock until a smooth soup is achieved.
2. Add Worcestershire sauce and pepper; whisk in mustard thoroughly.
3. Whisk egg yolks with cream and add gently to the soup, stirring briskly. Add lettuce and serve.

CALORIES: 319
CHOLESTEROL: 131 mg
VITAMIN A: 1096 IU

CARBOHYDRATE: 17 g
CALCIUM: 103 mg
VITAMIN C: 7 mg

PROTEIN: 8 g
SODIUM: 580 mg

FAT: 34 g
IRON: 2 mg

◆ *Pork with Apples and Ale*

BAKE: 35–40
minutes
OVEN: 350°F
YIELD: 50 pork
chops
PORTION: 5 oz.

17 lb. pork chops
12 oz. butter
3½ lb. onions, sliced
6 lb. apples, peeled, cored,
and sliced
6 oz. flour
1 gal. strong ale (apple cider may be
substituted)

2 T. salt
1 tsp. pepper
2 bay leaves
6 cloves
rind of 2 lemons

1. Trim pork chops and brown in some of the butter on both sides.
2. Fry onions and apples in remaining butter until golden brown. Stir in the flour and cook thoroughly.
3. Gradually add the ale and bring to a boil, stirring constantly. Season with salt and pepper.
4. Pour sauce over chops. Tie bay leaves, cloves, and lemon rind in cheesecloth and add to the chops. Cover tightly and bake.

CALORIES: 528
CHOLESTEROL: 123 mg
VITAMIN A: 245 IU

CARBOHYDRATE: 16 g
CALCIUM: 32 mg
VITAMIN C: 6 mg

PROTEIN: 31 g
SODIUM: 407 mg

FAT: 56 g
IRON: 2 mg

Colcannon (Mashed Potatoes with Cabbage and Scallions)

YIELD: 50 portions
PORTION: 5 oz.

15 lb. boiling potatoes, medium, peeled and quartered
10 oz. butter
1¼ qt. milk
10 lb. green cabbage, finely shredded

10 oz. butter
1 lb. scallions, chopped (include 2 inches of green portion)
3 T. salt
2 tsp. pepper
½ c. minced parsley

1. Boil potatoes until tender but not falling apart. Drain and return to pan. Shake pan over low heat until potatoes are dry and mealy. Mash to a smooth purée.
2. Beat in butter and milk, 1 cup at a time. Use enough milk to make a purée thick enough to hold its shape in a spoon. (Additional milk may be needed.)
3. Boil cabbage uncovered for 10 minutes. Drain thoroughly in colander.
4. Melt butter, add cabbage, and cook, stirring constantly, for a minute or two.
5. Stir cooked cabbage and scallions into mashed potatoes. Add salt and pepper. Sprinkle with parsley and serve.

CALORIES: 210
CHOLESTEROL: 29 mg
VITAMIN A: 684 IU

CARBOHYDRATE: 26 g
CALCIUM: 95 mg
VITAMIN C: 69 mg

PROTEIN: 5 g
SODIUM: 515 mg

FAT: 14 g
IRON: 1 mg

Pease Pudding

YIELD: 50 portions
PORTION: 4 oz.

5¼ lb. yellow split peas
¼ lb. carrots, peeled
¼ lb. bacon

¼ lb. onions, peeled
1 T. salt

1. Soak peas overnight in cold water. Drain and rinse. Put in pan and cover with cold water. Bring to a boil and boil for 10 minutes. Drain and return to pan.
2. Add carrots, bacon, and onions. Cover with cold water and bring to a boil. Skim, cover and simmer for 45 minutes until split peas are soft. Drain or boil rapidly to remove excess liquid. Discard carrots, bacon, and onions. Sieve or mash the peas. Season with salt.

CALORIES: 161
CHOLESTEROL: <1 mg
VITAMIN A: 305 IU

CARBOHYDRATE: 29 g
CALCIUM: 18 mg
VITAMIN C: <1 mg

PROTEIN: 11 g
SODIUM: 160 mg

FAT: 1 g
IRON: 2 mg

♦ Summer Pudding

14 lb. soft red fruit (cherries, strawberries, black or red currants, raspberries, etc.; see note)

1¾ lb. sugar

½ c. lemon juice

2 T. lemon rind

70 slices white bread, sliced thin

1 c. fresh red fruit

3 c. whipping cream

1. Clean fruit and simmer for a few minutes with sugar, lemon rind, and juice.
2. Remove crusts from bread and arrange slices around sides and base of greased 12″ × 20″ × 2″ pan. Fill with cooked fruit and arrange bread on top. Cover and chill overnight.
3. Serve garnished with fresh fruit and accompanied with softly whipped cream.

Note: If fruit is frozen, thaw and discard most of the juice. If fruit is fresh, reserve 1 cup for garnish.

CALORIES: 271   CARBOHYDRATE: 58 g   PROTEIN: 5 g   FAT: 6 g
CHOLESTEROL: 10 mg   CALCIUM: 68 mg   SODIUM: 224 mg   IRON: 2 mg
VITAMIN A: 264 IU   VITAMIN C: 30 mg

♦   ♦

M E N U
High Tea

Potted Beef

Welsh Rarebit

Scones

Lemon Curd Tartlets

Serving suggestions: Include other tea dishes such as small open-faced sandwiches and shortbread. Serve with butter, marmalade, jam, and tea, milk or cream, and sugar.

♦   ♦

High Tea

◆ *Potted Beef*

BAKE:
  approximately
  2 hours
OVEN: 325°F
YIELD: 50 portions
PORTION: 2 oz.

8 lb. beef, ground
1½ lb. bacon
2 tsp. salt
2 tsp. pepper
¼ tsp. mace
¼ tsp. nutmeg
¼ tsp. ginger

1 lb. butter
1 qt. red wine or beef stock
½ c. water
8 oz. butter
8 bay leaves
50 slices white bread

1. Combine beef, bacon, spices, and butter. Mix in a food processor or blender until a smooth paste forms. Slowly add wine or stock and water. Press mixture into four greased 2-quart loaf pans.
2. Dot tops with butter and place 2 bay leaves in each pan. Cover with foil and lids. Place pans in water, halfway up, and bake.
3. Drain and cool. Serve chilled with bread slices.

CALORIES: 332   CARBOHYDRATE: 17 g   PROTEIN: 19 g   FAT: 29 g
CHOLESTEROL: 82 mg   CALCIUM: <1 mg   SODIUM: 457 mg   IRON: 3 mg
VITAMIN A: 430 IU   VITAMIN C: 2 mg

◆ *Welsh Rarebit*

YIELD: 50 portions
PORTION: 6–8 oz.

12 oz. cornstarch
3½ qt. milk
2 T. mustard, ground
¼ tsp. cayenne pepper
1 T. salt

½ tsp. pepper
2 T. Worcestershire sauce
5¼ lb. Cheddar cheese, grated
50 slices white bread

1. Blend cornstarch with 2 cups of cold milk. Bring remaining milk to boil and stir in cornstarch paste. Simmer and stir for 1 minute. Reduce heat to low and add mustard, cayenne, salt, pepper, and Worcestershire sauce.
2. Stir in cheese. Cook until smooth, stirring often.
3. Toast bread and spread with cheese mixture. Brown under a hot grill.

CALORIES: 335   CARBOHYDRATE: 24 g   PROTEIN: 17 g   FAT: 25 g
CHOLESTEROL: 60 g   CALCIUM: 450 mg   SODIUM: 630 mg   IRON: 1 mg
VITAMIN A: 591 IU   VITAMIN C: <1 mg

◆ Scones

BAKE: 15–20
minutes
OVEN: 400°F
YIELD: 50 portions
PORTION: 1 scone

2 lb. flour
2 T. + 2 tsp. baking powder
½ lb. sugar
1 T. salt
12 oz. butter, cut into ¼″ bits and
   chilled

4 eggs
4 egg yolks
2 c. milk
4 egg whites

1. Sift the flour, baking powder, sugar, and salt together.
2. Cut in the butter bits until the mixture resembles coarse cornmeal.
3. Beat eggs and egg yolks together until frothy. Beat milk into egg mixture and pour over flour mixture. Mix until dough can be gathered into a compact ball. Dust lightly with flour and roll out ½ inch thick.
4. Cut scones using a 2-inch round cutter. Place an inch apart on greased baking sheet.
5. Beat egg whites briskly and brush top of the rounds before baking. Bake until light brown.

CALORIES: 150
CHOLESTEROL: 59 mg
VITAMIN A: 266 IU

CARBOHYDRATE: 18 g
CALCIUM: 45 mg
VITAMIN C: <1 mg

PROTEIN: 3 g
SODIUM: 242 mg

FAT: 10 g
IRON: 1 mg

◆ Lemon Curd Tartlets

BAKE: 10–12
minutes
OVEN: 350°F
YIELD: 48 portions
PORTION: 1 tartlet

Lemon Curd
4 lb. sugar
1½ lb. butter, unsalted
2¾ c. lemon juice

¼ c. grated lemon rind
36 eggs

1. Mix sugar, butter, lemon juice, and rind in top part of double boiler. Stir over simmering water until sugar is dissolved and the mixture is smooth. Cool.
2. Beat eggs until light and slightly thickened. Add butter mixture. Return to heat and cook until mixture is thick, stirring often, about 15 minutes. If mixture is not smooth, it may be strained.
3. Fill baked tartlet shells (recipe follows).

Tart Pastry

2 lb. flour
1 T. salt
1 lb. butter, unsalted

½ lb. vegetable shortening
¾–1 c. water, chilled

1. Combine flour and salt. Cut in butter and shortening until mixture has a mealy texture. Stir in water until dough forms a ball. Refrigerate 30–40 minutes.
2. Roll out dough on lightly floured board. Cut into 3-inch rounds. Place in small tart forms. Prick with a fork and bake until lightly browned.

CALORIES: 474	CARBOHYDRATE: 51 g	PROTEIN: 7 g	FAT: 39 g
CHOLESTEROL: 249 mg	CALCIUM: 32 mg	SODIUM: 185 mg	IRON: 2 mg
VITAMIN A: 920 IU	VITAMIN C: 5 mg		

·*8*· COOKING FROM
·*Greece and the Middle East*·

*Greek tiropetes
(flaky cheese-filled
turnovers).*

*T*he countries clustered at the eastern end of the Mediterranean Sea share a culinary tradition that has developed over thousands of years of friendly trade and hostile takeovers. There is little agreement on exactly where the geographic boundaries of the Middle East begin and end, but on the basis of cuisine, Greece, Turkey, Lebanon, Syria, Israel, Jordan, Iraq, Iran, Soviet Armenia, Saudi Arabia, Yemen, Sudan, Egypt, Algeria, Tunisia, and Morocco could all be included.

There is also little agreement on how to group regional cuisines. One approach is to recognize five major culinary areas: Greek/Turkish, Arabic, North African, Iranian, and Israeli. Nearly every nation in the region claims identical dishes found in Greece and the Middle East to be its own. The origins of these foods are actually difficult to determine because the cooking is remarkably similar throughout the area. Many common threads can be seen: lamb is the preferred meat, wheat and rice are the staple grains, olives and olive oil are used extensively, yogurt is an important part of the diet, and fresh fruit is popular.

Of all the cuisines, Israeli cooking contrasts most with the rest. The recent immigration of Jews from many countries, bringing traditional recipes from many diverse regions, has resulted in a collection of tremendously varied dishes. German, Russian, Yemenite, Moroccan, American, and many other influences are evident in Israeli cooking. In all, 80 nationalities are represented.

Religion also strongly influences the cuisine of the region. The Middle East is the birthplace of the three major Western religions: Judaism, Christianity, and Islam, each with many devout followers. Dietary laws may proscribe feasts, fast days, methods of food preparation, and proper food combinations.

Ingredients
MILK AND MILK PRODUCTS
Fermented milk products, such as yogurt and cheese, are used frequently in Greek and Middle Eastern dishes (fresh milk is used mostly for desserts).

Yogurt is used in sauces, salads, soups, drinks, and as a common ingredient in many main dishes. Frequently it is made at home. Cheese is usually made from goat's or sheep's milk. The mostly widely used is Greek feta, which is a salty, white, moist cheese that crumbles easily. Another popular cheese is kaseri, a firm, white, aged cheese (similar to Italian provolone).

MEAT AND MEAT ALTERNATIVES

Lamb is the most popular meat in the Middle East. Pork is prohibited for Jews and Muslims, but is eaten by Christians. Kid (goat) and camel are also eaten. Variety meats are consumed, especially tripe, brains, and liver. Chicken is popular, and game birds are hunted, including duck, geese, partridge, pheasant, and quail. Religious laws may dictate how meat must be prepared and may prohibit the eating of meat on certain days or in combination with certain foods.

Many types of fish and shellfish are available in coastal areas, including sturgeon, carp, herring, anchovies, sardines, red mullet, crayfish, lobster, shrimp, crab, scallops, clams, oysters, and mussels. Only fish with scales are considered kosher, and therefore observant Jews do not eat shellfish. Legumes are also an important source of protein. Chickpeas, fava beans, and lentils are among the most frequently consumed.

FRUITS AND VEGETABLES

Apricots, dates, figs, grapes, lemons, melons, oranges, pears, pomegranates, and quinces are some of the fruits featured in Middle Eastern dishes. Apples, bananas, cherries, mangos, peaches, plums, and strawberries are also cultivated.

Olives, such as the small, slightly bitter ripe black olives or the green Greek *kalamata* olives, accompany many meals. Olives are grown throughout the Middle East and are cured in many different ways; they are often marinated with spices. Artichokes, broccoli, cabbage, cauliflower, cucumbers, eggplant, green beans, okra, onions, tomatoes, turnips, and zucchini are other popular vegetables. Grape leaves are often used to wrap meat and rice fillings.

BREADS AND CEREALS

Wheat flour breads are made throughout the Middle East with many variations, depending on the region. However, the flat, round, "pocket" bread called pita is eaten nearly everywhere. Wheat doughs, such as the paper-thin pastry sheet called *filo*, are used for sweet and savory pastries. Cracked wheat, such as couscous (uncooked, finely cracked wheat pellets) and bulgur (steamed or boiled wheat kernels, which are then dried and cracked into fine, medium, or coarse granules), is also very popular.

Long-grain and basmati rice are used in many Middle Eastern dishes. In Iran, the country closest to Asia, rice is indispensable and is considered to be the main dish of the meal. Barley is an important grain in some countries.

OTHER INGREDIENTS

Olive oil is the most commonly used fat, especially in foods meant to be served cold. Butter is often preferred for hot dishes. In Israel, corn oil is used, and sesame oil is common in Egypt. Nuts and seeds, including sesame seeds (often in a paste form called *tahini*), almonds, pistachios, and walnuts, are often added to dishes, especially desserts.

Mixed fruit juices are consumed in many countries; oranges, lemons, pomegranates, raisins, and strawberries are common ingredients. However, tea and coffee are the most popular beverages in Middle Eastern countries. In Iran, sweetened tea is the favored hot beverage. In Israel, tea is served British style (strong, with milk) or Russian style (with sugar and sometimes lemon). In some areas, herb teas are served, especially those made from flowers and aromatic spices such as anise, chamomile, cinnamon, ginger, rose, saffron, and violet.

Coffee is native to Ethiopia and Arabia, and the southern Arabs are said to have introduced it to the rest of the Middle East. Turkish and Arabic coffees are both very strong, boiled coffees that may be heavily sweetened. Clove or cardamom is sometimes added. In some places, coffee is served unsweetened on sad occasions and very sweet on happy ones.

An anise-flavored apéritif distilled from grapes or other fruit is consumed in many Middle Eastern countries. Variously called *ouzo*, *arak*, and *raki*, it is always accompanied by food. In Greece, wine is the usual alcoholic beverage. The most commonly produced wine is the white *retsina*, which has a distinctive resin flavor.

Seasonings

Fresh herbs are used whenever possible, including mint, dill, and coriander. Flat-leaf parsley, oregano, basil, marjoram, bay leaves, and thyme are also used. Cumin seeds, black and cayenne pepper, cardamom, cinnamon, allspice, and aniseed are popular spices. Garlic is used in most countries, but in Iran, it is considered vulgar because of its overpowering flavor. Saffron and turmeric are valued for the color they add to foods. Other typical Middle Eastern spices include *mahlab*, made from black cherry kernels; *ajowan*, a small black seed; mastic; and sumac (ground from a nontoxic variety of the plant), which has a sour taste. To create a sour taste, *verjuice*, the juice of unripe grapes, lemons and dried, whole limes, are sometimes used. Salt is used to preserve foods as well as to flavor them. For sweet dishes, waters distilled from rose or orange petals give a distinctive perfume. Honey and sugar are both used as sweeteners.

Preparation

Ovens have been only recently introduced to the Middle East. Portable oil stoves were often used in the past, and dishes were simmered overnight. Anything that needed to be baked had to be taken to the village bakery. Long simmering is still done today, but grilling, frying, and roasting are also popular cooking methods.

Meat is frequently marinated and roasted, usually whole for special occasions. It is also cooked in cubes or slices. The traditional dish of skewered cubes of lamb and vegetables called *shish kebob*, meaning broiled lamb or mutton, originated over a thousand years ago and is still popular throughout the region. The Iranian national dish is *chelo kebob* — fragrant basmati rice with thin slices of well-marinated grilled lamb, raw egg, yogurt, and sumac. Very thin slices of meat are often mounded onto a rotisserie and roasted; this preparation is called *souvlaki* in Greece and *chawarma* in Lebanon.

Meat is also commonly ground and mixed with rice and spices. This mixture is used to stuff vegetables, grape leaves *(dolmas)*, and cabbage leaves. In Syria and Lebanon, ground meat is mixed with bulgur, and the resulting *kibbe* can be eaten raw, baked, or fried. Ground meat is also made into meatballs and is sometimes used as a filling for pastries. Chicken is usually grilled, fried, or stewed. Fresh fish is broiled, steamed, fried, or baked; sometimes it is smoked or dried and salted.

Sauces are a staple of Middle Eastern cookery. The most common is *avgolemono*, or egg-lemon, sauce, which is added to many soups. Yogurt-based sauces are also frequently used; yogurt with mint and yogurt with garlic are two of the simplest. Béchamel (white sauce) is said to have originated in Greece. Tomato-based sauces are also popular. To thicken sauces, nuts are often used.

Beans are eaten boiled, hot or cold. The national dish of Egypt is *ful medames*, cooked fava (broad) beans seasoned with oil, lemon, and garlic, and garnished with hard-boiled eggs and parsley. Cold beans with olive oil, lemon, and garlic are not uncommon for breakfast. Cooked, puréed chickpeas are the base for *hummus*, a spread or dip that can be used as an appetizer or a salad. Ground chickpeas or fava beans are mixed with spices, formed into balls, and deep-fried. The balls are served in pita bread *(falafel)* or as a main course *(ta´amia)*.

Bread is traditionally leavened, whether it is made in loaves, as in Greece, or baked flat, as in most other countries. Rather than slicing the flat bread, the diner tears off pieces and uses them as scoops, in place of a fork.

Bulgur can be used as a side dish or made into a refreshing salad called *tabouli*, by adding onions, parsley, and mint. Bulgur, as well as rice, is often made into pilaf; it is first sautéed in butter or oil in which chopped onions have been browned, then steamed in chicken or meat stock. In North Africa, couscous is commonly steamed and served with stews or broth.

Middle Eastern specialties: chicken with couscous flavored with almonds, raisins, and orange blossom water, and yakhini (stewed eggplant and zucchini with tomatoes).

Fresh fruits and vegetables are preferred, but when these are not available, fruit preserves and pickled vegetables are served. Vegetables are often eaten raw in salads, without lettuce, usually with a light dressing. They are also commonly cooked with tomatoes or tomato paste and onions, then steamed with a small amount of water, a method called *yakhini*.

Sweets are produced in great variety, many using the thin filo dough. The most well known of these is *baklava*, in which crushed walnuts, pistachios, or almonds and melted butter are layered between sheets of filo and baked. A sweet syrup flavored with honey, brandy, or rose or orange blossom water is poured over the baklava, which is served at room temperature or cold. Cakes, puddings, candied fruits, *halvah* (a sweet sesame seed paste), and Turkish delight, a sweet paste with pistachios, are other typical sweets. These are not usually served for dessert, but as a snack with midafternoon or late evening coffee and on special occasions.

Meal Patterns

Three meals a day are usually eaten, though the pattern may vary from one area to another. Breakfast is usually light, including coffee, bread, cheese, fruit or jam, and perhaps eggs or yogurt. An egg dish or a substantial soup is often served for lunch. A typical dinner menu might include a meat and vegetable stew or a meat-stuffed vegetable, accompanied by rice and bread. If the main dish does not contain a vegetable, a hot or cold vegetable dish, as well as a salad, may accompany it. Fruit is usually served for dessert. A formal dinner begins with anise liqueur and *meze*, or appetizers, which can include fresh and marinated vegetables, olives, fish, cheese, and eggplant preparations, and ends with a light dessert such as a pudding. Coffee completes the meal.

Kosher Food Preparation

Followers of Judaism belong to one of three congregations: Orthodox (who strictly observe all Jewish laws), Reform (who observe the moral laws), and Conservative (who observe a mix of Orthodox and Reform guidelines). All Orthodox, and some Conservative Jews, follow the Jewish dietary laws, called *Kashrut*. They are one of the pillars of Jewish religious life and are concerned with the fitness of food. *Kosher* or *kasher* means "fit" and is the popular term for the dietary laws.

The Kashrut defines the following food practices:

1. *Which animals are permitted for food and which are not.* Any mammal that has a complete cloven foot and also chews its cud is considered "clean" and can be eaten (including any milk products), such as cows, deer, goats, oxen, and sheep. "Unclean" mammals — pigs, rabbits, and carnivorous animals — are not to be eaten. Clean birds, such as chickens, ducks, geese, and turkeys, have a crop, gizzard, and an extra talon. Their eggs are also permitted. All fish that have fins and scales are permitted; all others, including catfish, eel, and shellfish, are considered unclean. All reptiles, amphibians, and invertebrates are also considered unclean.
2. *Method of slaughtering.* The meat of clean animals is permitted for consumption only if the life of the animal is taken by a special process known as *shehitah*. The *shohet* (person who kills the animal) must be trained and licensed to perform the slaughter, which is done by slitting the jugular vein and windpipe. If an animal dies of natural causes or for any other reason, it is not eaten.
3. *Examination of the slaughtered animal.* Any blemishes in the meat or organs of the slaughtered animal, or evidence of disease in any part, makes the whole animal unfit to eat.
4. *The parts of clean animals that are forbidden.* The blood and the separate layer of fat under the skin of the animal may not be eaten.

5. *The preparation of clean meat.* For meat to be kosher, the underlying fat, blood, blood vessels, and sciatic nerve must be removed.
6. *The law of meat and milk.* Meat and dairy products may not be eaten together. It is generally accepted that after eating meat a person must wait six hours before eating any dairy products. After eating dairy products, a person must wait an hour before consuming meat.
7. *Products of unclean animals.* The only product of an unclean animal that may be eaten is honey. All others (such as eggs) are forbidden.
8. *Examination of fruit and vegetables for insects and worms.* All plant foods are automatically kosher and since they are neither milk nor meat, can be eaten with both. But they must first be carefully examined in order to avoid accidentally consuming any insects or worms, which are unclean.

A processed product is considered kosher only if a Jewish authority's name or insignia is found on the package. The three most common insignias are the *U* (Union of Orthodox Jewish Congregations of America); *K* (Organized Kasrus Laboratories); or just a "K," indicating authorized Jewish supervision of the manufacturer.

<table>
<tr><td>

M E N U
Greek Dinner

Tiropetes
(flaky cheese turnovers)
Greek Salad
Pastitsio
(baked pasta with beef
and two sauces)
Baklava
(flaky nut-filled pastries)

Serving suggestions: Offer fruit juice, red wine, or cardamom-spiced coffee.

</td><td>

M E N U
Middle Eastern Dinner

Hummus bi Tahini
(chickpea dip)
Cacik
(cucumber and yogurt salad)
Chicken Baked with Couscous
Yakhini
(eggplant and zucchini
with tomatoes)

Serving suggestions: Offer fruit juice, white wine, coffee, or tea with mint. Serve fresh grapes or melon for dessert.

</td></tr>
</table>

Greek Dinner

◆ *Tiropetes (Flaky Cheese Turnovers)*

BAKE: 15–20
minutes
OVEN: 350°F
YIELD: 50–60
portions
PORTION:
1 tiropete

1 c. béchamel sauce (recipe
  follows), cooled
2 lb. feta cheese, crumbled
2 oz. Monterey Jack cheese, grated
3 egg yolks, beaten

2 T. parsley, chopped
3 T. unsalted butter, melted
2 lb. filo pastry sheets
1 lb. unsalted butter, melted

1. Stir cheeses, egg yolks, parsley, and butter into béchamel sauce.
2. Remove one sheet of filo at a time. (Cover remaining sheets with a damp
   cloth to prevent pastry from drying out.) Place sheet so that long sides are
   on top and bottom. Brush sheet with melted butter. Fold the sheet into
   thirds by overlapping right and left sides. Place one tablespoon of cheese
   mixture ¾ inch from bottom edge. Fold filo into a triangle over cheese.
   Continue until entire sheet is folded (as you fold a flag). Seal end with
   butter. Place triangles on buttered cookie sheet and brush with butter. Bake
   until golden brown.

Béchamel Sauce
1 T. unsalted butter
1½ T. flour
1 c. milk, hot

⅛ tsp. salt or to taste
⅛ tsp. white pepper

1. Melt butter. Add flour and stir until smooth.
2. Add milk gradually. Stir constantly and cook until smooth and thick.
   Season to taste.

CALORIES: 210
CHOLESTEROL: 57 mg
VITAMIN A: 475 IU

CARBOHYDRATE: 8 g
CALCIUM: 188 mg
VITAMIN C: <1 mg

PROTEIN: 7 g
SODIUM: 271 mg

FAT: 17 g
IRON: 1 mg

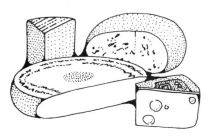

♦ *Greek Salad*

YIELD: 50 portions
PORTION: 1 c.

6 lb. romaine and iceberg lettuce, mixed
64 lb. tomatoes, cut into wedges
4 lb. cucumbers, peeled and sliced
1–2 lb. red onions, sliced thin

2 qt. Greek kalamata olives, drained
2–3 lb. feta cheese, crumbled
anchovy fillets and capers (optional)
1 qt. salad dressing (recipe follows)

1. Wash lettuce. Chop and drain excess water.
2. Depending on method of service, all ingredients may be tossed together with or without salad dressing. Or, salad fixings may be arranged on top of lettuce and dressing served on the side.

Salad Dressing

1 c. white wine vinegar
¾ qt. olive oil
1 T. salt
1½ tsp. pepper

1½ tsp. garlic, minced
1 tsp. basil, dried and crumbled
1 tsp. oregano, dried and crumbled

Combine and mix well.

CALORIES: 205
CHOLESTEROL: 12 mg
VITAMIN A: 1200 IU

CARBOHYDRATE: 6 g
CALCIUM: 125 mg
VITAMIN C: 18 mg

PROTEIN: 4 g
SODIUM: 445 mg

FAT: 34 g
IRON: 1 mg

◆ *Pastitsio (Baked Pasta with Beef and Two Sauces)*

BAKE: 1 hour
OVEN: 350°F
YIELD: 48 portions
PORTION: ¾ c.

2 lb. pastitsio noodles (hollow
  spaghetti or elbow macaroni
  may be substituted)
½ lb. butter
2 lb. Cheddar cheese, grated
12 eggs, beaten
7 lb. beef, ground
1½ lb. onions, chopped
1 T. garlic, minced
1 qt. tomato sauce

2 c. red wine (beef stock may
  be substituted)
1 T. cinnamon
½ tsp. allspice
½ tsp. nutmeg
2 T. salt
½ tsp. pepper
4 qt. béchamel sauce
  (recipe follows)

1. Cook pasta in boiling water for 8 minutes and drain well. Toss with butter
   and half the shredded Cheddar and eggs.
2. Brown beef, onions, and garlic. Drain and discard extra fat.
3. Add tomato sauce, wine, and spices to the meat mixture.
4. Grease two 12″ × 20″ × 2″ pans. Spread one quarter of the pasta mixture
   on the bottom of each pan. Cover with the meat mixture and sprinkle with
   half the remaining shredded cheese. Top with remaining pasta; cover with
   béchamel sauce and cheese. Bake.

Béchamel Sauce

1 lb. butter
1 lb. flour
1 gal. milk, hot

1½ T. salt
½ tsp. nutmeg
1 T. cinnamon

1. Melt butter. Add flour and stir until smooth.
2. Add milk gradually. Stir constantly until smooth and thick. Season to taste.

CALORIES: 553
CHOLESTEROL: 185 mg
VITAMIN A: 1035 IU

CARBOHYDRATE: 20 g
CALCIUM: 270 mg
VITAMIN C: 6 mg

PROTEIN: 30 g
SODIUM: 915 mg

FAT: 39 g
IRON: 4 mg

◆ *Baklava (Flaky Nut-filled Pastries)*

BAKE: 30 minutes;
30 minutes
OVEN: 350°F; 200°F
YIELD: 48 portions
PORTION: 1 piece

1½ lb. almonds and/or walnuts,
coarsely ground
2 oz. sugar
2 tsp. cinnamon
¼ tsp. cloves, ground

1 T. lemon peel, grated
½ lb. unsalted butter, melted
1 lb. filo pastry sheets
syrup (recipe follows)

1. Combine nuts, sugar, cinnamon, cloves, and lemon peel. Mix well and set aside.
2. Lightly butter a 12″ × 20″ × 2″ baking pan. Layer 6 sheets of filo in pan, brushing each with melted butter. Spread half the nut mixture on filo. Top with 6 more sheets of filo, brushing each with butter. Spread remaining nut mixture on filo. Top with remaining filo pastry, brushing each sheet with butter. Tuck edges inside pan to prevent curling while cooking. Cut into 1-inch diamond-shaped pieces prior to baking. Bake 30 minutes at 350°F. (You should begin making the syrup at this point.) Then reduce heat to 200°F and continue baking for another 30 minutes. Pour warm syrup over baklava. Cool before serving.

Syrup

1½ lb. sugar
2 c. water
⅛ tsp. cream of tartar

2 T. lemon juice
3 oz. honey

Prepare the syrup 30 minutes before baklava is finished baking. Combine all ingredients and boil for 20 minutes.

CALORIES: 250
CHOLESTEROL: 10 mg
VITAMIN A: 145 IU

CARBOHYDRATE: 35 g
CALCIUM: 43 mg
VITAMIN C: <1 mg

PROTEIN: 5 g
SODIUM: 3 mg

FAT: 12 g
IRON: 1 mg

Middle Eastern Dinner

◆ *Hummus bi Tahini (Chickpea Dip)*

YIELD: 50 portions
PORTION: ¼ c.

1 #10 can chickpeas, drained and
   rinsed (reserve liquid)
1½ c. lemon juice
3 cloves garlic
1 lb. tahini (sesame seed paste)

1 T. salt
1 c. olive oil
1 T. paprika
1 oz. parsley, chopped
2 lb. pita bread, sliced into wedges

1. Set aside one cup of liquid and one cup of chickpeas.
2. Purée remaining chickpeas, lemon juice, garlic, tahini, and salt until it has
   the consistency of a smooth, thick dip. Add reserved liquid if mixture is too
   thick. Season to taste.
3. Pour hummus into a serving dish, drizzle with olive oil, and garnish with
   paprika, parsley, and reserved chickpeas. Serve with pita bread.

CALORIES: 218   CARBOHYDRATE: 9 g   PROTEIN: 7 g   FAT: 23 g
CHOLESTEROL: 0 mg   CALCIUM: 48 mg   SODIUM: 246 mg   IRON: 3 mg
VITAMIN A: 107 IU   VITAMIN C: 4 mg

◆ *Cacik (Cucumber and Yogurt Salad)*

YIELD: 50 portions
PORTION: ½ c.

8–9 lb. cucumbers, peeled
   and chopped
2½ tsp. salt
5 lb. fresh tomatoes, chopped
   (optional)
25 eggs, hardboiled and quartered
3 T. garlic, minced

2 T. white pepper
1½ oz. fresh mint, chopped (¾ c.
   dried mint may be substituted)
3 T. white wine vinegar
6 qt. yogurt, plain
1 oz. mint leaves, fresh

1. Sprinkle cucumbers with salt. Place in colander and drain for 20 minutes.
2. Combine all ingredients. Refrigerate.
3. Garnish with mint leaves before serving.

CALORIES: 122   CARBOHYDRATE: 10 g   PROTEIN: 9 g   FAT: 7 g
CHOLESTEROL: 137 mg   CALCIUM: 236 mg   SODIUM: 442 mg   IRON: 1 mg
VITAMIN A: 358 IU   VITAMIN C: 12 mg

◆ Chicken Baked with Couscous

BAKE: 1 hour
OVEN: 350°F
YIELD: 48 portions
PORTION:
  1 chicken piece
  and 1 cup
  couscous

10 lb. precooked couscous
1 gal. water, tepid
5 qt. water, boiling
1 c. vegetable oil
¾ c. sugar
1 T. allspice
¼ c. cinnamon
1 c. orange blossom water
⅓ lb. raisins

1 lb. almonds, blanched, chopped
½ lb. butter
5 lb. onions, chopped
3 T. garlic, minced
1 T. ginger, ground
½ tsp. yellow food coloring
48 chicken quarters
1 lb. honey

1. Mix couscous with tepid water. Let stand until all liquid is absorbed. Stir to remove any lumps.
2. Add water, oil, sugar, allspice, cinnamon, orange blossom water, almonds, and raisins. Mix and divide into two 12″ × 20″ × 2″ pans.
3. Sauté onions and garlic in butter till soft. Add ginger and yellow food coloring. Arrange chicken over the couscous (24 pieces per pan); smother with onion and garlic mixture. Cover with foil and bake for ½ hour.
4. Remove foil, brush chicken with honey, and roast another ½ hour or until tender and golden brown.

CALORIES: 743
CHOLESTEROL: 104 mg
VITAMIN A: 270 IU

CARBOHYDRATE: 86 g
CALCIUM: 74 mg
VITAMIN C: <1 mg

PROTEIN: 42 g
SODIUM: 128 mg

FAT: 44 g
IRON: 7 mg

◆ Yakhini (Eggplant and Zucchini with Tomatoes)

YIELD: 50 portions
PORTION: ½ c.

5 lb. eggplant, peeled and sliced
8 lb. zucchini, sliced
rock salt
4 T. garlic, minced
2 c. oil (use olive oil if dish is
  served cold)

1 #10 can tomatoes, drained and
  chopped
1 oz. parsley, chopped
½ T. salt or to taste
1 tsp. pepper

1. Sprinkle eggplant and zucchini with salt and let stand ½ hour. Rinse and pat dry.
2. Heat garlic in oil, then add eggplant and zucchini. Sauté until tender.
3. Add tomatoes, parsley, salt, and pepper. Heat thoroughly and serve. This dish may also be chilled and served cold.

CALORIES: 116
CHOLESTEROL: 0 mg
VITAMIN A: 924 IU

CARBOHYDRATE: 8 g
CALCIUM: 33 mg
VITAMIN C: 29 mg

PROTEIN: 2 g
SODIUM: 161 mg

FAT: 17 g
IRON: 1 mg

·*9*· COOKING FROM
·*India*·

Indian vegetarian dinner featuring ekoori (spicy scrambled eggs), rice with dals, onion relish, coriander chutney, and mango chutney.

The cuisine of India is notable for its diversity and for its sophisticated seasoning. Because the geography of the country encompasses widely divergent climates, available foods vary from region to region, and only a few foods are eaten throughout all of India.

The northernmost part of India has a temperate climate, and fresh vegetables are available only on a seasonal basis. Nut and fruit orchards flourish, and sheep are raised. The northern plains just south of the Himalayan Mountains are irrigated by the Indus and Ganges rivers, producing a rich, fertile soil in which wheat and other grains, legumes, and a wide variety of vegetables grow easily. The southern part of India has a tropical climate suitable for the cultivation of rice. In coastal areas, fish and shellfish are abundant, as are coconuts, bananas, and an array of vegetables.

Indian diets are also strongly influenced by religion. Although most Indians follow Hinduism or its offshoots, others are Muslim, Christian, or Jewish, each with different food habits and restrictions that affect the cuisine. Hindus are prohibited from eating beef, while Muslims and Jews do not eat pork. Millions of Indians are strict vegetarians for religious reasons, excluding meat, poultry, fish, and/or eggs from their diets. Some also refrain from eating foods the color of blood, such as tomatoes and watermelon; vegetables grown underground; or vegetables with a shape resembling a head, such as mushrooms. Christian communities along the southwestern coast feature duck, boar, beef, and pork dishes, including Western-style sausage.

Ingredients

MILK AND MILK PRODUCTS
Cows are highly valued in India, and their milk — both fresh and evaporated — is widely consumed. Because refrigeration is not available in many areas,

fermented milk products such as yogurt are also very common. In the north, milk-based desserts, such as carrot pudding *(gajar halva)* and rice pudding with cardamom *(kheer)*, are popular.

MEAT AND MEAT ALTERNATIVES
There are fewer vegetarians in the north than in the south, and the region has been influenced by Muslim cuisine. Lamb and chicken are the most popular meats, and eggs are eaten often. Both freshwater and saltwater fish (including "Bombay duck," a strongly flavored dried fish) are accepted in coastal areas, as is seafood, such as clams, crabs, and shrimp.

Legumes (or pulses), called *dals*, especially after being hulled and split, are the common protein food in the south. Beans, lentils, and peas of many varieties — such as kidney and mung beans, chickpeas, and green peas — are found in main dishes, side dishes, breads, and desserts.

FRUITS AND VEGETABLES
Numerous fruits familiar to Westerners are eaten in India, including apples, coconuts, grapes and raisins, melons, peaches, pears, pineapples, oranges, strawberries, tangerines and many varieties of banana. Many other fruits, including mangoes, jackfruit, persimmons, pomegranate, and star fruit, are used as well.

More than two hundred vegetables are used in Indian cooking. Among them are okra; onions; squashes; the familiar brassicas — Brussels sprouts, cabbage, and cauliflower; the nightshades — eggplant, white potatoes, and tomatoes; greens such as mustard, turnip, beet, and spinach leaves; and root vegetables, including sweet potatoes, yams, beets, and turnips. Some more unusual vegetables, such as cassava and lotus root, are also used in Indian recipes.

BREADS AND GRAINS
Rice is the predominant grain throughout India, although it is eaten more in the south than in the north. Flavorful basmati rice is a favorite variety, although nearly a thousand different types of rice, classified by color, texture, and where and how long they were grown, are available. As an Indian girl grows up, she is initiated into the art of cooking rice. By the time she becomes a woman, she is expected to know at least 15 different ways to prepare rice.

Wheat grows well in the north, and flat, or unleavened, breads *(roti)* of whole wheat flour are popular. Crisp flat breads made from chickpea or lentil flour are also consumed, especially in the south.

OTHER INGREDIENTS
Ghee (pure, clarified butter) is the most popular fat, although it is usually too expensive for everyday cooking. Vegetable shortening is often used instead and is also called ghee (the butter type is usually referred to as *usli ghee*). Other

vegetable oils, such as those pressed from coconut meat, mustard seeds, and sesame seeds, are common as well. Nuts and seeds are added to many Indian dishes. Almonds, cashews, peanuts, walnuts, betel nuts, and sunflower seeds are among the most popular.

India is a major producer of tea, and this beverage is consumed throughout the country. Tea is often brewed in boiled milk, and is usually served with milk and sugar, rarely with lemon. Tea made from various spices provides variety. In the south where it is grown, coffee is also a popular beverage. Diluted yogurt (*lassi*) and fruit juices are other common beverages. Alcoholic beverages such as beer, rice wine, and fermented fruit juices are available, but are often avoided by devout Hindus and Muslims.

Seasonings

Indian cooking is known for its distinctive use of herbs and spices. However, not all Indian dishes are hot and spicy. Herbs and spices give foods their desired color, texture, and aroma, as well as their flavor. Many different spice blends are used in India. Curry powder, known as *garam masala* in India, is not a single spice, but a combination of spices, usually ground and mixed specifically for a single dish. Curry also refers to the method of stir-frying fresh vegetables with spices, common in southern India. Most curry powders contain coriander, cumin, fenugreek, turmeric, black and cayenne pepper, cloves, and mustard seed, as well as other spices.

Other herbs and spices used in Indian cooking include *ajwain* (carom or lovage seeds), *asafetida* (a pungent dried resin), cinnamon, coconut, fresh coriander, garlic, mint, parsley, saffron, and tamarind, which produces a sour taste. Both fresh and dried chili peppers also flavor many foods. As a general rule, aromatic seasoning is preferred in the north, and hot and spicy flavors predominate in the south.

Preparation

In the cool climate of northern India, fruits, vegetables, and herbs must be preserved for use during seasons when they are not available fresh. Fruits and vegetables are typically pickled or dried. Dried seasonings are mixed together to make *masalas* (including garam masala) — powders or pastes that are used to flavor aromatic dishes.

Braising, frying, steaming, and cooking in clay ovens are the favorite cooking methods in the northern regions. Braising, called *korma*, involves slowly simmering the choicest cuts of meat in a heavy pan using a small amount of marinade thickened with yogurt and nuts. Steaming, or *dum*, is done in a sealed pot with a generous amount of butter or other fat. The dum process is used for rice pilafs and for layered meat and rice casseroles called *biryani*.

A large clay oven called a *tandoor* is used to cook various meats on skewers and to bake whole wheat breads. Chunks of meat *(kebobs)* and meatballs *(kofta)* are broiled on skewers or fried. These are popular snacks. Breads, which are eaten daily, can be cooked in a tandoor or on a griddle, with or without oil. In addition, they are used to wrap spiced mixtures of vegetables and/or meats *(parothas* and *samosas)*. The finished packages are then fried or deep-fried.

In the southern region of India, fresh fruits and vegetables are used more commonly. Both pickles and masalas are made daily, and feature fresh ingredients. Chutney, a condiment that contains raw or cooked fruit (or a vegetable) in a spicy vinegar mixture, is very popular. Vegetables and fruits that flourish in the tropical climate of the south, such as jackfruit, bananas, and yams, are used extensively in curries and similar dishes. Frying and steaming are the most common methods of food preparation, the latter used for the ubiquitous rice. Other grains such as semolina and farina are cooked as a cereal known as *uppama*, which may contain vegetables. Dals (legumes) are used in a variety of ways and accompany nearly every meal, either as a spicy purée known as *sambar* or as thin, crisply fried *pappadums*. Fermented lentil flour is used for *idli*, which are steamed cakes, and for the spicy pancakes known as *dosas*.

Meal Patterns

Meal patterns in India, though not consistent across classes and regions, vary less than the foods themselves. A rich tea or coffee made with milk and sugar is enjoyed by early risers. Breakfast is usually eaten between nine and eleven and consists of rice or bread, a pickled fruit or vegetable, and a sambar, or lentil stew. These may be leftovers from the previous evening meal. At four or five in the afternoon, similar foods or sweet or spicy snack foods are eaten with coffee or tea. The evening meal is the main meal of the day and is eaten between seven and nine.

Texture, color, and balance of seasoning are very important in Indian meals. A typical dinner menu would include at least one rice dish; a main vegetable, legume, or meat dish; a vegetable or legume side dish; baked or fried bread; a fruit or pickled vegetable; and a yogurt *raita* or *pachadi* (yogurt with vegetables and spices). Sometimes dessert—usually fruit—is served. However, courses are not presented sequentially in traditional Indian meals—they are all placed on the table at once. People are then free to combine tastes and textures in any manner they please and may experiment with various combinations. After a meal, a tray with herbs; spices such as aniseed, cardamom, and fennel; and nuts (usually betel nuts) is passed. The ingredients are rolled into betel leaves *(paan)* and chewed to freshen breath and aid digestion.

Snacking is very popular in India. In cities and large towns, snacks are sold in numerous small shops and by street vendors. In villages, they are prepared at home. Snacks are considered different from meals unless traditional staples are prepared and served in a traditional manner, such as bread in the north and boiled rice in the south. Spicy snacks often consist of deep-fried, batter-coated vegetables, pancakes with or without filling, or fried seasoned dough made from lentils or wheat. These are served with chutneys and may be used as appetizers before large meals or eaten for breakfast or with afternoon tea. Sweet snacks are often milk-based, though nuts, coconut, sesame seeds, and lentil flour are also used. Since the ingredients are often costly in India and the sweets require elaborate preparation, they symbolize prosperity and are eaten particularly on special occasions, such as when a guest is entertained, and on feast days. When they are eaten with meals, sweets are served before or during, rather than after, the meal. They can also be eaten as an afternoon snack with tea.

Religion dictates many aspects of meal patterns, including fasting. Which and how many foods must be omitted is determined by the rules of each sect and, of course, by how devout a person is; fast days may include personal events (such as the anniversary of the death of one's father or mother) as well as religious occasions. Religious tradition also provides for holiday feasting, which often engages the entire community.

M E N U

Vegetarian Dinner

Samosas
(vegetable-stuffed turnovers)
Garam Masala
(spice mixture)
Onion Relish
Fresh Coriander Chutney
Ekoori
(spicy scrambled eggs)
Fried Okra
Rice with Dals

Serving suggestion: Offer fruit
juice or coffee.

M E N U

Indian Dinner

Pakoras
(chickpea fritters)
Tandoori Chicken
Puri
(fried whole wheat flat bread)
Raita
(yogurt with tomato and cucumber)

Serving suggestions: Accompany
meal with steamed rice (basmati,
if available), mango chutney, and
fruit juice or tea. Serve assorted
fruit for dessert (such as
bananas, litchis, loquats, mangos,
melon, or tangerines).

Vegetarian Dinner

◆ Samosas (Vegetable-Stuffed Turnovers)

DEEP-FAT FRY:
350°F
YIELD: 50 portions
PORTION: 1

5 lb. potatoes, boiled, peeled, and diced
¾ c. vegetable oil
1 lb. onions, chopped (about 3)
1 lb. peas, fresh or frozen
3 T. ginger root, grated
3 hot green chili peppers, chopped finely
½ c. fresh coriander, chopped

½ c. water
4 tsp. salt
3 tsp. coriander seeds
3 tsp. garam masala (recipe follows)
3 tsp. cumin seed, roasted and ground
¾ tsp. cayenne
6 T. lemon juice
50 egg roll wrappers

1. Heat oil and sauté onions until golden. Add peas, ginger, chili peppers, fresh coriander, and water. Cover and simmer until cooked. (Add more water if needed.)
2. Add potatoes, salt, coriander seeds, garam masala, cumin, cayenne, and lemon juice. Stir and cook over low heat for 4 to 5 minutes. Adjust seasonings to taste. Let mixture cool.
3. Cut wrapper in half diagonally. Pick one half up to form a cone. Glue edges together with water. Fill with approximately 2½ tablespoons or a heaping no. 30 scoop of potato mixture. Close top of cone by pressing edges together with water. Seams should be ¼ inch wide and they may be fluted.
4. Deep-fat fry until golden and crisp. The samosas may be served warm or at room temperature.

CALORIES: 161
CHOLESTEROL: <1 mg
VITAMIN A: 86 IU

CARBOHYDRATE: 22 mg
CALCIUM: 18 mg
VITAMIN C: 14 mg

PROTEIN: 3 g
SODIUM: 256 mg

FAT: 13 g
IRON: 1 mg

◆ Garam Masala (Spice Mixture)

YIELD:
approximately
1 c.

5 T. cardamom seeds
5 2-inch cinnamon sticks
5 tsp. black cumin seeds (regular cumin seeds can be substituted)

5 tsp. cloves, whole
5 tsp. black peppercorns
1 nutmeg, whole

1. Place all ingredients in a grinder or food processor. Grind until the mixture becomes a fine powder.
2. If tightly sealed, this masala may be stored for several months.

♦ *Onion Relish*

YIELD: 50 portions
PORTION:
  approximately
  2 T.

3¼ lb. onions
2 T. salt
6 oz. lemon juice

1 T. paprika
1½ tsp. cayenne

Use a slicer to cut onions crosswise into paper-thin rings. Combine with remaining ingredients. Let mixture stand for 30 minutes before serving.

CALORIES: 10	CARBOHYDRATE: 3 g	PROTEIN: <1 g	FAT: <1 g
CHOLESTEROL: 0 mg	CALCIUM: 11 mg	SODIUM: 267 mg	IRON: <1 mg
VITAMIN A: 118 IU	VITAMIN C: 5 mg		

♦ *Fresh Coriander Chutney*

YIELD: 50 portions
PORTION:
  1 heaping T.

2 lb. fresh coriander
4 oz. green chili peppers (canned),
  diced

1 c. lemon juice
4 tsp. salt
5 tsp. pepper or to taste

Combine all ingredients. Blend into a smooth paste using a food processor or blender. Store in a glass or other nonmetallic bowl.

CALORIES: 8	CARBOHYDRATE: 2 g	PROTEIN: 0.9 g	FAT: <1 g
CHOLESTEROL: 0 mg	CALCIUM: (26 mg)	SODIUM: (179 mg)	IRON: (1.2 mg)
VITAMIN A: (958 IU)	VITAMIN C: (19 mg)		

♦ *Ekoori (Spicy Scrambled Eggs)*

YIELD: 50 portions
PORTION: 3 oz.

½ lb. unsalted butter (or 1 c.
  vegetable oil)
½ lb. onions, chopped
5 tsp. ginger root, grated
½ c. fresh coriander, chopped
1¼ tsp. turmeric

5 tsp. cumin
½ tsp. cayenne or to taste
2½ lb. tomatoes, peeled, seeded,
  and chopped
6 dozen eggs, beaten
salt and pepper, to taste

1. Melt butter and sauté onions until soft. Add ginger, fresh coriander, turmeric, cumin, cayenne, and tomatoes. Cook for 5 minutes.
2. Add eggs. Stir gently until they begin to set. Cook to preferred consistency. Season with salt and pepper.

CALORIES: 153	CARBOHYDRATE: 2 g	PROTEIN: 9 g	FAT: 17 g
CHOLESTEROL: 389 mg	CALCIUM: 48 mg	SODIUM: 87 mg	IRON: 2 mg
VITAMIN A: 700 IU	VITAMIN C: 6 mg		

♦ Fried Okra

FRY: 4–5 minutes
DEEP-FAT FRYER:
  350°F
YIELD: 50 portions
PORTION: 3 oz.

12 lb. okra (fresh or frozen)
salt and pepper, to taste
1 tsp. cayenne or to taste

2 T. garam masala (page 108)
  or to taste

Wash okra and pat dry. Slice in rounds ⅛ inch thick. Deep-fat fry until the okra turns crisp and slightly brown. Drain and season to taste.

CALORIES: 113
CHOLESTEROL: 0 mg
VITAMIN A: 548 IU

CARBOHYDRATE: 7 g
CALCIUM: 103 mg
VITAMIN C: 22 mg

PROTEIN: 2 g
SODIUM: 134 mg

FAT: 17 g
IRON: 1 mg

♦ Rice with Dals

YIELD: 50 portions
PORTION: 4 oz.

1 lb. yellow split peas
3 lb. long-grain rice
12 oz. ghee (clarified unsalted
  butter or vegetable oil can be
  substituted)

5 tsp. cumin seed
5 tsp. garam masala (page 108)
2 T. salt or to taste
1 oz. fresh coriander, chopped
1 gal. chicken stock

1. Soak split peas in water and cover for 2 hours. Add rice to water and soak an additional hour. Drain.
2. Heat ghee. Add cumin and toast the seeds. Add drained rice and split peas. Sauté for 3 minutes, stirring to coat grains. Add garam masala, salt, and coriander.
3. Add chicken stock, bring to a boil, and reduce heat to low. Cook for 25 minutes. Remove from heat and let sit for another 15 minutes. (To cook in the oven, place sautéed rice and peas in a 12″ × 20″ × 4″ pan. Pour boiling chicken stock over the rice and peas. Cover with foil and bake at 350°F 30–45 minutes.)

CALORIES: 192
CHOLESTEROL: 15 mg
VITAMIN A: 223 IU

CARBOHYDRATE: 29 g
CALCIUM: 22 mg
VITAMIN C: 3 mg

PROTEIN: 6 g
SODIUM: 520 mg

FAT: 9 g
IRON: 1 mg

♦ *Pakoras (Chickpea Fritters)*

FRY: 4–5 minutes
DEEP-FAT FRYER:
  360°F
YIELD: 50 portions
PORTION: 3 fritters

5 c. chickpea flour
2½ tsp. baking soda
1½ c. cold water
2 lb. onions
5 c. (2¼ lb.) uncooked potatoes,
  peeled and finely chopped

1 c. fresh coriander, finely chopped
1½ T. ground cumin
1 T. cayenne
2 T. salt

1. Combine chickpea flour, baking soda, and water. Stir to make a smooth batter.
2. Cut onions in half lengthwise, then slice lengthwise into paper-thin slivers.
3. Add onions, potatoes, coriander, cumin, cayenne, and salt to batter. Stir well.
4. Use a no. 60 scoop and drop fritters into hot oil. Fry until golden brown. Drain. Pakoras may be served hot or at room temperature.

CALORIES: 110
CHOLESTEROL: 0 mg
VITAMIN A: 65 IU

CARBOHYDRATE: 12 g
CALCIUM: 30 mg
VITAMIN C: 7 mg

PROTEIN: 3 g
SODIUM: 272 mg

FAT: 11 g
IRON: 1 mg

♦ *Tandoori Chicken*

BAKE: 45 minutes
OVEN: Grill or
  400°F
YIELD: 50 portions
PORTION: 1 breast

15–16 lb. halved chicken breasts,
  skinned
¾ c. lemon juice
½ c. salt
2 oz. fresh ginger root
2 cloves garlic
2 T. water
2¼ tsp. coriander powder

½ tsp. ground cumin
1 tsp. cayenne or to taste
4 T. paprika
2 tsp. garam masala (page 108)
1 tsp. pepper
3 c. plain yogurt
1 lb. lemons, sliced
1 lb. onions, sliced (optional)

1. Rub chicken with lemon juice and sprinkle with salt.
2. Purée ginger root and garlic with water. Combine with spices and yogurt. Add chicken and mix well. Cover and refrigerate overnight.
3. Remove chicken from yogurt and grill for 45 minutes or until chicken is done and has a red glaze. (Chicken may be baked for 45 minutes at 400°F.) Garnish with the lemon and onions.

CALORIES: 152
CHOLESTEROL: 71 mg
VITAMIN A: 27 IU

CARBOHYDRATE: 1 g
CALCIUM: 42 mg
VITAMIN C: 1 mg

PROTEIN: 27 g
SODIUM: 600 mg

FAT: 5 g
IRON: <1 mg

Tandoori chicken with puri (fried whole wheat flat bread).

◆ *Puri (Fried Whole Wheat Flat Bread)*

FRY: 3–4 minutes
DEEP-FAT FRY:
  360°F–375°F
YIELD: 50 portions
PORTION: 1

4¼ lb. whole wheat flour
5 tsp. salt

1¾ qt. water
½ c. vegetable oil

1. Combine flour, salt, water, and oil and mix into a dough. Let dough sit for 20 minutes. Roll dough into small balls, press flat into 3- to 4-inch circles. (A tortilla press can be used.)
2. Deep-fat fry until both sides are puffed and golden brown. Adjust heat so puris puff up when placed in hot oil.

Note: Purchased pappadums can be substituted for the puri.

CALORIES: 220
CHOLESTEROL: 0 mg
VITAMIN A: <1 mg

CARBOHYDRATE: 26 g
CALCIUM: 16 mg
VITAMIN C: 0 mg

PROTEIN: 5 g
SODIUM: 221 mg

FAT: 21 g
IRON: 2 mg

Raita (Yogurt with Tomato and Cucumber)

YIELD: 50 portions
PORTION: 4 oz.

5 lb. cucumbers, seeded and cubed
2 lb. onions, chopped
2½ T. salt
5 lb. tomatoes, cubed

¾ c. fresh coriander, chopped
2 qt. plain yogurt
3 T. cumin seed, roasted

1. Combine cucumbers, onions, and salt. Let sit for 15 minutes, then squeeze out excess moisture.
2. Add tomatoes and coriander.
3. Combine yogurt and cumin and pour over vegetables. Adjust seasoning to taste and chill before serving.

CALORIES: 45
CHOLESTEROL: 2 mg
VITAMIN A: 406 IU

CARBOHYDRATE: 8 g
CALCIUM: 92 mg
VITAMIN C: 18 mg

PROTEIN: 3 g
SODIUM: 365 mg

FAT: 1 g
IRON: 1 mg

*Zuppa di pesce, a
southern-style
Italian fish and
seafood stew.*

Italians have contributed many Mediterranean and Asian foods to the rest of the Western world. Artichokes, asparagus, grapes, ice cream, pasta, rice, and marzipan (sweetened almond paste) are a few examples.

The Romans created the foundations for Italian cuisine, drawing inspiration from the Middle East and Greece. Arab invaders brought sugar cane. Rice was introduced to Italy in the 12th century, and it became especially popular in the north. In the 13th century, pasta was introduced, and became a mainstay of the diet by the late 15th century. Tomatoes were a late addition, brought from the New World in the mid-16th century. Other New World foods adopted by the Italians included corn, potatoes, chili and sweet peppers, kidney and related beans, and turkey.

Because Italy did not become a unified nation until relatively recently, Italian cuisine remains a collection of regional specialties. The broadest culinary division is between the country's fertile north and its arid south. The Italian cuisine best known outside of Italy is the southern style because the majority of emigrants have been from that part of the country. Southern cooking is known for its use of olive oil, tomatoes, and garlic in pizza and stuffed pastas, while northern cuisine uses more butter and cream, especially in delicate sauces served over pasta.

Northern Italian cooking is strongly influenced by the city of Bologna and the surrounding region. *Mortadella*, the forerunner of American bologna, was first made here, and Parmesan cheese was originally made in nearby Parma. The cuisine of this area is known for delicate pasta, herbed vinegars, and processed pork products such as the uncooked, smoked ham called *prosciutto*.

Northeastern Italy borders on Austria and Yugoslavia and its cuisine is dominated by the city of Venice. Fish and seafood, such as *scampi* (a type of shrimp), are characteristic ingredients in Venetian cuisine. Rice dishes are also very popular. Along the Austrian border, sausages, sauerkraut, and strudel are featured. Lombardy, in the north central part of Italy, borders on Switzerland. The cuisine here features lavish use of butter and slow-cooking techniques. Regional dishes include *risotto*, a creamy rice dish; *polenta*, cooked cornmeal topped with cheese or sauce; *panettone* (a fruit-studded cake); and a spicy mixture of candied fruits in mustard sauce known as *mostarda*.

The Piedmont area in the northwest borders on France and is known for its truffles, especially white ones; its cheeses, which include Fontina; and its game, which includes wild goat and boar. Wine, brandy, and vermouth are also produced in this region. Many herbs are grown near the coast and are used extensively in dishes and sauces.

Excellent produce is grown in central Italy (deep-fried baby artichokes are a specialty); Chianti wine and *sambucca* (anise liqueur) are produced. *Fettucine Alfredo* is one of the region's best-known dishes. Invented in a Roman restaurant, it consists of egg noodles tossed with butter, cream, and freshly grated Parmesan cheese. Florence is famed for dishes made with spinach.

Naples dominates the cuisine of southern Italy. The food is heartier here than in the north. Less meat is eaten, but chickens and legumes are readily available. Oysters are cultivated, and swordfish, eel, sardines, and anchovies are common. Eggplants, artichokes, tomatoes, and sweet peppers are used. Ricotta, provolone, and mozzarella cheeses are popular. Bread and pasta are used extensively and pizza is frequently eaten. This region is also known for its desserts, especially ice cream and flavored ices know as *gelati*.

On the island of Sicily, citrus fruits, wheat, grapes, olives, and a variety of vegetables are grown. Sicily is known for its bread and pastries. Pasta is used commonly, and little meat is eaten, mostly sausage. Tuna, sardines, and dried salt cod are eaten often. Northwest of Sicily, on the island of Sardinia, sheep and goats are raised and eaten; beef and cheese are also used. Game is available, and as in Sicily, fish is very popular. Pasta and bread are also widely used.

Ingredients

MILK AND MILK PRODUCTS

Cows, sheep, goats, and water buffalo are kept as milk-producing animals in various regions. Milk is not usually consumed as a beverage, but is used in many dishes, particularly desserts. Cream is especially popular in northern Italy. About half of the milk that is produced is made into cheese, which comes in numerous forms: mild Fontina; blue-veined Gorgonzola; mozzarella (a fresh curd cheese originally made with buffalo milk); provolone (sweet to sharp, depending on aging; may be smoked); hard, tangy Parmesan and Romano; and ricotta (creamy, fresh cheese) are but a few.

MEAT AND MEAT ALTERNATIVES

Veal and pork are the most commonly eaten meats; pork is often cured in hams and sausages (including the well-known salami). Pork variety cuts (such as feet and knuckles) are also popular, especially in the north. Beef and lamb are available regionally, while chicken is a favorite throughout the country. Turkey is also eaten, and eggs are used in many dishes.

Fish and shellfish are prevalent, particularly in coastal regions. Common varieties include calamari (squid), octopus, clams, mussels, sole, cod (especially dried), anchovies, sardines, tuna, swordfish, scampi, and langustino (spiny rock lobster).

Legumes are an important source of protein, especially in the south. Cannellini (white beans), fava beans, chickpeas, and green peas are some of the types used.

FRUITS AND VEGETABLES

Fruit, both fresh and candied, is especially popular for dessert. Grapes, cherries, dates, figs, melons, and strawberries are a few native examples. A wide variety of vegetables are grown and eaten in Italy. While tomatoes are probably most often associated with Italian cuisine, these were not widely used until about 1700. Other typical Italian vegetables include artichokes, asparagus, broccoli, cabbage, cauliflower, eggplant, cardoons (an edible thistle), fennel, olives, peas, sweet peppers, zucchini, green beans, potatoes, and spinach and other greens. Wild mushrooms (*porcini* are a favorite) and truffles are collected.

BREADS AND CEREALS

Corn, rice, and wheat are all grains common in Italy. Cornmeal is used to make the northern specialty known as polenta. Rice is an ingredient in many dishes, especially in the north. Wheat is used for making bread, which is an important part of the diet, and the granules of hard durum wheat, called *semolina*, are processed into pasta. Pasta, the mainstay of Italian cuisine, comes in dozens of shapes and flavors to provide variety, but only two basic doughs are used: with and without egg. The egg dough is eaten more commonly in the north, while the eggless pasta is eaten more commonly in the south. There are more than 500 types of pasta, including *fettucine* (like spaghetti), *tagliatelle* (thinner than fettucine), *trenette* (very thin fettucine), ravioli, *agnolotti* (small ravioli), *tortellini* (little filled rings), *lasagna* (flat wide noodles), *gnocchi* (dumplings), *spaghettini* (thinner than spaghetti), *manicotti* (tubes to be filled), *rigatoni* (smaller tubes), *farfalle* (butterflies), *conchiglie* (shells), and *fusilli* or *vermicelli* (very thin strands in coils).

OTHER INGREDIENTS

Butter is favored in northern regions, while olive oil is preferred in the south. But both can be found in dishes throughout the country. Pork fat is commonly used in Bologna.

Nuts are added to many dishes. Almonds, filberts (hazelnuts), chestnuts, pignoli (pine nuts), and walnuts are common.

Italians typically drink wine with meals. Many wines are produced in Italy, including table wines, most notably chianti; aperitif wines, such as Italian vermouth; and marsala, a sweet wine used mostly in cooking. Fruit and/or nut-flavored syrup sodas (such as *orzata*) are also popular. Coffee is the most popular hot beverage, especially strong, dark espresso. *Caffé latte* or *cappuccino* is espresso mixed with steamed milk. Espresso flavored with brandy, liqueur, or spices is also popular.

Seasonings

Garlic, the strong seasoning most often associated with Italian cooking, is used liberally in the south. But in the north, seasoning is more subtle. Herbs, including parsley, oregano, and basil, frequently flavor the dishes. These herbs are used fresh in green sauces, such as *pesto* (herbs and nuts pulverized with olive oil and Parmesan). Throughout the country, fennel seeds, juniper berries, borage, coriander, saffron, and shallots are some of the more distinctive seasonings. Lemon juice, along with many other familiar herbs and spices including marjoram, thyme, rosemary, tarragon, mint, cloves, and onions, are also used.

Preparation

Soups, stews, and mixed dishes are common; *minestrone* (vegetable and pasta soup) and *zuppa di pesce* (fish stew) are classic examples. Many dishes feature bread, dumplings, pasta, polenta, or rice flavored with meats, vegetables, or sauces. Bread is used for pizza, which can have either a white sauce or the well-known tomato sauce, and for *calzone*, in which the dough is folded over the toppings to make something like a turnover. Dumplings and pasta are often added to soup. Pasta can be served with a sauce, as in *vermicelli alle vongole* (pasta with clam sauce) or *spaghetti alla carbonara* (pasta with salt pork, eggs, and Parmesan). Sauces are an important part of the cuisine. The best known of these include tomato sauce, pesto, cream sauces, and *ragú*, a sauce of finely chopped meat, onions, carrots, celery, butter, and tomatoes. Cream sauces are preferred in the north, while tomato sauces are more prevalent in the south. Many types of pasta, such as ravioli and manicotti, are filled with ground meat, cheese, or vegetables. Meat and cheese are also used to stuff vegetables. Stuffed pasta may be served with or without sauce.

Fish is usually steamed, gently sautéed, or grilled. Fennel stalks are sometimes added to charcoal during grilling to give fish a unique flavor. Meats are commonly included in sauces or casseroles. When they form the basis of an entrée, they are usually fried or simmered. Examples include *osso buco* (veal shanks in wine) and the mixed boiled meats served with parsley sauce, *bollito misto*. Vegetables are picked young and cooked gently, sautéed, boiled, or both, but care is taken not to overcook them.

A traditional Italian meal of mixed boiled meats (bollito misto) served with salsa verde (a green herb sauce), and sliced polenta.

Cakes and pastries are popular. The best-known pastry is undoubtedly *cannoli*—fried pastry tubes filled with sweetened ricotta and cream flavored with nuts, citron, and chocolate. Cakes can be elaborate, using liqueur flavorings, cheese, marzipan, candied fruit, and nuts; *cassata* and *tiramisu* are examples. Cookies such as *amaretti* (almond macaroons) and *biscotti* (twice-baked cookies) are also popular. Many desserts are egg-based, including meringues and *zabaglione*, a custard made with eggs, sugar, and marsala.

Meal Patterns

Eating three meals a day is typical in Italy. Breakfast is light, usually just bread and jam with caffé latte, tea, or hot chocolate. The midday meal is usually the largest, and is served in courses beginning with antipasti. Antipasti are combinations of fish, meat, and/or vegetables served in small portions as appetizers. These are served on plates at the table. Next, soup or a pasta or rice dish is served. A meat or fish entrée follows, usually accompanied by a vegetable. A salad course is served after the main course. At home, fruit and cheese is served for dessert; on special occasions or in restaurants, cakes, puddings, or pastries are eaten. Finally, coffee is served, usually very sweet espresso. In a poorer family, the pasta dish would be the main course and would contain some meat or fish. Supper is generally a smaller meal, consisting of a soup or *frittata* (similar to an omelet), a salad, and cheese and fruit. Bread and wine are served with lunch and supper. Often, an aperitif is served with antipasti. When work schedules demand it, lunch is lighter and supper becomes the main meal.

M E N U
Italian Dinner I

Polenta
(cornmeal porridge)
Bollito Misto
(mixed boiled meats)
Herb-Baked Tomatoes
Biscotti
(almond cookies)

Serving suggestions: Start the meal with purchased spinach tortellini served in broth, if desired. Offer crusty Italian bread and hearty red wine with the entrée. Serve fresh fruit with the biscotti.

◆ Polenta (Cornmeal Porridge)

YIELD: 50 portions
PORTION: ½ c. or
  2″ × 4″ piece

3 gal. water
3 T. salt

4 lb. polenta or yellow cornmeal,
  finely ground

1. Bring water and salt to a boil.
2. Pour cornmeal slowly into boiling water, stirring constantly. Simmer, stirring frequently, for 20 to 30 minutes, or until thick enough to support a spoon.
3. Scoop into serving dishes or pour into two 12″ × 20″ × 2″ pans. Chill 2 hours and cut contents of each pan into 24 pieces. Reheat before serving.

CALORIES: 132   CARBOHYDRATE: 28 g   PROTEIN: 3 g   FAT: 1 g
CHOLESTEROL: 0 mg   CALCIUM: 2 mg   SODIUM: <1 mg   IRON: 2 mg
VITAMIN A: 160 IU   VITAMIN C: 0 mg

◆ Bollito Misto (Mixed Boiled Meats)

YIELD: 50 portions
PORTION: 4–6 oz.

8 lb. beef brisket
8 lb. beef tongue
1 lb. celery stalks with leaves
2½ lb. carrots
4 lb. onions
1 lb. turnips, medium
2–3 lb. plum tomatoes
2 T. salt

1 T. black peppercorns
2 T. marjoram
2 T. thyme
12 bay leaves
15 lb. chicken, cut into serving
  pieces
5–8 lb. Italian sweet or hot sausage
salsa verde (recipe follows)

1. Combine brisket, tongue, celery, carrots, onions, turnips, and tomatoes. Add enough cold water to cover.
2. Add salt and peppercorns and bring to a boil. Scoop off any froth that forms. Add herbs, reduce heat, and simmer for 1 hour.
3. Add chicken and simmer 1 hour.
4. Prick skin of sausage on all sides. Simmer in water for 2 hours.
5. Slice meats (skin tongue), chicken (reserve stock), and sausage into serving pieces. Baste with hot stock and serve with salsa verde.

CALORIES: 634   CARBOHYDRATE: 6 g   PROTEIN: 58 g   FAT: 63 g
CHOLESTEROL: 223 g   CALCIUM: 63 g   SODIUM: 865 g   IRON: 6 mg
VITAMIN A: 2682 IU   VITAMIN C: 11 mg

Salsa Verde (Green Sauce)

4 slices white bread
1 c. wine vinegar
8 c. Italian parsley, finely chopped
1 T. garlic, minced
4 egg yolks, hard boiled, cold

1 qt. olive oil
1 tsp. salt
½ tsp. pepper
2 T. capers (optional)

6. Pour vinegar over bread and soak for 20 minutes. Squeeze dry.
7. Mix parsley, garlic, and egg yolks well. Combine with bread.
8. Slowly add olive oil and beat until sauce has a creamy texture.
9. Add salt, pepper, and capers. Cover and refrigerate at least 1 hour before serving.

CALORIES: 162   CARBOHYDRATE: < 1 g   PROTEIN: < 1 g   FAT: 32 g
CHOLESTEROL: 21 mg   CALCIUM: 28 mg   SODIUM: 50 mg   IRON: < 1 mg
VITAMIN A: 841 IU   VITAMIN C: 17 mg

◆ Herb-Baked Tomatoes

BAKE: 25–35
  minutes
OVEN: 375°–400°F
YIELD: 50 portions
PORTION:
  ½ tomato

25 tomatoes, large and firm
rock salt
1½ T. garlic
8 c. fresh basil, coarsely chopped
8 c. Italian parsley, coarsely
  chopped

1 tsp. salt
½ tsp. pepper
1 c. bread crumbs
1½ c. olive oil

1. Cut tomatoes in half horizontally and remove seeds.
2. Sprinkle inside of halves with salt and let stand 20–25 minutes.
3. Combine garlic, basil, parsley, salt, and pepper.
4. Rinse tomatoes to remove salt and accumulated liquid. Wipe dry. Fill with herb mixture.
5. Top with bread crumbs and place on greased baking pan.
6. Sprinkle a teaspoon of oil over each tomato and bake until soft but not overcooked.

CALORIES: 85   CARBOHYDRATE: 5 g   PROTEIN: 2 g   FAT: 14 g
CHOLESTEROL: 0 mg   CALCIUM: 63 mg   SODIUM: 252 mg   IRON: < 1 mg
VITAMIN A: 2187 IU   VITAMIN C: 47 mg

◆ *Biscotti (Almond Cookies)*

BAKE: 35 minutes;
15 minutes
OVEN: 350°F; 325°F
YIELD: 50 portions
PORTION: 2 cookies

1 lb., 14 oz. flour
2½ lb. sugar
6 eggs
4 egg yolks
2 tsp. baking powder

½ tsp. salt
2 tsp. vanilla flavoring
1 lb., 5 oz. blanched almonds,
toasted
2 eggs, beaten

1. Pour flour in bowl and make well in center. Add sugar, eggs, baking powder, salt, and vanilla and gradually mix until smooth.
2. Add almonds. Knead 4–5 minutes. Dough should be stiff. Add flour if necessary.
3. Divide dough into eight parts. Roll each piece on a floured board into a log 2 to 2½ inches wide. Place on a greased and floured cookie sheet.
4. Brush tops of dough with egg. Bake in 350°F oven for 35 minutes. Remove; reduce oven temperature to 325°F. Cut dough diagonally into ¾- to 1-inch slices. Place cut side of cookie on sheet. Return to oven for another 15 minutes and bake until lightly browned.

CALORIES: 222
CHOLESTEROL: 63 mg
VITAMIN A: 67 IU

CARBOHYDRATE: 39 g
CALCIUM: 34 mg
VITAMIN C: 0 mg

PROTEIN: 5 g
SODIUM: 43 mg

FAT: 11 g
IRON: 1 mg

◆   ◆

M E N U
Italian Dinner II

Antipasti
Finocchio all'Olio
(fennel salad)

Frittata di Carciofi
(artichoke omelet)

Zuppa di Pesce
(fish and seafood stew)

Torta di Ricotta
(ricotta cheese tart)

Serving suggestions: Other antipasti, such as marinated vegetables or prosciutto, may be provided. Serve stew with a green salad and crusty Italian bread; offer white wine, fruit juice, or coffee.

◆   ◆

Italian Dinner II

◆ *Finocchio all'Olio (Fennel Salad)*

YIELD: 50 portions
PORTION: ⅓ c.

20 lb. fennel bulbs, chilled*
2 c. olive oil
1 T. salt or to taste

½ T. pepper or to taste
3 T. wine vinegar

1. Cut off stalks of fennel, and remove tougher outer layers if necessary. Cut into quarters and discard core. Slice into thin wedges. Wash in cold water; drain thoroughly.
2. Add olive oil, salt, and pepper. Toss gently. Add vinegar and toss again.

CALORIES: (100)
CHOLESTEROL: 0
VITAMIN A:

CARBOHYDRATE: (10 g)
CALCIUM:
VITAMIN C:

PROTEIN: 1 g
SODIUM: 130 mg

FAT: 7 g
IRON:

*Nutritional composition of fennel is unknown; energy nutrient analysis was based on celery.

◆ *Frittata di Carciofi (Artichoke Omelet)*

BAKE: 35–45
  minutes
OVEN: 325°F
YIELD: 48 portions
PORTION: one
  2″ × 2½″ piece

6 lb. artichoke hearts, quartered
  (frozen or canned)
½ c. lemon juice
1½ c. olive oil

56 eggs, beaten
3 T. salt or to taste
3 oz. Parmesan cheese, grated

1. Toss thawed or drained artichoke hearts in lemon juice. Sauté in oil until tender.
2. Combine artichokes, eggs, salt, and Parmesan. Pour into 2 greased 12″ × 20″ × 2″ baking pans. Cook until firm and golden brown.

CALORIES: 181
CHOLESTEROL: 296 mg
VITAMIN A: 370 IU

CARBOHYDRATE: 6 g
CALCIUM: 71 mg
VITAMIN C: 4 mg

PROTEIN: 9 g
SODIUM: 300 mg

FAT: 23 g
IRON: 2 mg

♦ Zuppa di Pesce (Fish and Seafood Stew)

BAKE: 45 minutes
OVEN: 350°F
YIELD: 50 portions
PORTION: 1 c.

10 lb. mixed white fish fillets
(cod, shark, flounder, etc.)
2 lb. shrimp, unshelled
4 lb. mussels
1 lb. onions, cut into fine slivers
1 oz. parsley, chopped
1 qt. black or green olives,
Italian or Greek

1 T. garlic, minced
1 T. black peppercorns
1 tsp. Tabasco sauce (optional)
2 bay leaves
2 c. olive oil
2 oz. salt
1½ qt. dry white wine
(fish stock may be substituted)

1. Clean fish, cut into 2- to 3-inch chunks, and put in bottom of casserole pan.
2. Layer shrimp on top of fish.
3. Scrub and debeard mussels, and put on top of all other fish.
4. Sprinkle onions, parsley, olives, garlic, peppercorns, and Tabasco over fish.
5. Insert bay leaves among fish.
6. Pour olive oil over fish to coat. Sprinkle with salt and add wine.
7. Cover tightly and bake.

CALORIES: 251   CARBOHYDRATE: 2 g   PROTEIN: 30 g   FAT: 20 g
CHOLESTEROL: 157 mg CALCIUM: 148 mg   SODIUM: 725 mg   IRON: 4 mg
VITAMIN A: 211 IU   VITAMIN C: 3 mg

♦ Torta di Ricotta (Ricotta Cheese Tart)

BAKE: 45–50
minutes
OVEN: 350°F
YIELD: 48 portions
PORTION: ⅛ pie

1 lb. raisins, golden
1¼ c. marsala wine (orange juice
may be substituted)
6 lb. ricotta cheese
1½ lb. sugar
7 T. flour
24 egg yolks
1½ c. cream

1½ c. sour cream
2 tsp. cinnamon
5 tsp. vanilla flavoring
24 egg whites
1 tsp. salt
6 9½" unbaked pastry shells
(tart pastry, page 87)*

1. Prepare tart pastry as directed except roll dough to fit six 9½-inch pie plates; bake 25–30 minutes until light brown.
2. Soak raisins in wine for 15 minutes. Drain and reserve wine.
3. Press ricotta through sieve. Add sugar and flour and beat until smooth and light. Blend in egg yolks, cream, sour cream, wine, cinnamon, and vanilla. Add raisins.
4. Beat the egg whites and salt until stiff. Fold gently into the ricotta mixture. Fill pastry shells and bake until golden. Turn off the oven and let stand with oven door open for 30 minutes. Chill well before serving.

CALORIES: 420   CARBOHYDRATE: 41 g   PROTEIN: 12 g   FAT: 23 g
CHOLESTEROL: 185 mg CALCIUM: 195 mg   SODIUM: 355 mg   IRON: 2 mg
VITAMIN A: 820 IU   VITAMIN C: <1 mg

*Purchased pastry shells may be substituted.

·11· COOKING FROM
·Japan·

Japanese sushi rolls
(kappa maki and
California roll)
served with pickled
ginger and wasabi
(green horseradish).

Japanese food is known both for its simplicity and its aesthetic appeal. Each meal is a demonstration of how artfully the cook can present Nature's wares to the diner. In Japan a complex system of rules and etiquette is applied to the preparation, serving, and eating of food. A great deal of attention is paid to the combination of food textures and shapes, and the Japanese emphasis on harmony with nature is reflected in both the selection of ingredients that are in season, and the use of garnishes in shapes and colors that match the season. The choice of trays, bowls, and dishes in which food is served is also governed by the seasons.

Throughout Japan's history, food has often been scarce, and Japanese cooking developed around these shortages. Rice has long been a staple in the diet, supplemented by fish, seafood, and seaweed, which, because of Japan's long coastline, have always been abundant. Historically, meat has been scarce due to lack of grazing land. Fruits and vegetables are important, but preference is given to growing rice on the limited amount of plowable land.

Japanese cuisine has been greatly influenced by that of China. Contact with China in the 7th and 8th centuries brought soybeans and tea to Japan, two ingredients that have assumed major importance in the diet. Sugar was also introduced by the Chinese at this time, but it was not generally used except as a medicine until the mid-19th century. Today, sugar is included as an ingredient in many savory dishes, but the Japanese have very few sweets that resemble sweets eaten in the West.

In the 16th century, the Portuguese landed in Japan, and soon afterward Catholic missionaries began to arrive. The Japanese adopted very little of the Portuguese cuisine, but they did try to provide batter-fried shrimp on the religious fast days when the Portuguese were not allowed to eat meat. The *tempura* that resulted has a more delicate batter and is fried in a lighter oil than the Portuguese version. It is one of the Japanese foods best known by foreigners today. During the rule of the Shoguns from the 1600s to the 1800s, Europeans were evicted, and Japan was isolated from the Western world. The character of Japanese cuisine developed during this time without imported ingredients or foreign influence. After World War II, Western foods, especially American dishes, were incorporated into Japanese cuisine and are very popular today.

Ingredients

MILK AND MILK PRODUCTS
Almost no milk foods are used in the traditional cooking of Japan.

MEAT AND MEAT ALTERNATIVES
Fish and seafood are available in a multitude of varieties. Tuna, swordfish, salmon, cod, sardines, oysters, clams, and shrimp are but a few of the more familiar types. Many others, including cuttlefish, shark, eel, sea urchin, and the poisonous *fugu* blowfish, are also eaten. The toxin found in certain organs of the blowfish can kill the consumer in a matter of hours, and no antidote is known. Therefore, they are prepared by specially licensed blowfish cooks in restaurants that serve nothing but this potentially deadly delicacy. Beef, pork, and horsemeat are available, but costly. Poultry is popular, including chicken, duck, goose, and small game birds. Eggs from both chicken and fish are also consumed.

Legumes, such as adzuki and soybeans, figure prominently in Japanese diets and are employed in many ways. *Tofu*, a soybean "cheese"; *miso*, a soy paste; and *shoyu*, or soy sauce, are commonly used.

FRUITS AND VEGETABLES
Several types of fruit are available, including strawberries, persimmons, apples, plums, dates, and citrus fruits such as the winter tangerines called *mikan*. Although these could be grown in hothouses or imported year round, it is important to the Japanese to eat them in their proper season. Thus, when strawberries become available in the spring, they are sold and served everywhere, but once their season has passed, they are nowhere to be found.

Distinctively Japanese vegetables include *gobo* (burdock root), *daikon* (a long, white radish), chrysanthemum leaves, and several varieties of mushrooms such as *enoki* and *shiitake*. Bean sprouts, lotus root, snow peas, and bamboo shoots, common in China, are also used in Japan. In addition, many vegetables used in other parts of the world are found, including broccoli, carrots, corn, green and red peppers, onions, peas, spinach, squash, and turnips. As with fruits, importance is placed on eating vegetables in their natural seasons. However, both fruits and vegetables may be pickled for use at other times.

Seaweed is used extensively in Japanese cooking. There are several varieties, each with its own texture, flavor, and uses. *Nori* is a thin, flat sheet of dried seaweed used as a wrapper for rice and other fillings. *Aonoriko* is a seasoning powder made from the same seaweed. *Kombu* or kelp is used in making fish stock called *dashi*, which is used in the preparation of many dishes. *Wakame* and *hijiki* are used in soups and salads.

BREADS AND CEREALS

Short-grain rice is the staple food of Japan. It is eaten three times a day, every day, in all seasons, and can be served hot or cold. There are several grades of rice available, and the best is considered to be that eaten soon after it is harvested. Steamed rice can be pounded into a dough to make the traditional New Year's cake known as *mochi*. Many types of noodles are also popular, including *somen* and *udon* (made from wheat), *soba* (made from buckwheat), *chasoba* (soba with the addition of green tea), and *harusame* or cellophane noodles (made from sweet potato starch). Chilled noodle dishes are eaten in the summer.

OTHER INGREDIENTS

Little fat is used in Japanese cooking, as most foods are cooked with water or steam rather than oil. For deep-fried foods, such as tempura and *tonkatsu*, a fried pork dish, a mixture of oils is used, usually sesame and one or more vegetable oils. Peanut, corn, olive, and cottonseed oils are commonly used.

Nuts and seeds, such as chestnuts, *ginkgo* nuts, peanuts, walnuts, poppy seeds, and sesame seeds are sometimes added to dishes, especially at the time of harvest.

When tea was first introduced, it was used primarily as a medicine; it was a beverage only for priests and aristocrats. Later, the tea ceremony, brought to Japan by Chinese Buddhists but then forgotten in China, was raised to an art form. In this ritual, a small group of friends enjoy tea, and often snacks, served gracefully in a tranquil atmosphere. The surroundings must be beautiful but simple, and the concepts of serenity, harmony with nature, and respect between people are exalted. Even apart from the tea ceremony, brewing and drinking tea are considered an art form in Japan. Today, tea is the most common beverage, usually green tea. *Mugicha* is iced tea made from roasted unhusked barley. Sake (rice wine) is popular, warmed in winter and chilled in summer. Beer and soft drinks are also consumed.

Seasonings

Japanese seasonings, unlike those in some parts of Asia, are generally mild. The Japanese feel that the essential nature of foods should not be overpowered. Ginger, garlic, seaweed, sesame seeds, mustard, chives, chili peppers, scallions, sugar, salt, and pepper are used. Sauces such as soy *(shoyu)*, sweet rice wine *(mirin)*, *teriyaki* (shoyu and mirin), vinegar, and sake flavor many foods. Bean paste *(miso)* and fish paste are added to some dishes. Pickled ginger and the hot green horseradish called *wasabi* traditionally accompany many meals.

Preparation

Japanese dishes are divided according to how they are prepared. *Yaki* indicates broiling; *teriyaki* is broiled with a marinade, and *shioyaki* means broiled after being salted. *Sukiyaki* originally meant broiled on a hoe or plow blade because the dish was made by farmers or hunters who killed wild animals and cooked the meat over an open fire in whatever utensils they had. As it is known today, sukiyaki is a combination of vegetables and meat, usually beef, simmered in seasoned broth. Foods cooked this way are known as *nimono*.

Rice is always steamed. Today, electric rice cookers are very popular, giving more reliable results than older methods. Other foods, such as the popular unsweetened egg custard known as *chawanmushi*, are also steamed, using a method called *mushimono*. Fried foods are called *agemono* and include *karaage* (fried in a small quantity of oil after being lightly coated with cornstarch) as well as tempura. There are two basic types of salad: vinegared salad *(sunomono)* and mixed foods with a thick dressing *(aemono)*. Sliced raw fish, called *sashimi*, is popular. It is often served with *sushi* (rice mixed with rice wine vinegar), formed into artistic mounds or bundles.

A combination of miso, soy sauce, vinegar, salt, the residue from sake production, and sometimes sugar is used to preserve fish, seafood, fruits and vegetables for later use. These pickles, called *tsukemono*, are eaten at almost every meal. So important are they to the Japanese diet that, before they were commercially available, the test of a bride's worthiness was her ability to make pickles.

Some foods, including sukiyaki, are cooked at the table, a procedure called *nabe*. In some nabe dishes, each diner picks up the raw ingredients in bite-size pieces and holds them in a pot of bubbling broth with chopsticks until they are cooked.

Meal Patterns

Three meals a day and a snack are typical in Japan. Breakfast usually includes rice with nori (sometimes topped with egg), soup, pickled plums, and pickled vegetables. Lunch is often rice with leftovers from the night before. Tea or soup stock is often added to the rice to make a complete meal. Another popular lunch dish is hot noodles with bits of meat and vegetables.

Three dishes are essential at dinner: soup, rice, and pickled vegetables. Except for special occasions, when so many foods are served that they are offered in courses, all dishes are served at once. Etiquette requires that a little rice be tasted; then the broiled, steamed, or deep-fried meat, poultry, fish, or seafood is eaten with the vegetables and rice. Pickled vegetables are traditionally saved for last, to be eaten with the remaining rice. Soup may be served with the meal (if so, it is consumed first, to stimulate the appetite), or it may be offered at the end of the meal. If dessert is served, it consists of fresh fruit. Green tea accompanies meals, and beer or sake may be offered at dinner.

Chopsticks are the only utensils used at the table; soups are drunk from the bowl. Spoons are permissible only for chawanmushi. Therefore, food is always cut into bite-size pieces before being served. Each dish is served in small quantities, but many dishes can be included. Many Japanese dishes are served at room temperature.

Snacks are often fresh fruit, although rice crackers and confections such as sweet bean jelly or rice cakes are also enjoyed. Sweet bean paste is the main ingredient in confections, which are eaten only at teatime, never for dessert. Picnics are also popular with the Japanese, with the food arranged in small boxes as beautifully as it is on plates or trays indoors.

Specialized restaurants that serve only one type of food are common. Extensions of the street vending tradition, these eateries include sushi bars, tempura houses, noodle shops, sukiyaki restaurants, blowfish restaurants, and tea houses.

M E N U
Japanese Dinner

Miso Udon
(noodle soup with miso)
Cucumber and Bean Sprout Salad
Tempura
(batter-fried shrimp and vegetables)
Tempura Dipping Sauce
Pickled Turnips

Serving suggestions: Serve
steamed short-grain rice, fresh
fruit for dessert, and tea.

M E N U
Japanese Appetizers

Sushi
(seasoned rice)
Kappa Maki
(cucumber sushi roll)
Pickled Ginger
California Roll
(crab and avocado sushi roll)

Serving suggestions: Serve with
green tea, beer, or rice wine.

◆ *Miso Udon (Noodle Soup with Miso)*

YIELD: 50 portions
PORTION: 1½ c.

10 lb. chicken with bone, cut into 1-inch pieces
2½ gal. water
1 lb. (16 large) dried shiitake mushrooms

20 lb. fresh udon (thick wheat flour noodles) or 10 lb. dried
3–4 c. miso (soy bean paste)
2½ lb. scallions, chopped

1. Cover chicken with water and bring to a boil. Skim, reduce heat, cover, and simmer for about 45 minutes.
2. Soak mushrooms in warm water for 30 minutes. Drain. Discard stems and cut caps into quarters. Add to chicken.
3. Cook fresh noodles in boiling water, drain, and set aside. (Follow the directions on package for dried noodles.)
4. Mix about 1 cup of chicken stock with bean paste until smooth. Stir it back into the soup. Add noodles and scallions. Simmer gently for 3 minutes and serve.

CALORIES: 270   CARBOHYDRATE: 19 g   PROTEIN: 29 g   FAT: 8 g
CHOLESTEROL: 68 mg   CALCIUM: 41 mg   SODIUM: 659 mg   IRON: 2 mg
VITAMIN A: 1223 IU   VITAMIN C: 11 mg

◆ *Cucumber and Bean Sprout Salad*

YIELD: 50 portions
PORTION: ⅓–½ c.

5 lb. fresh bean sprouts
5 lb. cucumber, peeled, seeded, and sliced
2 T. salt

¾ c. rice vinegar
¾ c. sesame oil
1½ c. soy sauce
3 oz. sesame seeds, toasted

1. Blanch bean sprouts. Drain and cool.
2. Sprinkle cucumbers with salt. Let stand 20 minutes; rinse and pat dry.
3. Combine vinegar, sesame oil, and soy sauce. Toss with bean sprouts and cucumbers. Adjust seasoning. Before serving, sprinkle with sesame seeds.

CALORIES: 72   CARBOHYDRATE: 4 g   PROTEIN: 3 g   FAT: 10 g
CHOLESTEROL: 0 mg   CALCIUM: 22 mg   SODIUM: 271 mg   IRON: <1 mg
VITAMIN A: 13 IU   VITAMIN C: 9 mg

Tempura (Batter-Fried Shrimp and Vegetables)

FRY: 1–2 minutes
DEEP-FAT FRYER:
    400°F
YIELD: 50 portions
PORTION: 3–4
    shrimp; 2 slices
    each of eggplant,
    sweet potatoes,
    carrots; 2–3
    snowpeas or
    green beans

7 lb. raw shrimp, shelled and deveined
½ lb. flour
3 lb. eggplant (Japanese), peeled, leaving a few strips of purple skin, and sliced ¼" thick
1½ lb. snow peas, fresh or frozen, thawed and patted dry
  or
1½ lb. green beans, cut 3 inches long

5 lb. sweet potatoes, peeled, sliced ¼" thick
2 lb. carrots, peeled and cut into ¼" × 3" strips
10 egg yolks
1 gal. water, ice-cold
2½ tsp. baking soda, dissolved in 1 T. cold water
4 lb. flour
1 gal. dipping sauce (see recipe)

1. Toss shrimp in flour to lightly coat.
2. Prepare batter by combining egg yolks, ice water, and baking soda. Slowly stir the flour into the egg mixture and mix well. The batter should be very thin. Adjust consistency with the addition of water or flour.
3. Dip vegetables or shrimp in batter and quickly fry until lightly golden. Drain. This dish is best when eaten immediately or when cooked to order. Serve with dipping sauce.

CALORIES: 459
CHOLESTEROL: 148 mg
VITAMIN A: 8671 IU

CARBOHYDRATE: 54 g
CALCIUM: 270 mg
VITAMIN C: 19 mg

PROTEIN: 23 g
SODIUM: 171 mg

FAT: 30 g
IRON: 5 mg

Tempura Dipping Sauce

YIELD: 1 gal.

2 c. mirin (sweet sake)
2½ c. soy sauce
½ c. lime juice

1 c. preflaked katsuobushi (dried bonito)
2½ qt. water
1 tsp. salt

1. Heat mirin until lukewarm. Turn off heat and ignite. Shake gently until flames die.
2. Add soy sauce, lime juice, katsuobushi, water, and salt. Bring to a boil over high heat, then strain through a fine sieve. Cool to room temperature and season to taste.

*Tempura with dip-
ping sauce, featur-
ing shrimp, pea
pods, and slices of
sweet potatoes, egg-
plant, and carrots.*

♦ *Pickled Turnips*

YIELD: 50
PORTION: 1–1½ oz.

5 lb. turnips with greens
⅓ c. salt

1 tsp. lemon peel (fresh), grated

1. Cut off greens; wash, dry, chop finely, and set aside.
2. Wash turnips; peel and julienne.
3. Combine turnips and greens in a bowl; mix in salt. Let stand 1 minute. Squeeze out excess liquid.
4. Mix in lemon peel. Cover and weight. (If there is no cover that fits inside of bowl or pot, a heavy plastic bag may be placed over the turnips and then filled with water to serve as a weighted cover.) Let stand for at least 1 hour at room temperature. May be refrigerated for up to one week.

CALORIES: 11   CARBOHYDRATE: 2 g   PROTEIN: <1 g   FAT: <1 g
CHOLESTEROL: 0 mg   CALCIUM: 27 mg   SODIUM: 717 mg   IRON: <1 mg
VITAMIN A: 0 IU   VITAMIN C: 14 mg

M E N U *Japanese Appetizers*

♦ *Sushi (Seasoned Rice)*

YIELD: 3 gal.

9 lb. short-grain rice
6½ qt. water
2½ c. rice vinegar

6 oz. sugar
3 T. salt

1. Wash rice and drain. Add water to rice and bring to a boil. Cover pot and steam over low heat for 20 minutes. Remove from heat and let stand, covered, for 10 to 15 minutes.
2. Heat rice vinegar, sugar, and salt, stirring until sugar is completely dissolved.
3. Slowly pour vinegar mixture over rice while folding with a large wooden spoon. Rice will cool and become shiny as it is mixed. Rice may be left covered at room temperature for several hours until ready to use.

◆ Kappa Maki (Cucumber Sushi Roll)

YIELD: 50 rolls
PORTION: two or three 1-inch rounds

3 gal. sushi (see preceding recipe)
10 cucumbers, peeled and seeded
25 standard sheets nori

2¼ c. tezu "hand vinegar" (made by mixing 2¼ c. water and 3 T. rice vinegar)
¾ c. prepared wasabi

1. Cut cucumber into ¼-inch wide strips, 7–8 inches long.
2. Cut nori in half lengthwise. Place shiny side down onto a bamboo mat or slightly damp cloth.
3. Moisten hands with tezu. Spread enough rice over ¾ of a nori sheet so that rice layer is ⅛ to ¼ inch thick. The top of the sheet should not be covered with any rice.
4. Spread a small amount of wasabi across the center of the rice. Lay the cucumber strip along the wasabi.
5. Starting at the rice covered end, roll up nori firmly, using the mat or cloth to help lift and roll. Nori edges should overlap slightly. (It should not look like a jelly roll.) Seal edges with water.
6. Using a sharp knife dipped in water, cut each roll into 1½-inch pieces. May be served with soy sauce.

CALORIES: 318   CARBOHYDRATE: 72 g   PROTEIN: 6 g   FAT: <1 g
CHOLESTEROL: 0 mg CALCIUM: 31 mg   SODIUM: 427 mg   IRON: 4 mg
VITAMIN A: 80 IU   VITAMIN C: 3 mg

Note: Nutritional information is for one roll.

◆ Pickled Ginger

YIELD: 50 portions
PORTION: 2 T.

1½ lb. ginger root, peeled
2 T. salt
3 c. rice vinegar

1 c. water
½ c. sugar

1. Sprinkle ginger with salt and let stand overnight. Drain.
2. Combine vinegar, water, and sugar, stirring until sugar dissolves. Pour over ginger. Refrigerate for 7 days. Ginger will become pink. May be stored for several months if refrigerated.
3. Cut into paper-thin slices before serving.

CALORIES: 19   CARBOHYDRATE: 5 g   PROTEIN: 0.2 g   FAT: 0.1 g
CHOLESTEROL: 0 mg CALCIUM: 4 mg   SODIUM: 257 mg   IRON: <1 mg
VITAMIN A: 0 IU   VITAMIN C: <1 g

♦ *California Roll (Crab and Avocado Sushi Roll)*

YIELD: 50
PORTION: two or three 1-inch rounds

3 gal. sushi (see recipe)
5–6 lb. avocados
4 lb. crabmeat, cooked
1 lb. scallions, green part only, chopped

25 standard sheets nori
2¼ c. tezu "hand vinegar" (made by mixing 2¼ c. water and 3 T. rice vinegar)
¾ c. wasabi, prepared

1. Cut nori in half lengthwise. Place shiny side down onto a bamboo mat or slightly damp cloth.
2. Moisten hands with tezu. Spread enough rice over ¾ of a nori sheet so that rice layer is ⅛ to ¼ inch thick. The top of the sheet should not be covered with any rice.
3. Spread a small amount of wasabi across the center of the rice. Lay the avocado and crabmeat along the wasabi. Sprinkle with scallions.
4. Starting at the rice-covered end, roll up nori firmly, using the mat or cloth to help lift and roll. Nori edges should overlap slightly. (It should not look like a jelly roll.) Seal edges with water.
5. Using a sharp knife dipped in water, cut each roll into 1½-inch pieces. May be served with soy sauce.

CALORIES: 418
CHOLESTEROL: 21 mg
VITAMIN A: 767 IU

CARBOHYDRATE: 74 g
CALCIUM: 52 mg
VITAMIN C: 8 mg

PROTEIN: 13 g
SODIUM: 540 mg

FAT: 8 g
IRON: 5 mg

Note: Nutritional information is for one roll.

·*12*· C O O K I N G F R O M
·*Korea*·

Sanchek (fried beef, pork, cabbage, and scallion skewers) and kimchi (spicy pickled cabbage), specialties of Korea.

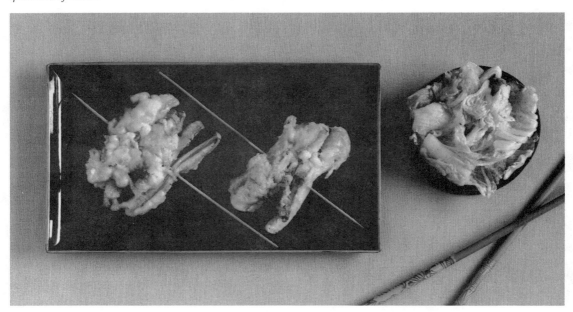

*N*orth and South Korea lie between China and Japan, bordered by the Sea of Japan, the East China Sea, and the Yellow Sea. Korea shares elements of both Japanese and Chinese cuisines and cultures. The Chinese, who first settled Korea in the second century B.C., brought Buddhism and Confucianism to the country. These remain the two major religions in Korea, although there are also many Christians in South Korea. The Japanese made repeated attempts to gain control over the country, and succeeded in ruling Korea from 1910 until 1945. Missionaries from the United States, Great Britain, and other countries have also brought their influences to bear on the country. Despite these pressures, however, Korean cooking has retained a distinct character, and imitates neither Japanese nor Chinese cuisine.

As in other Asian countries, rice is the mainstay of the diet. Soybean products and noodles are used extensively. Many types of fish and shellfish are eaten. Most of the vegetables that grow in China and Japan are also available in Korea, and many are pickled. Unique to Korean cooking are hearty dishes featuring beef and an abundant use of garlic, ginger, chili peppers, sesame seeds, hot mustard, and other seasonings.

A balance of flavors is important in Korean cooking. Sweet, sour, bitter, hot, and salty tastes are combined in meals, and foods are often spiced both before and after cooking. Five colors—white, red, black, green, and yellow—are also important considerations in the preparation and presentation of dishes.

Ingredients
MILK AND MILK PRODUCTS
Milk and milk products are generally not consumed or used in cooking.

139

MEAT AND MEAT ALTERNATIVES

Beef and beef variety cuts such as heart, liver, and tongue are especially popular. Pork and chicken are also eaten. Eggs are used as ingredients and as garnishes for many dishes. Fish and shellfish are eaten throughout the country, as most of Korea is not far from fresh or salt water. Inland, dried and salted fish products are used more than fresh fish, while both are used in coastal areas. Popular fish include cod, mackerel, whiting, and shad. Commonly eaten shellfish include abalone, crab, oysters, scallops, and shrimp. Octopus, cuttlefish, squid, and sea cucumbers are also consumed. *Mysid*, a tiny shrimplike crustacean, is fermented in salt to make *saewu-jeot*, which is used to flavor many foods.

Soybean products, primarily soy sauce, soy paste, and bean curd, are added to many dishes. Mung beans, *adzuki* beans, and other legumes are steamed and used in both savory and sweet preparations. Mung and soy beans are sprouted, and mung beans are made into cellophane noodles. In rural areas, soy sauce and soy paste are made in each household, traditionally in the spring.

FRUITS AND VEGETABLES

Asian pears (which differ from European pears and are called "apple-pears" in the United States) are popular. In addition, apples, cherries, *jujubes* (red dates), plums, melons, grapes, oranges, tangerines, and persimmons are commonly eaten.

Chinese cabbage (both bok choy and napa) and a long white radish (a type of daikon) are the most important vegetables. Lettuce, spinach, eggplant, bamboo shoots, water chestnuts, onions, cucumbers, carrots, potatoes, lotus root, winter melon, and sweet potatoes are other commonly used vegetables. Seaweeds including kelp and laver (called *kim*) are also eaten. Kim is brushed with sesame oil, salted, and toasted to make a condiment.

BREADS AND CEREALS

Rice is without question the most important component of the Korean diet. Short-grain varieties are usually used, both a regular and a glutinous (sticky) type, the latter for sweets. Millet and barley are also used, but mainly to extend the rice rather than for their own merits. Noodles are also an important staple and are made from wheat, buckwheat, and mung beans. The buckwheat variety is often used in cold dishes. Wheat flour is used in some baked goods.

OTHER INGREDIENTS

Foods are cooked in vegetable oils, usually peanut or sesame. Animal fat is rarely used.

Nuts and seeds are frequent additions. Pine nuts, hazelnuts (filberts), chestnuts, and peanuts are commonly used, while sesame is the most popular seed. Sesame seeds are often toasted and crushed, whether used as garnish or ingredient.

Soup or a thin barley-water is used as a beverage. On special occasions, wine might be served. Wines are made from rice (called *sui*) and other grains; some include various flower blossoms or ginseng as flavorings. Beer is also a popular beverage.

Herb teas are popular in Korea, and ginseng tea flavored with cinnamon and ginger is a favorite. Ginger, cinnamon, or citron can also be used separately to make spice teas. A common drink is rice tea, made by pouring warm water over toasted, ground rice or by simmering water in the pot that rice has been cooked in. These beverages would be served after the meal. For special occasions, Koreans make a thick drink of persimmons or dates, nuts, and spices, and a drink flavored with molasses and magnolia that is served with small, edible flowers floating on top.

Seasonings

Garlic, ginger root, black pepper, chili peppers, soy sauce, scallions, and toasted sesame in the form of oil or crushed seeds are the seasonings most often used. Fresh coriander, hot mustard, rice wine and rice vinegar, and pine nuts are also used.

Both red and green chili peppers are used. Red peppers are dried in the fall, then flaked, powdered, or cut into very fine threads to be used as a garnish. Almost all the powder is made into chili sauce or chili paste. Known as *kochujang*, chili paste is made from powdered chili peppers, rice flour, soy paste, and malt or sugar. The mixture is fermented and used to flavor vegetables, fish, and soups. Marinades and dipping sauces are often used. Combinations of vinegar, lemon juice, and soy sauce; bean paste, chili peppers, and soy sauce; or soy sauce, sugar, sesame seeds, and sesame oil are just a few of the frequently used mixtures.

Preparation

Foods are typically steamed, braised, simmered, stir-fried in a wok, pan-fried, deep-fried, or charcoal grilled. Some vegetables, meat, and seafood are served uncooked. Little baking is done. Foods are often preserved by drying, salting, and fermenting.

Since chopsticks and soup spoons are the only eating utensils, food must be cut into bite-size pieces before being served. Often, ingredients are very finely chopped. Ground meat (usually beef) is commonly used. It is cooked with vegetables as a topping for rice or noodles, used to stuff sweet peppers or lettuce leaves, or made into meatballs.

Soups are made from soy paste, which is similar to the Japanese miso, with added vegetables and fish or meat, or they can be made from meat or chicken braised in sesame oil and soy sauce, then simmered.

Barbecuing is a favorite method for cooking meat. Cubes or thin slices of marinated meat, usually beef or chicken, are grilled over charcoal, either outdoors for a picnic or at the table on a small brazier for a special occasion. Sometimes the meats are skewered with vegetables to make kebobs before barbecuing. Another Korean specialty prepared at the table is the fire pot or *sinsullo*. Similar to the dish found in northern China, thinly sliced meats such as beef and liver, fish, egg strips, vegetables (including mushrooms, carrots, bamboo shoots, and onions), as well as meatballs and walnuts, are cooked in seasoned broth in a charcoal-heated pot. When the morsels of food have been eaten, the broth is served as a soup.

Vegetables are popular. They can be cooked individually and served hot or cold, or they can be added to soups and stews. Salads of julienned vegetables are often eaten, sometimes mixed with meats. Pickled vegetables are eaten at every meal, usually in the form of *kimchi*. There are many types of kimchi, but most are made with Chinese cabbage and white radish, heavily seasoned with garlic, onions, and red pepper, and fermented. Cucumber, eggplant, turnip, and even pickled shellfish can be added. Some types are mild, others hot. Rural families make their own kimchi every autumn, and it is a big event, with relatives coming to help out. In the past, a family's wealth was determined by the ingredients in their kimchi, and the well-to-do used the rarest vegetables and even fruits to display their affluence.

Rice is most often served just boiled, though it can also be added to mixed dishes. Since rice is such an important part of the diet, rice cooking is an important skill: It must be neither underdone nor overcooked and mushy. Rice sandwiches called *kim bap* are made with a little meat or vegetables in the center, and the whole thing is wrapped in a sheet of seaweed, very much like the Japanese *sushi*.

Sweets are made for snacks and special occasions. Cakes are made from a dough of glutinous rice and shaped into balls around fillings, or rolled out and filled. Fillings usually consist of sweetened pastes of beans, chestnuts, dates, or sesame seeds. Cakes are either fried or steamed. Cookies or candies can be made from nuts and sesame seeds or roasted rice.

Meal Patterns

Rice is considered the main dish of each meal. Everything else is served as an accompaniment to the rice and is called *panch'an*. At least one meat or fish dish is included, and two or three vegetables are usually served. Kimchi is always included. Soup is very popular and is served at most meals. Dessert is seldom eaten, but if there is any, it is fresh fruit. On special occasions, however, cakes or candies are served. A beverage such as rice tea follows the meal. All the dishes are served at the same time. Individual bowls of rice and soup are served to each diner. Panch'an dishes are served on trays in the center of the table and everyone eats from these communal dishes.

Traditionally, breakfast is the main meal of the day. Modern city dwellers, however, may eat a light breakfast. Soup is almost always served at breakfast, along with rice (which may be a gruel at this meal), kimchi, meat or fish, vegetable dishes, and dipping sauces. For lunch, noodles are often served in a broth of beef, chicken, or fish and garnished with shellfish, meat, or vegetables. Supper more closely resembles breakfast. Snacks are usually rice cookies, dried fruits, or nuts.

Appetizers may be served as an accompaniment to wine before dinner. Batter-fried vegetable slices, seasoned bean curd, pickled seafood, meatballs, steamed dumplings, and similar tidbits are served. These foods can also be included in a meal, but they are served at the same time as the other dishes, not before.

Historically, Korean cooking was divided into everyday fare and cuisine for royalty. The traditions of palace cooking and food presentation, including the use of numerous ingredients in elaborate dishes, are seen today in meals for special occasions. At a meal celebrating a birthday or holiday, or one shared with guests, more dishes are served and both wine and dessert are offered.

M E N U

Korean Dinner

Pear Salad
Bul Koki
(grilled sirloin strips; grilled spareribs)
Sanchek
(fried meat and cabbage skewers)
Kimchi
(pickled cabbage)

Serving suggestions: Offer with steamed short-grain rice, hot mustard, and fruit juice.

Korean Dinner

◆ *Pear Salad*

YIELD: 50 portions
PORTION: 2½–3 oz.

2½ lb. carrots, peeled and julienned
5 lb. cucumbers, peeled, seeded, and
  julienned
2½ lb. cabbage, shredded
1 lb. celery, julienned

3 lb. pears or apple pears, peeled,
  seeded, and julienned
1½ lb. scallions, chopped
3 oz. ground sesame seeds
  (page 145)
¾ c. salad dressing (recipe follows)

Combine carrots, cucumber, cabbage, celery, pears, and scallions. Toss with sesame seeds and salad dressing.

Salad Dressing
¼ c. vinegar
1 c. lemon juice
3 oz. sugar

¾ c. sesame seed oil
5 tsp. salt

Combine all ingredients and refrigerate.

CALORIES: 83
CHOLESTEROL: 0 mg
VITAMIN A: 3464 IU

CARBOHYDRATE: 11 g
CALCIUM: 67 mg
VITAMIN C: 17 mg

PROTEIN: 1 g
SODIUM: 248 mg

FAT: 8 g
IRON: 1 mg

◆ *Bul Koki I (Grilled Sirloin Strips)*

YIELD: 50 portions
PORTION: 4 oz.

15 lb. beef, sirloin, sliced very thin
2½ c. soy sauce
10 oz. sugar
½ lb. scallions, minced
4 T. garlic, minced
¾ c. ground sesame seeds (recipe
  follows)

1 c. toasted sesame seed oil
½ c. dry sherry
2 tsp. pepper
vinegar-soy sauce (page 145)

Combine all ingredients. Grill or pan-broil until beef is cooked medium rare. Serve with vinegar-soy sauce.

Ground Sesame Seeds

2 oz. sesame seeds, white, hulled

Pan-roast sesame seeds in dry pan till they become golden and start to pop. Grind in food processor or blender until mealy but not pasty.

CALORIES: 436	CARBOHYDRATE: 6 g	PROTEIN: 23 g	FAT: 60 g
CHOLESTEROL: 90 mg	CALCIUM: 17 mg	SODIUM: 445 mg	IRON: 3 mg
VITAMIN A: 114 IU	VITAMIN C: 1 mg		

◆ Bul Koki II (Grilled Spareribs)

YIELD: 50 portions
PORTION: 2–4 pork ribs; 1–2 beef ribs

25 lb. spareribs, pork or beef
2½ c. soy sauce
2 oz. scallions, chopped
4 T. garlic, finely chopped
¼ c. fresh ginger root, finely chopped
1½ T. bean paste
1½ T. cayenne
1½ T. soy sauce
3 oz. ground sesame seeds (see preceding recipe)
1 c. sesame oil
½ c. vegetable oil
2 tsp. pepper
½ c. dry sherry
vinegar-soy sauce (recipe follows)

1. Separate ribs and marinate for at least one hour in the following mixture.
2. Combine all other ingredients except vinegar-soy sauce.
3. Grill or broil meat until cooked through. Serve with vinegar-soy sauce.

Vinegar-Soy Sauce

1¾ qt. soy sauce
3½ c. rice vinegar
2¼ c. lemon juice

Combine all ingredients.

CALORIES: 427	CARBOHYDRATE: 2 g	PROTEIN: 11 g	FAT: 63 g
CHOLESTEROL: 99 mg	CALCIUM: 17 mg	SODIUM: 577 mg	IRON: 2 mg
VITAMIN A: 139 IU	VITAMIN C: 1 mg		

♦ *Sanchek (Fried Meat and Cabbage Skewers)*

FRY: 5–6 minutes
DEEP-FAT FRYER:
  350°F
YIELD: 50 portions
PORTION: 1 skewer

4 lb. beef round
4 lb. boneless pork
4 lb. bok choy, white parts
10 oz. scallions
1 T. garlic, finely chopped
¾ c. sesame seed oil
¾ c. vegetable oil
1½ c. soy sauce

1½ tsp. sugar
3 oz. ground sesame seeds
  (page 145)
15 eggs
1¼ lb. flour
1 T. water
1 T. salt or to taste

1. Cut beef, pork, bok choy, and scallions into 3″ × ½″ × ¼″ strips.
2. Mix together garlic, oil, soy sauce, sugar, and sesame seeds. Combine with meat mixture.
3. Skewer meat, cabbage, and scallions on bamboo sticks. Mix together eggs, flour, water, and salt to form a batter. Dip prepared skewers into batter; fry flat. Drain. Remove sticks before serving.

CALORIES: 521   CARBOHYDRATE: 15 g   PROTEIN: 23 g   FAT: 70 g
CHOLESTEROL: 150 mg   CALCIUM: 103 mg   SODIUM: 675 mg   IRON: 4 mg
VITAMIN A: 1905 IU   VITAMIN C: 21 mg

◆ *Kimchi (Pickled Cabbage)*

YIELD: 60–120 portions
PORTION: 1–2 oz.

8 lb. napa cabbage
¾ c. rock salt
¾ qt. water
3 T. sugar
3 tsp. salt

3 T. fresh ginger root, finely chopped
1½ lb. scallions, chopped
3 oz. garlic, crushed and peeled
½ c. crushed red pepper

1. Cut cabbage into 1- to 1½-inch square pieces and separate layers. Add rock salt and water. Let mixture stand for 1–1½ hours, stirring occasionally. Drain.
2. Combine cabbage with remaining ingredients. Mix well and place weight on top of mixture. Keep in a warm place for 8 hours, then refrigerate.

CALORIES: 21
CHOLESTEROL: 0 mg
VITAMIN A: 2666 IU

CARBOHYDRATE: 4 g
CALCIUM: 145 mg
VITAMIN C: 24 mg

PROTEIN: 1 g
SODIUM: 2789 mg

FAT: <1 g
IRON: 1 mg

◆ *13* ◆ C O O K I N G   F R O M
◆ *Mexico* ◆

*Mexican chilaquiles
(chicken tortilla
casserole garnished
with cheese, sour
cream, and pickled
onion rings) served
with simmered
beans and jicama,
orange, and
cucumber salad.*

Six thousand years before the Spaniards arrived in what is now Mexico, the native Indians, among them the predecessors of the Mayans and the Aztecs, were engaged in agricultural pursuits. At first, they grew squash, beans, and corn, later adding tomatoes and chili peppers. These foods formed the basis of the Indian diet and are still staples in Mexican cooking today. The Mexican Indians also made use of other fruits, vegetables, and herbs indigenous to the region. They fished and hunted deer, rabbits, and a variety of birds.

When the Spaniards came, they introduced many new foods, including rice, sugar cane, wheat, and some fruits and vegetables, such as onions. They also brought with them domesticated cows, pigs, and chickens. The blending of native and Spanish foods resulted in some of the dishes most characteristic of Mexican cooking today: rice and beans; chopped tomatoes, onions, and chili peppers (salsa); and corn tortillas fried in lard. Other hybrid foods evolved, such as wheat flour tortillas.

Mexico has a variety of climates, and the cuisine varies accordingly. The coastal regions support rain forests and tropical crops. At higher elevations, the temperate zone is ideal for growing many fruits and vegetables. Even higher up in central Mexico, grains such as wheat are easily grown. The northern part of the country is arid, but suitable for grazing cattle.

Coastal areas include seafood and tropical fruits and vegetables in their repertoire. A pickled raw fish dish called *seviche* is popular, as are regional specialties such as octopus prepared in its ink, sea turtle soup, and iguana.

In northern Mexico, beef is eaten much more frequently than in the rest of the country. The state of Sonora is famed for its *menudo*, or tripe stew. In the central plateaus, lamb and grains are featured in dishes that combine Indian and Spanish influences. In southern regions, tropical fruits and vegetables are enjoyed and colorful, spicy sauces are typical. In Yucatán, the Mayan heritage

149

is evident; steamed foods, squash seed sauces, and delicate seasonings are used to produce dishes that contrast strongly with those from the rest of the country.

Ingredients

MILK AND MILK PRODUCTS

Milk and milk products began to be included in the cuisine of Mexico after the introduction of cows by the Spanish settlers around 1530. Although milk and cheese appear in many dishes today, they have not been so integrated that they form an indispensable part of the diet. Milk itself is rarely drunk by adults. Sweetened milk drinks are popular, however, such as *café con leche* (coffee with milk), hot chocolate, *licuado* (fresh fruit juice with milk and sugar) and *atole* (warm milk thickened with corn flour and flavored with sugar and fruit or spices). Fresh, unripened cheeses and mild, aged cheeses are common in the northern regions but can be found in dishes throughout the country. The cheese most frequently used is white *(queso blanco)*, with a mild flavor and a crumbly texture.

MEAT AND MEAT ALTERNATIVES

Legumes are one of the most important protein sources in Mexico. Pinto, kidney, and pink beans are used most. They are eaten daily, sometimes at every meal.

Beef is common in the plains of the north. A specialty of the area is the strongly flavored dried beef called *cecina*. All cuts, including the variety meats and organs, are used. Pork is widely available, and most parts are consumed. It is made into sausages, both *chorizo*, which is hot, and the milder *longanzina*. Turkey (which originated in the New World), chicken, and kid (goat) are featured in some dishes. Eggs are very common for breakfast.

Fish and shellfish are important components of the diet in coastal regions. Specialties include shrimp, oysters, tuna, crabs, crayfish, octopus, pompano, and red snapper.

FRUITS AND VEGETABLES

Citrus fruits, bananas and plantains, *cherimoya* (custard apple), mangos, papayas, pineapple, *guanabana* (soursop), *mameys*, *granadillas* (passion fruit), *zapote* (sapodilla), and guavas are grown in the tropical regions. Peaches and apricots were brought by the Spaniards. The fruit of the prickly pear cactus, called *tuna*, is also eaten, especially in the north.

Several types of squash, pumpkin, potato, tomato, sweet potato, and onion are among the most commonly eaten Mexican vegetables. Other popular vegetables include *tomatillo*, a small, green relative of the tomato; *jicama*, a root with crisp, white flesh reminiscent of green peas; *chayote*, a green squash; *cassava*, a root also known as *yuca* and *manioc*; and *nopales*, leaves of the prickly pear cactus. Squash blossoms are consumed as well as the fruit. Avocados are widely eaten. Chili peppers are native to the region; as many as 90 varieties are grown, from the very mild to the fiery hot.

BREADS AND CEREALS

Corn is the native grain, though wheat and rice introduced by the Spaniards are also frequently used. Corn is typically soaked in a slaked lime solution to remove the hulls, resulting in *pozole*, identical to some types of hominy. It is then mashed into a fresh dough called *masa*, which is used to make foods such as *tamales* (baked or steamed portions of masa with sauce) and *tortillas*, the round, flat bread made throughout Mexico. The fresh masa can also be dried and stored as a flour known as *masa harina*. This flour is sometimes used as a thickening agent. Tortillas are also made from wheat, especially in the north. Raised breads made from wheat flour are also eaten.

OTHER INGREDIENTS

Lard is the favored fat; olive and other vegetable oils are sometimes used. Butter is served with breads.

Pecans, piñons (pine nuts), and pumpkin and amaranth seeds were used by Mexican natives. Spaniards brought walnuts, almonds, filberts, and sesame seeds. Finely ground nuts and seeds are used as thickening agents in some dishes.

Coffee, which is grown in the mountainous regions of Mexico, is the favorite hot drink, although hot chocolate and other hot milk drinks are also popular. Fruit juice and soft drinks are frequently consumed. Beer is the most popular alcoholic drink, although the Mexican wine industry is growing. *Pulque*, the fermented drink made from the sap of the *maguey*, or century plant, is still common in some regions. More often, pulque is distilled to produce the spirit *mescal*; the most famous variety is the twice-distilled mescal known as *tequila*.

Seasonings

Besides the chili peppers that are used to flavor many dishes, one of the most popular herbs is *epazote*, which has a distinctive pungent flavor. Other native seasonings are chocolate and vanilla. Cilantro, or fresh coriander, is used extensively; the coriander seeds are also used. Marjoram, oregano, bay leaves, mint, and parsley are commonly used herbs. Popular spices include cinnamon and cloves, which were brought by the Spaniards, and anise and allspice. The red seeds known as *achiote* or *annatto* are used to color foods, especially in the Yucatán peninsula.

Preparation

The traditional cookware of Mexico is earthenware; the *comal*, for example, is an unglazed griddle used for making tortillas, and the *cazuela* is a glazed casserole. A stone *metate* is used to grind corn into meal. A mortar and pestle is used to grind other ingredients, and special implements are available to mash beans and to whip chocolate drinks. A tortilla press is sometimes used to form round tortillas with uniform thickness.

One-dish meals are very popular in Mexico, usually served with warm *tortillas*. Hearty soups or stews known as *caldos* are favorite family entrées, and casseroles using tortilla pieces (such as *chilaquiles*), rice, or macaroni, called *sopa seca* ("dry soup"), are common. Mexico is also famous for its "stuffed" foods, such as tacos, enchiladas, tamales, quesadillas, and burritos. These are found throughout the country with regional variations.

Tortillas are used in a myriad of ways in Mexico. They can be cut into triangles and fried, resulting in a tortilla chip or *tostadita*, which is used like a spoon to transfer food from plate to mouth. Tortillas can be topped with shredded meat, vegetables, cheese, and sauces, and eaten flat *(tostadas)* or folded *(tacos)* — the Mexican equivalent of sandwiches. If wheat tortillas are used, as they often are in the north, the result is a *burrito*, usually filled with beans and salsa. *Enchiladas* are tortillas softened in hot lard or sauce and filled with a seasoned meat, poultry, seafood, cheese, or egg mixture. For *tamales*, masa is folded into corn husks (in the north) or banana leaves (in the south) and baked in hot ashes or steamed over boiling water. The tamale may be unflavored masa, may have a savory meat or vegetable filling, or may be sweetened for dessert. *Quesadillas* are tortillas filled with a little cheese, sausage, leftover meat, or vegetables, then folded in half and crisply fried. Dried-out tortillas can be ground up, moistened, and formed into balls to become dumplings.

Meats are usually cooked over high heat, such as the grilled beef strips called *carne asada* and the fried pork skin called *chicharrónes*. When meat is used as a filling — in tacos, for example — it is usually shredded.

The most common way to prepare beans in Mexico is to fry previously boiled beans, called *frijoles refritos* (incorrectly known as refried beans in the United States), in lard. Simmered beans *(frijoles de olla)* are also served as a side dish or used as a filling for stuffed foods.

Vegetables are usually served as part of the entrée or as a substantial garnish rather than as a side dish. Chili peppers are used frequently, in seasonings, sauces, and even stuffed, as in the cheese-filled, batter-fried chile dish called *chiles rellenos*.

Preparation of chili peppers requires some caution as contact with the hottest peppers can irritate and even burn the skin. Both fresh and dried chili peppers are "cleaned" by the removal of the stem, the seeds, and the veins inside the pepper. The seeds are the hottest part, so thorough removal of the seeds also keeps the piquancy to a minimum. The smaller, dried peppers are often crumbled directly into the food being prepared, but the larger dried types must be soaked and puréed before they are added. Red chili peppers can often be purchased as a powder, not to be confused with the familiar chili powder, a

Tex-Mex spice. Both peppers and tomatoes are often roasted before use, which can be done over open coals or on a griddle.

Sauces play an important part in Mexican cuisine. Salsa, a mixture of tomatoes, onions, and chili peppers, accompanies meals. Guacamole, mashed avocado flavored with chili peppers and lemon juice, sometimes with the addition of onions, tomatoes, and cilantro, is commonly served. In southern parts of the country, *moles* are prepared in which the spices are ground to a paste and sautéed before liquid is added. Moles are made with numerous ingredients, including chili peppers, nuts, raisins, and even unsweetened chocolate.

Meal Patterns

Throughout Mexico, the poorest families may eat only two meals a day, consisting mostly of corn, beans, and squash. In families with ample income, four or five meals are often eaten. The day begins with *desayano*, which comprises coffee with milk and sweet rolls or breads. *Almeurzo*, eaten later in the morning, is a more substantial breakfast, including fresh fruit, eggs, beans, tortillas, salsa, and coffee. *Comida* is the largest meal of the day and can be eaten any time from 2:00 to 5:30 in the afternoon. Traditionally it has several courses, including a light soup; the main course, which is a meat or fish dish plus salad or vegetables; beans served with tortillas and rolls; and dessert, which may be fresh or stewed fruit, *flan* (a custard), or a pudding such as *capirotada* (bread pudding) or *huevos reales* (egg yolks and sugar seasoned with sherry, cinnamon, pine nuts, and raisins). *Merienda* is the evening meal, which may be eaten by children at 6:00 or 7:00 P.M., and by adults as late as 9:00 P.M. It consists of coffee, hot chocolate, or atole, and light snacks, such as sweet breads with jam, sandwiches, or tacos. *Cena*, or dinner, is usually eaten only for special occasions with guests. It is a large meal eaten between 8:00 P.M. and midnight. Recently, many Mexicans have adopted the American habit of eating a light lunch and a heavy supper. Snacking is very common; fresh fruit, pastries, or grilled meats can be purchased from street vendors located at every corner in urban areas.

Tex-Mex Cooking

The cooking of the southwestern United States has been greatly influenced by the foods of Mexico, especially in Texas. Some dishes that Americans assume are Mexican are actually adaptations developed in Texas. These include *chili con carne*, which is beans and ground beef seasoned with another Texas invention: chili powder (ground chili peppers mixed with cumin, oregano, and sometimes garlic). Many Tex-Mex dishes are flavored with chili powder or chili peppers and are preferred spicy hot, although as in Mexican cuisine, there are also many dishes that are mildly seasoned.

Nachos (tortilla chips topped with cheese and chili peppers), a casserole made with cheese-stuffed chiles (chiles rellenos), grilled chili-spiced meat kebobs called *anacuchos*, barbecued kid (goat), and capirotada with whiskey sauce ("drunken pudding") are other examples of Tex-Mex creations. In addition, enchiladas, tacos, tamales, and refried beans are widely available in Texas and the rest of the Southwest. Many Mexican-style dishes served in the United States are from the northern border regions of Mexico, featuring grilled meats, especially beef, and wheat products such as flour tortillas. An example is *fajitas*, grilled marinated beef or poultry strips served in wheat tortillas.

M E N U
Mexican Dinner

Chilaquiles
(tortilla casserole)
Simmered Beans
Salsa Verde
(green sauce) *
Jicama, Orange, and
Cucumber Salad
Layered Nut Cake

Serving suggestions: Offer beer or
fruit drinks with the meal; serve
coffee with dessert.

*Purchased red salsa may be sub-
stituted, if desired.

M E N U
Tex-Mex Dinner

Chili con Queso
(cheese dip)
Anacuchos
(spicy meat kebobs)
Tex-Mex Rice
Fresh Mango Ice Cream

Serving suggestions: Accompany
entrée with refried beans or corn
bread; offer beer or fruit juice.

◆ *Chilaquiles (Tortilla Casserole)*

FRY: 1–2 minutes
DEEP-FAT FRY:
  350°F
YIELD: 50 portions
PORTION: 1–1½ c.

8 lb. whole chicken breasts
3 T. salt
10 garlic cloves, peeled
1 lb. onions, sliced
1 oz. fresh coriander (cilantro), chopped
1 oz. mint, chopped
1¼ gal. cold water
1 #10 can tomato sauce
3 c. tomato paste
1½ T. garlic, finely chopped

2 tsp. cayenne or to taste
3 qt. chicken stock
10 dozen corn tortillas, each cut in 6 sections
2 qt. prepared sour cream
7–8 lb. avocados, cubed and tossed with lemon juice (to prevent browning)
2 c. pickled onion rings (recipe follows)
2 lb. farmer's cheese

1. Combine chicken, salt, garlic, onion, cilantro, mint, and water. Bring to a boil and simmer until chicken is tender, approximately 20–30 minutes. Remove chicken and cool. Remove meat from bones and shred. Strain stock and set aside.
2. Combine tomato sauce and paste, garlic, cayenne, and chicken stock. Cook until heated through. Adjust seasoning. Remove from heat.
3. Deep-fat fry the tortillas until crisp, but not brown. Drain.
4. Reheat tomato sauce until it begins to boil. Add tortillas and toss until most of the sauce is absorbed and the tortillas begin to soften. Stir frequently to prevent sticking.
5. Put the tomato mixture into a pan or serving tray. Top with the shredded chicken, sour cream, avocado, onion rings, and cheese. Serve immediately.

Pickled Onion Rings

2 lb. onions, sliced
2 qt. boiling water
2 c. white vinegar

2 c. cold water
4 tsp. salt

Put onions in a colander and pour boiling water over them. Drain. In a nonmetallic bowl, combine onions, vinegar, water, and salt. Pickle 30 minutes, stirring occasionally. Pickled onions will keep for several days if refrigerated but will lose their crispness.

CALORIES: 715
CHOLESTEROL: 72 mg
VITAMIN A: 2139 IU

CARBOHYDRATE: 63 g
CALCIUM: 491 mg
VITAMIN C: 18 mg

PROTEIN: 26 g
SODIUM: 1217 mg

FAT: 69 g
IRON: 4 mg

◆ *Simmered Beans*

YIELD: 50 portions
PORTION: 3 oz.

3½ lb. pinto beans, dried
4 oz. lard

1 lb. onions, chopped
1 T. salt

1. Rinse beans. Add water until beans are covered by several inches. Soak beans overnight. Drain.
2. Add enough fresh water until beans are covered by 1½ inches. Add fat, onions, and salt. Simmer for 1–2 hours, or until beans are tender. Add more water if necessary. Stir occasionally to prevent sticking.

CALORIES: 105
CHOLESTEROL: 13 mg
VITAMIN A: 7 IU

CARBOHYDRATE: 16 g
CALCIUM: 34 mg
VITAMIN C: 1 mg

PROTEIN: 5 g
SODIUM: 156 mg

FAT: 5 g
IRON: 2 mg

◆ *Salsa Verde (Green Sauce)*

YIELD: 50 portions
PORTION: 2½ T.

3 lb. tomatillos, husked
1 lb. onions, chopped
4 oz. can jalapeño chiles, drained, or to taste

2 oz. fresh coriander (cilantro), chopped
1 T. salt or to taste

1. Boil tomatillos in water until just tender (about 10 minutes). Drain.
2. Combine tomatillos, onions, chiles, and coriander. Lightly purée in a food processor or blender. Add salt. If mixture is too thick, it can be thinned with water.

CALORIES: 10
CHOLESTEROL: 0 mg
VITAMIN A: 109 IU

CARBOHYDRATE: 2 g
CALCIUM: 9 mg
VITAMIN C: 7 mg

PROTEIN: <1 g
SODIUM: 162 mg

FAT: <1 g
IRON: <1 mg

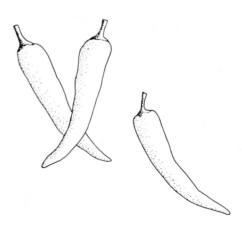

♦ Jicama, Orange, and Cucumber Salad

YIELD: 50 portions
PORTION: ½ c.

7 lb. jicama, peeled and cubed
6 lb. cucumbers, peeled and chopped
10 lb. oranges, peeled and cubed
1 c. lemon juice
1 tsp. cayenne

1 tsp. cumin powder
1 T. salt
4 lb. lettuce, rinsed and divided into leaves
2 oz. fresh coriander (cilantro), chopped

1. Combine jicama, cucumbers, and oranges.
2. In a separate bowl, combine lemon juice, cayenne, cumin powder, and salt. Pour over salad.
3. Arrange ½ cup of salad on a large lettuce leaf. Chill at least 2 hours. Garnish with fresh coriander.

CALORIES: 71   CARBOHYDRATE: 16 g   PROTEIN: 2 g   FAT: <1 g
CHOLESTEROL: 0 mg   CALCIUM: 79 mg   SODIUM: 156 mg   IRON: 1 mg
VITAMIN A: 913 IU   VITAMIN C: 70 mg

♦ Layered Nut Cake

BAKE: 15–20 minutes
OVEN: 350°F
YIELD: 48 portions
PORTION: 3″ × 4½″ piece

3 qt. milk
8 cinnamon sticks
3 lb. sugar
16 egg yolks, lightly beaten
4 oz. cornstarch

4 lb. almonds or pecans, toasted and finely ground
2½ c. sweet sherry
8 lb. pound cake, thinly sliced
1½ lb. sour cream (optional)

1. Combine milk, cinnamon sticks, and sugar. Cook over medium heat, stirring often, until sugar is dissolved.
2. Mix egg yolks with cornstarch until smooth. Add to milk mixture and cook over low heat, stirring constantly, until slightly thickened.
3. Add nuts to custard. Continue cooking, stirring frequently, until very thick. Stir in 2 cups of sherry. Cool slightly.
4. Place a layer of cake slices in three greased 12″ × 18″ pans. Sprinkle with a third of the remaining sherry. Spread with half of the nut mixture. Repeat. Top with cake; sprinkle with the last of the sherry. Bake until lightly browned. Cool. Serve topped with 1 tablespoon sour cream.

CALORIES: 812   CARBOHYDRATE: 76 g   PROTEIN: 15 g   FAT: 89 g
CHOLESTEROL: 179 mg   CALCIUM: 203 mg   SODIUM: 199 mg   IRON: 4 mg
VITAMIN A: 495 IU   VITAMIN C: 1 mg

◆ *Chili con Queso (Cheese Dip)*

YIELD: 50 portions
PORTION: ¼ c.

6 oz. butter, melted
3 oz. flour
1½ qt. evaporated milk
1 #2½ can tomatoes, peeled
and drained

1 #2½ can green chiles, drained
and chopped
2 tsp. garlic, finely chopped
6 lb. Monterey Jack cheese, grated
4 lb. tortilla chips

1. Cook flour in butter until thickened. Slowly add milk; continue cooking
   until mixture is slightly thickened.
2. Combine tomatoes, chiles, and garlic. Cook over medium heat, stirring,
   until mixture thickens and no liquid remains. Add white sauce.
3. Add cheese. Melt over low heat, stir until smooth.
4. Serve warm with tortilla chips.

CALORIES: 402	CARBOHYDRATE: 22 g	PROTEIN: 18 g	FAT: 38 g
CHOLESTEROL: 68 mg	CALCIUM: 603 mg	SODIUM: 405 mg	IRON: 1 mg
VITAMIN A: 967 IU	VITAMIN C: 12 mg		

Chili con queso, a spicy Tex-Mex cheese dip.

◆ Anacuchos (Spicy Meat Kebobs)

YIELD: 50 portions
PORTION: 3–4 oz.

1 qt. red wine vinegar
1½ c. vegetable oil
2 T. chili powder
2 T. garlic, finely chopped
½ tsp. cayenne or to taste

6 tsp. salt
10 lb. beef, chuck, cut into
  1½" cubes
10 lb. boneless pork, cut into
  1½" cubes

Combine all ingredients. Marinate, refrigerated, for 48 hours. Skewer kebobs and reserve marinade. Grill or broil, basting with marinade occasionally, until meat is cooked, about 15–20 minutes.

CALORIES: 571
CHOLESTEROL: 124 mg
VITAMIN A: 188 IU

CARBOHYDRATE: 1 g
CALCIUM: 16 mg
VITAMIN C: <1 mg

PROTEIN: 28 g
SODIUM: 335 mg

FAT: 77 g
IRON: 3 mg

◆ Tex-Mex Rice

YIELD: 50 portions
PORTION: ½ c.

1½ c. vegetable oil
5 lb. onions, chopped
3 T. garlic, finely chopped
1 T. chili powder
4 lb. rice

1 #10 can tomatoes, chopped,
  undrained
2¼ qt. beef stock
2½ lb. peas, cooked
1 T. salt or to taste

1. Sauté onions and garlic in oil over medium heat; add chili powder and rice. Cook, stirring often, until rice is golden brown.
2. Add tomatoes with juice and stock. Simmer, covered, over very low heat until all liquid is absorbed, about 30 minutes.
3. Stir in peas and season with salt.

CALORIES: 238
CHOLESTEROL: 1 mg
VITAMIN A: 763 IU

CARBOHYDRATE: 41 g
CALCIUM: 31 mg
VITAMIN C: 16 mg

PROTEIN: 5 g
SODIUM: 440 mg

FAT: 13 g
IRON: 2 mg

◆ Fresh Mango Ice Cream

YIELD: 50 portions
  (1 gal.)
PORTION: 2½–3 oz.

3 lb. mangoes, peeled and seeded
2 T. lime juice
8 egg yolks

1 lb. sugar
2 qt. half-and-half, scalded

1. Purée mangoes with lime juice.
2. Beat egg yolks with sugar until fluffy.
3. Add hot half-and-half slowly to yolk mixture. Continue mixing until sugar is dissolved. Stir in 2 cups of mango purée. Place in ice cream freezer and process according to manufacturer's directions.

CALORIES: 100
CHOLESTEROL: 58 mg
VITAMIN A: 475 IU

CARBOHYDRATE: 12 g
CALCIUM: 46 mg
VITAMIN C: 2 mg

PROTEIN: 2 g
SODIUM: 17 mg

FAT: 7 g
IRON: <1 mg

·*14*· COOKING OF THE
·*Native Americans*·

A typical Native American meal of lamb stew with fry bread.

The traditional Native American diet has made many important contributions to American cuisine. Historians suggest that early European colonists would not have survived without the agricultural and culinary expertise of the Indians. Beans, blueberries, squash, corn, cranberries, and turkey are just some of the indigenous foods used by Native Americans. Squash and pumpkins were cultivated in North America before 1000 B.C., and corn and beans were planted later. However, many of the plant and animal foods used by the Indians were gathered or hunted. In some cases it is difficult to say exactly which plants were indigenous, as no records were kept before contact with Europeans, and many plants introduced by the settlers quickly spread and became "wild."

Native American cooking before the arrival of European settlers differed greatly from region to region and can be divided into five broad geographic areas: the Northeast, the South, the Great Plains, the Southwest, and the Pacific Northwest, including Alaska. Native Americans in New England cultivated beans, corn, and squash and collected mustard, dandelion, and other greens, nuts, and a wide variety of fruits and berries. Many of the foods associated with New England cuisine have their origins in northeastern Indian recipes. Along the coast, the Narragansett and Penobscot Indians gathered clams and lobsters and baked them in a beach pit lined with hot rocks and covered with seaweed, creating the clambake. Boston baked beans evolved from the Indian method of simmering dried beans for days with maple syrup. Clam chowder, brown bread, corn pudding, pumpkin pie, and the dessert called Indian pudding are all variations of Native American recipes.

In the South, the staple food was hominy, made from cultivated corn. Hominy was made into fried, baked, or boiled breads. Hominy, grits, and these breads were introduced to the settlers and slaves by the Indians, and survive as typical southern foods today. The dish we know as succotash was originally a stew of corn, often hominy, with lima or other beans, plus other ingredients

161

such as fish or game when available. Variations of this meal were prepared by most Native Americans. Southeastern Indians hunted deer, bear, squirrels, wild turkey, and other birds; they gathered persimmons, grapes, pawpaws, and berries; and collected nuts, greens, and roots, including the wild sweet potato. Sassafras leaves were dried and ground and used as a thickener for soup. This powder was later introduced to the black slaves and the French; today it is called *filé* and is used in Creole and Cajun cooking.

The Native Americans of the Great Plains were mostly nomadic hunters, following the great herds of buffalo across the flat plains. They also hunted deer, rabbit, and game birds and gathered wild rice and roots, such as Indian breadroot and hog peanut. Almost all parts of the buffalo were consumed, from the meat and marrow to the organs and hump. Farther west, in what is now Colorado, Utah, Nevada, and Wyoming, food was scarce. The Indians hunted mountain sheep, deer, and antelope, but roots, seeds, berries, and nuts were the mainstays of their diet.

Like the Native Americans of the eastern United States, the Indians of the Southwest grew beans, squash, and the corn that was their primary staple food. Up to 20 different varieties and colors of corn were cultivated; some of the more unusual, like blue corn, were used for ceremonial dishes. Indians in this region hunted deer, rabbit, and antelope; they gathered pine nuts and berries; and ate many types of cactus. They occasionally used chili peppers, onions, and honey to flavor food. Seeds, beans, and corn were commonly ground into meal before being used, and it was important for every young girl to become proficient at grinding. Another important food plant was *mesquite*, the pods yielding a sweet pulp that could be eaten fresh, made into bread, or fermented into beer. The seeds, flowers, and resinous gum were also eaten.

In the Pacific Northwest, food was abundant, and the Indians had little need for agriculture. Fishing was a major source of food. Large numbers of salmon were caught annually in the spring and summer, and the eggs, known today as red caviar, were a favorite spread. Many other types of fish were caught, as well as seals, whales, and otter. Ducks, geese, gulls, and other birds were eaten, and deer, elk, bear, and wild goats were abundant. Many nuts, greens, berries, and roots were gathered. In Alaska, few plant foods were available, and more emphasis was placed on hunting and fishing. Salmon and seal were among the most important foods. Other fish, plus caribou and other large mammals (of which all parts were used), migrating birds and their eggs, several kinds of berries, a few greens and roots, and seaweeds completed the diet.

When Europeans arrived in the New World, they brought wheat, sheep, pigs, cattle, and horses. Subsequently, pork and mutton were raised and consumed by many Native Americans. Wheat was used to make traditional foods such as fried bread. New fruits and vegetables were added to the diet. As the Europeans took over, many Indians were relocated and restricted from access to some of the wild food they were accustomed to eating. Over the years, many traditional Native American recipes have been altered or lost.

Today, most Native Americans consume a fairly typical American diet. Some never eat the traditional dishes of their ancestors; others prepare them only for special occasions. Some Native Americans are working to revive and preserve Indian cooking as an important part of their heritage.

Ingredients

MILK AND MILK PRODUCTS

No source of milk was available to Native Americans before the introduction of cows and sheep from Europe.

MEAT AND MEAT ALTERNATIVES

Large and small game were plentiful in many parts of the United States, including bear, elk, goat, opossum, moose, rabbit, squirrel, and venison. Game birds, such as duck, goose, partridge, passenger pigeon, and turkey were also widely available. Catfish, frogs, sturgeon, trout, and turtle were some of the freshwater foods caught in some areas. The sea gave the Indians halibut, herring, cod, eel, sole, and other fish; clams, oysters, crab, shrimp, and other shellfish; and seal, whale, and walrus.

Before the Europeans came, animals were not domesticated, although in some areas deer were semidomesticated. Later, pigs and sheep were raised.

Legumes, especially beans such as lima, navy, kidney, and pinto, provided a reliable source of protein for many Native Americans.

FRUITS AND VEGETABLES

A wide selection of berries was available to Native Americans all over the United States, including blueberries, blackberries, raspberries, salal, elderberries, currants, strawberries, buffalo berries, gooseberries, cranberries, beach plums, and many more. Other fruits gathered were crab apples, persimmons, pawpaws, chokecherries, and the fruits of cacti and palm trees.

Many types of leaves were gathered for use as greens; some of the more familiar are alfalfa, clover, cress, sorrel, and lamb's quarters or pigweed. Young shoots were used as vegetables; wild lettuce, ferns of several kinds, and cattails are some of the plants used this way. Pumpkins, squashes, and tomatoes were cultivated in many areas. The blossoms of squashes were eaten, as were the flowers of other plants, such as cattails. Mushrooms of several types were eaten. Bulbs, including those from several types of lily, wild onion, wild garlic, and wild leek; and roots, such as Jerusalem artichoke, potato, sweet potato, and many others played an important part in Indian diets. Europeans introduced apples, carrots, peaches, canteloupes, and watermelons, which became popular.

BREADS AND CEREALS

Corn was the staple grain for many Native Americans. It was eaten green, on the cob, in soups and stews, and as hominy and grits. Indian pudding and steamed bread were made from cornmeal in the Northeast; cornmeal was used in flat breads such as tortillas and *piki*, a lacy, flat bread made from blue cornmeal, in the Southwest. Popcorn was eaten. Barley, wild oats, wild rye, and other wild grasses were gathered as grain foods in various parts of the country.

California Indians did not grow corn but made meal from acorns, which had to be processed before use to remove their tannic acid. Acorns were also used by Indians of the Southeast when their corn crop was insufficient. Wild rice was collected by the tribes of the northern Great Plains, who likewise did not raise corn. Some of the roots used as vegetables were also processed into fine meal, and the pollen of the cattail was used as flour.

OTHER INGREDIENTS

Animal fats from game were extensively used. Bear fat was common in the Southeast, buffalo fat in the Great Plains, and seal fat in Alaska. Fish oil was also used in the cooking of the Northwest. Many nuts were eaten, including beechnuts, acorns, chestnuts, hickory nuts, pecans, walnuts, black walnuts, maple seeds, and piñon seeds, or pine nuts. Squash, pumpkin, and sunflower seeds were also eaten.

Tea was brewed from many plant parts, including sassafras roots, wild mint leaves, hemlock leaves, pine needles, rose hips, corn, and acorns. The sap collected from maple trees was drunk. Maple sap, and the sap of the century plant, were fermented into beverages. However, alcoholic beverages seem not to have played a major role in Native American life until the arrival of the Europeans.

Seasonings

Native American dishes were not usually spicy. Common seasonings included indigenous roots and herbs such as wild onions. Pine and other nuts, animal fats, and berries were used to flavor some dishes. Chili peppers in small amounts seasoned many foods in the Southwest. Some areas had salt, while the ash of certain plants was used in other regions to provide a salty taste. Sweeteners included honey and maple syrup.

Preparation

Native Americans made cookware from wood, bones, shells, and gourds. Animal skins and woven baskets were also used as containers. In the Southwest, pottery eventually replaced gourds and baskets as cooking vessels.

Hot Indian pudding topped with ice cream.

Many cooking methods were employed. The simplest was roasting over an open fire. Boiling was accomplished by dropping hot rocks into a basket or other container of water. Foods were baked in underground pits or in ashes. Some foods were wrapped in leaves prior to baking or steaming. Food preparation also involved grinding, soaking, and sometimes leaching with ashes to remove toxins. Soups and stews were popular. In some areas, particularly Alaska, meat and fish were often eaten raw.

In many areas food preparation emphasized preservation of seasonal foods, either by drying them in the sun or smoking them over a fire. For meat, fish, and oysters, special wood was often used to impart a distinctive flavor to the food. Dried meat was usually pounded or shredded before being used. Breads were often dried and became so hard they had to be soaked before eating. Many foods were dried in pieces with a hole in them so they could be carried on a string. Other foods were ground into meal and carried in a bag. Fruits were dried, pounded into a paste, or made into jam or syrup. In Alaska, greens and berries were preserved in fermented blubber.

Extra buffalo meat was preserved by cutting it into thin strips, then dehydrating it in the sun or over a fire. This tough, dried meat would keep for several years and was known as jerked buffalo, or jerky (probably from the Spanish word *charqui*, meaning "sun-dried"). Both fresh meat and jerky would commonly be "stone-boiled," with fire-heated stones added to the stew until it boiled. Jerky was also shredded and mixed with buffalo fat and berries, then formed into cakes called *pemmican*.

Meal Patterns

Meal patterns varied from one area to another. In the Southeast, there were often no specific mealtimes and members of the group did not eat together, each person eating when hungry. In the Southwest, breakfast was prepared before dawn, and supper preparation began in the midafternoon; supper was usually eaten before sunset. In the Northeast, one large meal was eaten before noon, with snacks available the rest of the day. In the Pacific Northwest, two meals were eaten each day. In Alaska, four meals were eaten: a very light breakfast, a meal at 11:00 A.M., supper around 5:00 P.M., and a late evening snack.

In all areas, variety in meals and between meals depended on supplies. For those Native Americans who did not cultivate plants, meals often consisted primarily of whatever was in season for as long as it was available. They then moved to a locale where another food would be in season. In other regions, the native food supply was sufficient to permit permanent settlement. Crops usually provided a consistent diet for Native Americans who cultivated the land.

M E N U

Native American Dinner

Lima Bean Soup
Lamb Stew
Indian Fry Bread

Serving suggestions: Serve squash or corn with the stew along with fruit juice or mint tea. Offer sliced melon for dessert.

Native American Dinner

◆ *Lima Bean Soup*

YIELD: 50 portions
PORTION: 1 c.

4 lb. lima beans
3 gal. water
¼ oz. parsley
2 lb. onions, sliced

1 lb. salt pork or bacon, cubed
3 lb. tomatoes, cubed
2 tsp. crushed red pepper
3 T. salt or to taste

1. Soak beans in 1½ gallons of water for at least 4 hours. Drain.
2. Combine beans with 1½ gallons water and other remaining ingredients. Add more water if beans are not covered. Bring to a boil and simmer, covered, for 1 hour. Remove cover and continue to simmer until beans are tender, about 1 hour.

CALORIES: 103
CHOLESTEROL: 18 mg
VITAMIN A: 560 IU

CARBOHYDRATE: 14 g
CALCIUM: 22 mg
VITAMIN C: 20 mg

PROTEIN: 5 g
SODIUM: 127 mg

FAT: 5 g
IRON: 2 mg

◆ *Lamb Stew*

YIELD: 50 portions
PORTION: 3 oz.

20 lb. lamb shoulder, or beef chuck, cut into 1½" cubes
vegetable oil
1 lb. onions, peeled and chopped
4 garlic cloves, peeled and crushed

12 juniper berries, dried and crushed
1½ gal. water or beef stock
2 T. salt or to taste
2 tsp. pepper

1. Heat oil; add lamb and brown.
2. Add onions, garlic, and juniper berries. Sauté until onions are golden.
3. Add water and seasonings. Bring to a boil. Simmer, covered, until lamb is tender, about 2 hours. Stir occasionally.

CALORIES: 508
CHOLESTEROL: 160 mg
VITAMIN A: 4 IU

CARBOHYDRATE: 1 g
CALCIUM: 21 mg
VITAMIN C: 1 mg

PROTEIN: 32 g
SODIUM: 352 mg

FAT: 58 g
IRON: 2 mg

◆ *Indian Fry Bread*

FRY: 3–4 minutes
DEEP-FAT FRYER:
  350–375°F
YIELD: 50 portions
PORTION: 1 fry
  bread

4½ lb. flour, sifted
6 T. baking powder

1 T. salt
1½ qt. warm water

1. Combine dry ingredients.
2. Slowly mix in warm water. Knead. Dough should be soft, not sticky. Add more flour or water if necessary. Cover and let dough rest 15 minutes.
3. Roll 2- to 3-inch balls of dough and roll into circles ¼ inch thick. Make a hole in center of each round and pierce the dough several times with a fork.
4. Fry until dough puffs and is golden brown on both sides. Drain. Serve warm.

CALORIES: 230 CARBOHYDRATE: 31 g PROTEIN: 4 g FAT: 17 g
CHOLESTEROL: 0 mg CALCIUM: 60 mg SODIUM: 222 mg IRON: 2 mg
VITAMIN A: <1 IU VITAMIN C: 0 mg

M E N U

Dishes of Native American Origin

Oyster Fritters
Pumpkin Soup
Turkey with Wild Rice Stuffing
Jerusalem Artichoke Salad
Indian Pudding

Serving suggestions: Offer succotash or stewed tomatoes and cranberry sauce with the turkey.

◆ *Oyster Fritters*

FRY: 2–3 minutes
DEEP-FAT FRY:
   350°F
YIELD: 50 portions
PORTION: 2 fritters

5 lb. canned oysters
   or
8 lb. fresh, shucked oysters
14 oz. flour
2 T. baking powder
2 oz. sugar

4 oz. yellow cornmeal
1 T. salt
1 tsp. pepper
2½ c. milk
2 eggs, lightly beaten

1. Drain oysters; reserve liquid.
2. Combine dry ingredients and mix.
3. Stir in milk and eggs. The batter should be thick, like heavy cream. If too thick, add small amounts of oyster liquid. Fold in oysters.
4. Using a #60 dipper, and making sure to include at least 1 oyster per fritter, fry until golden brown. Drain.

CALORIES: 189   CARBOHYDRATE: 8 g   PROTEIN: 5 g   FAT: 27 g
CHOLESTEROL: 44 mg   CALCIUM: 47 mg   SODIUM: 349 mg   IRON: 3 mg
VITAMIN A: 123 IU   VITAMIN C: <1 mg

◆ *Pumpkin Soup*

YIELD: 50 portions
PORTION: 1 c.

2 lb. onions, chopped
14 oz. butter or margarine, melted
2 oz. flour
1½ gal. chicken stock
1½ gal. pumpkin purée
1 c. dry sherry or white wine

2 T. salt
1 tsp. pepper
3½ c. cream, whipped
1½ c. pumpkin seeds, toasted
   (optional)

1. Sauté onions in butter until soft.
2. Stir in flour and cook 2–3 minutes.
3. Slowly add chicken broth, stirring briskly. Mix in pumpkin purée. Cook over low heat for 15 minutes.
4. Add sherry, salt, and pepper. Adjust seasoning.
5. Serve warm, garnished with a heaping tablespoon of whipped cream and a few toasted pumpkin seeds.

CALORIES: 196   CARBOHYDRATE: 13 g   PROTEIN: 5 g   FAT: 21 g
CHOLESTEROL: 37 mg   CALCIUM: 56 mg   SODIUM: 716 mg   IRON: 1 mg
VITAMIN A: 7968 IU   VITAMIN C: 8 mg

Turkey with Wild Rice Stuffing

YIELD: 60 portions
(2 gal.)
PORTION: ½ c.

1 lb. bacon, sliced and chopped
2 lb. onions, chopped
¾ lb. celery, finely chopped
3 lb. mushrooms, sliced
1 oz. parsley, chopped
3 T. sage, dried
1 lb. wild rice, cooked

2 lb. cornbread stuffing mix
3 lb. chestnuts, shelled, peeled, and
   quartered
1 lb., 4 oz. butter, melted
3 c. chicken stock
½ tsp. pepper
3 15-lb. turkeys

1. Brown bacon; remove and drain. Add onions and celery to fat and sauté
   until light brown.
2. Add mushrooms, parsley, and sage. Continue cooking for 8–10 minutes.
   Stir occasionally.
3. Combine above mixture with remaining ingredients. Stuff the turkeys;
   cook as desired.

CALORIES: 230
CHOLESTEROL: 31 mg
VITAMIN A: 432 IU

CARBOHYDRATE: 30 g
CALCIUM: 60 mg
VITAMIN C: 6 mg

PROTEIN: 5 g
SODIUM: 241 mg

FAT: 16 g
IRON: 2 mg

Note: Nutritional analysis is for stuffing only.

Jerusalem Artichoke Salad

YIELD: 50 portions
PORTION: 1 c.

1 qt. vegetable oil
1¾ c. white vinegar
½ lb. scallions, finely chopped
¾ c. honey
1 T. salt

1 tsp. pepper
8 lb. Jerusalem artichokes, peeled
   and diced
5 lb. lettuce

1. Combine oil, vinegar, scallions, honey, salt, and pepper. Mix.
2. Add artichokes and toss. Marinate at room temperature for at least 1 hour.
   Toss before serving. Serve on lettuce leaves.

CALORIES: 191
CHOLESTEROL: 0 mg
VITAMIN A: 35 IU

CARBOHYDRATE: 11 g
CALCIUM: 16 mg
VITAMIN C: 2 mg

PROTEIN: 1 g
SODIUM: 134 mg

FAT: 32 g
IRON: 2 mg

◆ *Indian Pudding*

BAKE: 20 minutes;
 2 hours
OVEN: 350°F; 275°F
YIELD: 48 portions
PORTION: ½ c.

½ lb. cornmeal
3 qt. milk
6 oz. butter
2 T. salt
4 T. ginger
2 lb. molasses, dark

2 lb. apples, peeled, cored, and
 grated
3 c. milk
6 eggs, beaten
3 c. milk
ice cream*

1. In a heavy saucepan, slowly beat milk into the cornmeal. Add butter, salt, ginger, and molasses; bring to a boil. Add grated apples. Boil mixture, stirring, until it begins to thicken, about 10 minutes. Transfer cornmeal mixture to a 3-gallon pot and bake, uncovered, for 20 minutes at 350°F.
2. Combine milk and eggs. Stir into cornmeal mixture.
3. Pour milk on top of cornmeal mixture. Do not mix in. Bake, uncovered, for 2 hours at 275°F. Pudding will form a crust. Serve warm with ice cream.

CALORIES: 160　　CARBOHYDRATE: 20 g　　PROTEIN: 4 g　　FAT: 7 g
CHOLESTEROL: 54 mg　　CALCIUM: 246 mg　　SODIUM: 367 mg　　IRON: 3 mg
VITAMIN A: 277 IU　　VITAMIN C: 1 mg

*Not included in nutritional analysis.

•15• COOKING FROM THE
•*Philippines*•

Ukoy (shrimp, sweet potato, and squash fritters) and empanadas (deep-fried meat turnovers), Filipino appetizers or snacks.

*M*any foreign influences have affected the cuisine of the Philippines. Long ago, Chinese, Asian Indian, and Malay trading ships frequented the port of Manila. For nearly 400 years, Spain dominated much of the Philippines, with the exception of the southern portion, which was already under the influence of Islam. Spanish missionaries established the Roman Catholic church in the Philippines, making it the only primarily Christian country in Asia. Brief occupation by the United States during the 20th century added yet another cultural influence.

Thus, beginning with native foods such as coconuts and seafood, the Filipinos forged a cuisine that incorporated both Chinese and Spanish cooking techniques and ingredients as well as a smattering of Indonesian, Asian Indian, and American ideas. Today, Filipinos produce an array of dishes found nowhere else in the world. Rice has been eaten in the Philippines for about 2,000 years and is the backbone of the diet. No meal is complete without it, and snacks can be distinguished from meals by the fact that rice is not served with them. Aside from the reliance on rice, the Chinese influence can be seen in Filipino dishes such as *lumpia*, very similar to an egg roll, and in the use of soy sauce, bean curd, bean sprouts, and noodles.

The Spanish introduced pork and olive oil, and brought a taste for rich desserts. Many Spanish dishes have been adapted for use with Filipino ingredients. The *empanada*, a spicy turnover, uses typically Spanish ingredients. Variations of the Spanish rice *paellas* are also made. Indonesian influence, particularly strong in the south, can be seen in the use of fish sauce, coconut milk, and peanuts. Americans brought cola drinks, steak, and hot dogs, which are now popular. As might be expected, cuisine varies among the approximately 7,000 islands that comprise the Philippines.

Ingredients
MILK AND MILK PRODUCTS
Fresh milk from goats or *caraboa* (water buffalo) is sometimes consumed or used in cooking. Evaporated milk is more popular. One of the few native cheeses made in Asia is the Filipino white cheese made from caraboa milk. Western-style cheese is now processed locally, and cheese is imported from Australia.

173

MEAT AND MEAT ALTERNATIVES

Pork (including all the variety meats, as well as blood and entrails) is the most popular meat, with chicken second. Beef, kid (goat), and deer are also eaten. Eggs are eaten and used frequently in cooking.

Fish and shellfish are commonly eaten, including crabs, shrimp, herring, anchovies, crayfish, tuna, carp, squid, and many more. *Bangus* (milkfish) is the national dish of the Philippines. Legumes such as black beans, mung beans, soybeans, chickpeas, and peanuts are used in some dishes, even desserts. Chinese-style bean products, including bean sprouts, soybean paste, soy sauce, and bean curd, are also popular.

FRUITS AND VEGETABLES

Many tropical fruits are available. More than a hundred varieties of bananas and plaintains are grown, and even banana blossoms are used in some dishes. Breadfruit, custard apples, guavas, limes, mandarin oranges, papayas, persimmons, pineapples, star fruit, and tangerines are some of the other fruits commonly used. Java plum (a small, sour fruit), *rambutan* (related to litchis), and *durian* (a strong-smelling fruit with an exquisite creamy pulp) are other fruits that grow in the Philippines.

Many of the vegetables used are similar to those found in China: bamboo shoots, long beans, water chestnuts, bitter melon, Chinese cabbage, bean sprouts, and snow peas, for example. Tropical roots such as taro, cassava, sweet potato, and many types of yam are found, as well as white potatoes. Several types of squash, both summer and winter, are grown. Lettuce, cabbage, green beans, hearts of palm, tomatoes, peas, onions, winged beans, and many other vegetables are also common.

BREADS AND CEREALS

Rice is the staple food of the Philippines. The long-grain type is used in most dishes, although short-grain, glutinous rice is preferred for sweet dishes. Rice flour is used in the popular bread *pan de sol*. Noodles are also common and can be made from wheat, rice, or mung beans. Today, wheat flour bread is becoming more popular.

OTHER INGREDIENTS

Lard and olive oil are the most commonly used fats, though coconut oil and peanut oil are used in some dishes. Coconuts are an important part of Filipino cuisine. Recipes may call for coconut milk, coconut cream, or unsweetened shredded coconut. Immature coconuts are a popular delicacy. Other nuts used include almonds, betel nuts, cashews, and pili nuts.

Coffee, tea, and hot chocolate are the favored hot beverages; soy and coconut milk are served cold. Water is usually served with meals. Filipino beer is popular, as is *tuba*, a fermented drink made from the sap of palms.

Seasonings

Filipino foods are often spicy, although the types of seasonings used are limited. Garlic, onions, and chili peppers season many dishes. Sour tastes are also prominent in Filipino cooking and are attained through the use of mild palm vinegar, *kamias* (a sour cucumberlike fruit), *calamansi* (a small lime), and tamarind pulp. Tiny fish and shrimp are salted and fermented to make the condiments *bagoong* (fish paste) and *patis* (fish sauce). Annatto, saffron, and turmeric are used to color foods yellow or orange. Bay leaves and ginger root, lemon grass, and cilantro flavor some foods, and vanilla is used in some desserts.

Preparation

Three principles govern most of Filipino cooking: first, no food should be cooked by itself; second, foods should be flavored with fried garlic or onion; and third, tart ingredients should be used to impart a cool, sour taste to dishes. An example is *adobo*, in which pork and/or chicken is marinated in vinegar with garlic, bay leaves, salt, and peppercorns. Then it is simmered till tender, the garlic and meat are removed from the marinade and sautéed in lard, and finally they are returned to the marinade and simmered until a thick sauce is produced.

Frying, stewing, and roasting are the most common ways of cooking meat and fish; ingredients are often sautéed before being added to a stew. Clay pots as well as metal pans resembling woks are used.

Dishes that combine ingredients are popular. In fact, rice and certain types of fish are the only foods cooked alone. Other fish, meat, chicken, vegetables, noodles, and even fruits are combined in soups, stews, and other mixed dishes that are served as accompaniments to the rice. There is no central or essential ingredient in mixed dishes. The combination of available ingredients, as well as the spices and cooking method used, determine what the dish will become. Examples are *sinigang*, a soup that can be made with either fish or meat, containing sour fruit, tomatoes, and other vegetables, and *puchero*, which combines beef, chicken, sometimes pork, and a variety of vegetables in a garlicky eggplant sauce.

A whole pig may be roasted for a special occasion, and some dishes feature roast meat or poultry, such as *chicken relleno*, a chicken stuffed with boiled eggs, pork, and sausage. Snack foods such as empanadas, lumpia, and *ukoy* (fritters made with vegetables and shrimp) are fried.

Filipino desserts often feature glutinous rice and coconut milk. *Halo-halo* is a liquid dessert containing shaved ice and coconut milk with a variety of other ingredients such as mung beans, corn kernels, and pineapple jelly added. Cakes, fruit fritters, and custards are also made; a popular dessert is *leche flan*, a Spanish-style custard. Ice cream is made with such unusual flavors as avocado and purple yam.

Meal Patterns

Filipinos eat three meals a day. Breakfast traditionally consists of garlic-flavored fried rice and fish or sausages. Fried eggs can be added, and bread may be substituted for rice; coffee or hot chocolate is usually served. Lunch and dinner are similar in size and composition; often both are large meals. Soup, a fish and/or meat dish, rice, and fresh fruit or a rich dessert are usually served either in courses (Spanish style) or all at once (Filipino style). Traditional condiments are bagoong, patis (which is even poured on salad), and calamansi juice. It is not unusual, however, for ketchup and other American condiments to join these.

In addition to meals, a mid-morning snack is often eaten. A favorite snack is hot chocolate and *ensaimadas*, a sweet dough with a filling of aged cheese. In the afternoon, a snack called *merienda* is eaten. Traditionally consisting of sweets, the merienda today consists of almost anything, with the exception of rice, which is served only at meals.

M E N U

Filipino Dinner

Ukoy
(shrimp, sweet potato, and squash fritters)
Empanadas
(deep-fried meat turnovers)
Adobo
(chicken stew)
Pineapple-Stuffed Tomatoes
Banana Fritters

Serving suggestions: Offer adobo with steamed long-grain rice along with coffee or tea.

◆ *Ukoy (Shrimp and Squash Fritters)*

FRY: 5–6 minutes
DEEP-FAT FRYER:
  350°F
YIELD: 50 portions
PORTION: 1 fritter

2½ c. boiling water
1½ T. salt
1½ T. annatto seeds
2½ lb. medium shrimp, unshelled
1 lb. flour
4 c. cornstarch

2 lb. sweet potatoes, peeled and
  coarsely grated
3 lb. acorn squash, peeled, halved,
  seeded, and coarsely grated
½ lb. scallion tops, finely chopped
garlic sauce (recipe below)

1. Add salt and annatto seeds to water. Add shrimp and bring to a boil. Reduce heat and simmer about 3 minutes or until shrimp are firm and pink. Remove shrimp with slotted spoon and drain, cool, shell, and devein. Strain cooking liquid and add enough water to make 5 cups.
2. Combine flour and cornstarch. Add cooking liquid and mix until batter is smooth.
3. Add grated sweet potatoes, squash, and scallions to batter. Mix thoroughly.
4. Using ⅓ cup of batter mixture, form a patty on a small plate. Lightly press a shrimp into the center. Fry patty shrimp-side up for about 5 minutes (spoon hot oil over patty while cooking). Serve with garlic sauce (1 tablespoon per ukoy).

Garlic Sauce
5 T. garlic, finely chopped
5 tsp. salt

1¼ qt. white vinegar

Crush garlic and salt together until the consistency of smooth paste. Pour in vinegar and mix thoroughly.

CALORIES: 237	CARBOHYDRATE: 25 g	PROTEIN: 11 g	FAT: 18 g
CHOLESTEROL: 25 mg	CALCIUM: 53 mg	SODIUM: 700 mg	IRON: 1mg
VITAMIN A: 1599 IU	VITAMIN C: 5 mg		

◆ Empanadas (Deep-Fried Meat Turnovers)

FRY: 4–6 minutes
DEEP-FAT FRYER:
  375°F
YIELD: 50 portions
PORTION: 1
  turnover

1¼ lb. flour
1 tsp. salt
1¼ c. water
2½ T. sugar

2 egg yolks
6 oz. butter or shortening, melted
2 egg whites, lightly beaten
meat filling (recipe below)

1. Sift flour and salt into a bowl. Combine water, sugar, and egg yolks. Beat into flour and salt until smooth. Let dough rest 10 minutes.
2. On lightly floured surface, roll out dough. Brush with butter. Tightly roll pastry into a long, thin tube. Cut into ¾-inch pieces. Roll each slice into a 3-inch circle.
3. Fill with 1 tablespoon of meat mixture. Seal with egg white. Fry until golden brown. Drain. Serve hot.

Meat Filling

4 oz. bacon, chopped
2 T. vegetable oil
1 T. garlic, minced
1 lb. onions, finely chopped
½ lb. pork, ground
½ lb. beef, ground
½ lb. chicken, ground

1 tsp. salt
½ tsp. pepper
3 oz. tomato sauce
6 eggs, hard-boiled, chopped
3 oz. pickled gherkins, chopped
½ c. black olives, chopped

1. Fry bacon until crisp. Reserve.
2. Sauté garlic and onions in oil and remaining bacon fat.
3. Add pork, veal, and chicken; brown meats. Mix in salt, pepper, and tomato sauce. Cook over low heat for 15 minutes.
4. Mix in eggs, gherkins, olives, and reserved bacon. Adjust seasonings and cool.

CALORIES: 242
CHOLESTEROL: 47 mg
VITAMIN A: 148 IU

CARBOHYDRATE: 12 g
CALCIUM: 14 mg
VITAMIN C: 2 mg

PROTEIN: 5 g
SODIUM: 253 mg

FAT: 34 g
IRON: 1 mg

◆ Adobo (Chicken Stew)

YIELD: 50 portions
PORTION: 3 oz.

20 lb. whole chicken
2 c. vinegar
6 oz. garlic, finely chopped
6 bay leaves

2 T. salt or to taste
1 tsp. pepper
¾ c. oil
3 c. coconut milk, unsweetened

1. Cut chicken into 18 pieces. Cut breasts in fourths and wings, drumsticks, and thighs in half. Combine vinegar, garlic, bay leaves, salt, and pepper. Add to chicken. Add enough boiling water to cover. Simmer, uncovered, until chicken is tender and water has evaporated.
2. Add oil and fry chicken until brown. Add coconut milk to chicken, heat, and serve.

CALORIES: 339
CHOLESTEROL: 115 mg
VITAMIN A: 87 IU

CARBOHYDRATE: 2 g
CALCIUM: 40 mg
VITAMIN C: <1 mg

PROTEIN: 38 g
SODIUM: 368 mg

FAT: 38 g
IRON: 2 mg

◆ Pineapple-Stuffed Tomatoes

YIELD: 50 portions
PORTION: 1 tomato

50 medium tomatoes, skinned
3 T. salt
1 #10 can pineapple, drained and shredded (or 2½ qt. fresh, shredded pineapple)

1½ lb. roasted peanuts, chopped
1 c. patis (French dressing may be substituted)
2 lb. lettuce leaves

1. Slice off top of each tomato; remove pulp. Sprinkle with salt and let stand 10 minutes; rinse.
2. Combine pineapple, peanuts, and patis. Stuff tomatoes.
3. Arrange stuffed tomatoes on lettuce leaves and serve.

CALORIES: 137
CHOLESTEROL: 0 mg
VITAMIN A: 1175 IU

CARBOHYDRATE: 17 g
CALCIUM: 36 mg
VITAMIN C: 34 mg

PROTEIN: 4 g
SODIUM: 544 mg

FAT: 13 g
IRON: 1 mg

◆ Banana Fritters

FRY: 4–6 minutes
DEEP-FAT FRYER: 375°F
YIELD: 50 portions
PORTION: 2 fritters

2 lb. flour
2 qt. evaporated milk

1 lb. sugar
25 bananas, ripe

1. Mix flour, milk, and sugar to make a smooth batter.
2. Peel and quarter bananas. Dip in batter and deep-fry until brown. Drain. May be served hot or cold.

CALORIES: 261
CHOLESTEROL: 2 mg
VITAMIN A: 206 IU

CARBOHYDRATE: 40 g
CALCIUM: 124 mg
VITAMIN C: 6 mg

PROTEIN: 6 g
SODIUM: 48 mg

FAT: 17 g
IRON: 1 mg

·16·COOKING FROM
·*Polynesia*·

*Haupia, a sweet
Polynesian coconut
dessert.*

*P*olynesia comprises several widely separated, small groups of islands, including the Hawaiian Islands, the Society Islands (including Tahiti), the Cook Islands, and the Samoas. The origins of the Polynesian people are uncertain. It is known that voyagers from elsewhere in Polynesia settled the Hawaiian Islands around A.D. 500. They found yams, birds, a few small animals, and fish as possible sources of food. They introduced breadfruit, taro, and probably pigs and chickens. Bananas and coconuts were probably brought from Indonesia around A.D. 1000.

Europeans began to settle the islands in the late 1700s. The Spanish brought oranges, figs, grapes, and pineapples. They also introduced techniques for refining sugar from cane. Since few Hawaiians wanted to tend the sugar cane fields, a succession of plantation workers from China, Japan, Korea, and the Philippines were brought to Hawaii. Each nationality brought their own native foods with them, so that ingredients and cooking methods from many cultures were soon added to the Hawaiian repertoire.

Today, the cuisine of Hawaii is a mixture of Asian, European, American, and native Polynesian foods, but these have not been melded into a single style. Instead, each recipe retains its traditional character, and dishes from several different cultures may be served at the same meal. Outside the Hawaiian Islands, fewer foreign influences have been brought to bear on the cuisine, and the food reflects more of its Polynesian background. In 1842, after France claimed the Society Islands, Tahiti's cuisine took on a French character. Samoan cuisine was more strongly influenced by the early British missionaries.

181

Ingredients

MILK AND MILK PRODUCTS

Milk was brought to the islands by European settlers, but it is not frequently consumed, and is seldom used in cooking. Polynesia's hot climate and limited grazing land discourage farmers from keeping cattle.

MEAT AND MEAT ALTERNATIVES

Fish and shellfish are staples in Polynesian diets, and are eaten at every meal on some islands. Mullet is one of the most popular fish, but many others, including *mahimahi* (dolphinfish), salmon, shark, tuna, and sardines, are consumed. The variety of shellfish is tremendous: in addition to all the types familiar in the West—clams, crab, lobster, scallops, and shrimp—there are crayfish, giant clams, sea urchins, and many others that have no English names. Eel, octopus, squid, and sea cucumbers are also eaten.

Poultry, particularly chicken, is widely available, as are eggs. Pork, is the most popular meat, especially for festive occasions. Beef stew and corned beef dishes became popular after they were introduced by New Englanders, but beef is not eaten frequently. Soybean products are used, particularly by Asian residents, and winged beans are an important protein source on some islands.

FRUITS AND VEGETABLES

Many types of fruit are available, including bananas, citrus fruits, pineapples, guavas, litchis, jackfruits, mangos, papayas, melons, and passion fruit.

Starchy vegetables are a mainstay of the Polynesian diet. These include the root vegetable *taro*, which is a little denser and more glutinous than the white potato, and breadfruit, actually a fruit that grows on trees and has a fluffy, breadlike interior. Yams, sweet potatoes, and white potatoes are also used. The green vegetable most commonly eaten in traditional Polynesian diets is the taro leaf. Leaves from other plants such as the sweet potato and the *ti* plant are also used.

Various settlers introduced many vegetables, including Chinese cabbage, bitter melon, bean sprouts, onions, tomatoes, squash, watercress, and snow peas. More than 40 varieties of seaweed are also available.

BREADS AND CEREALS

Since the arrival of the Chinese, Japanese, and Koreans, both long- and short-grain rice have become popular. Noodles and soybean products were also introduced by the Asians, and are commonly used in Asian-influenced dishes. Wheat flour breads and crackers are also widely consumed. Arrowroot and cornstarch are used to thicken puddings and other dishes.

OTHER INGREDIENTS

Coconut oil and lard are the preferred fats in Polynesia. Some dishes use special fats or oils, including butter, peanut oil, sesame oil, or turtle fat. The water or juice inside coconuts is a traditional beverage, and it is also used to make a fermented drink. Fermented beverages are also made from breadfruit, pineapple, ti root, and other tropical plants. Fruit juices, coffee, which grows in Hawaii, and tea are also very popular.

Almonds, candlenuts (*kukui* nuts), and peanuts are eaten. Macadamia nuts, for which Hawaii is famous, were introduced from Australia less than 100 years ago. The most frequently used nut, though, is the coconut. Coconuts provide juice for drinking, sap for brewing, and milk and cream used in baking, sauces, stews, and even in coffee. Coconut milk can be baked into a custard and made into substances resembling cheese and buttermilk. Immature coconuts provide a soft food for babies, and are considered a delicacy for adults. Grated coconut is added to many dishes.

Seasonings

Lime and lemon juice, coconut milk, garlic, ginger, tamarind, scallions, rock salt, and pepper flavor many dishes. Brown sugar, soy sauce, curry powder, and other seasonings associated with the various imported cuisines are also used. Traditional Polynesian food is not highly seasoned.

Preparation

Polynesian cuisine developed without benefit of metal pots, pans, or utensils. On some islands, cooking was traditionally done in a pit lined with stones (called an *imu* in Hawaii and a *hima'a* in Samoa), in which a fire was built and kept burning for two or three hours until the rocks were thoroughly heated. Then, the coals were removed and a layer of banana leaves or palm fronds was set on top of them. Food was placed on the leaves and covered with more leaves and a layer of dirt. In some cases, water was added to the rocks just before the pit was sealed, steaming the foods rather than baking them. The pit was left sealed for several hours until the food was done. Many foods were baked in an imu: taro, breadfruit, bananas, and sweet potatoes were often included, as well as fish and chicken. For special occasions, a whole pig was cooked. The Hawaiian luau, or feast, is still cooked in an imu. Similar feasts are held on other islands, but have different names.

Foods are often stewed or steamed in Polynesian cuisine. Historically, boiling was accomplished by placing hot stones in a bowl containing water and the food to be cooked. Today, soups and chowders remain common, featuring fish and shellfish, coconut milk, and sometimes breadfruit or green papayas. Packets of fish, chicken, or pork with chopped taro leaves and coconut milk wrapped in ti leaves (called *laulaus* in Hawaii and *palusami* in Samoa) were traditionally cooked in the imu, but today they are prepared in a steamer.

Fruits and cooked root vegetables are often pounded into a paste. In Hawaii, taro root prepared this way and eaten either fresh or slightly fermented is called *poi*, which originally referred to the pounding method. In Tahiti, the word *poe* survives as the name for a sweet dessert made of pounded guavas, papayas, bananas, and other fruit. Poi is a staple of the traditional Hawaiian diet; when food was scarce, people survived on salted poi or poi with a little fish or seaweed. In Samoa, although taro is the most important staple vegetable, it is not made into poi.

Many foods are eaten raw; not only fruits and nuts, but fish as well. Throughout the Polynesian islands, fish chunks of various kinds are marinated in lime or lemon juice, which denatures the fish protein, turning it white just as cooking does. *Lomi-lomi* is a well-known Hawaiian dish adapted from the salt fish introduced by New Englanders. Lomi means "massage" in Hawaiian, and the thin, salted fillets were "massaged" in water to remove some of the salt and break down the fibers. Today, this dish is most often made with fresh salmon. Then tomatoes and onions are added and it is served with poi or alone as an appetizer. Other seafood is also eaten raw; in Tahiti, raw sea urchins are a delicacy.

Few traditional vegetables are edible or palatable in a raw state, and salads have never formed a part of the traditional cuisine. Even today, vegetables, and fruits used as vegetables, such as bananas, are usually served cooked. Puddings are popular, and are made from coconut milk with banana, breadfruit, taro, sweet potato, or cornstarch.

Many dishes now found in Polynesia come from American, Asian, European, or Southeast Asian recipes. Marinated beef skewers, beef jerky, curried dishes, *rumaki* (chicken liver with a slice of water chestnut wrapped in bacon and deep-fried), fried wontons, *sushi*, and sweet Portuguese-style bread are a few examples. Traditional ingredients have been prepared in unconventional ways, as in crackers and chips made from taro, breadfruit, bananas, and soybeans.

Meal Patterns

Traditional meals included poi or boiled taro, breadfruit, or green bananas; fish or pork; and greens or seaweed, with the evening meal being largest. Little distinction was made between the foods served at the two or three meals eaten daily. Since cooking in an imu is a lengthy project, enough food to feed a family for two or three days was cooked at one time, and then leftovers were eaten for several meals. Today, breakfast is more likely to be a generic American breakfast, as bread replaces poi and rice, and coffee becomes more popular than tea. Traditional foods may still be offered at lunch and dinner; some Hawaiians still eat poi at least twice a day and Asians may eat Asian-style food at lunch and dinner. More beef and canned fish is consumed, however, and fresh fruit appears more often as part of a meal rather than as a snack. *Saimin*, created by adding pork to a Japanese noodle dish, has become a very popular quick lunch in Hawaii.

M   E   N   U   *Polynesian Dinner*

◆ *Lomi-lomi (Marinated Salmon)*

YIELD: 50 portions
PORTION: 2–3 oz.

8 lb. salmon fillets, cut into 1" cubes
8 lb. tomatoes, peeled, seeded,
   and chopped
1 qt. lime juice
12 oz. scallions, chopped

½ tsp. Tabasco sauce
2½ T. sugar
3½ T. salt
2 tsp. pepper

Combine all ingredients. Marinate in the refrigerator for at least 6 hours, turning salmon occasionally, until fish is more opaque and appears "cooked."

CALORIES: 161
CHOLESTEROL: 51 mg
VITAMIN A: 909 IU

CARBOHYDRATE: 6 g
CALCIUM: 44 mg
VITAMIN C: 24 mg

PROTEIN: 14 g
SODIUM: 502 mg

FAT: 16 g
IRON: 1 mg

◆ Green Papaya Chowder

YIELD: 60 portions
PORTION: 1 c.

1 lb. bacon, chopped
1½ lb. onions, sliced
8 lb. unripe (green) papayas, cubed

2 T. salt
2 gal. water
3 qt. milk

1. Fry bacon until crisp. Add onions and sauté until soft.
2. Add papaya, salt, and water to onion mixture. Simmer until vegetables are tender.
3. Add milk and heat (do not boil).

CALORIES: 100
CHOLESTEROL: 13 mg
VITAMIN A: (1279 IU)

CARBOHYDRATE: (9 g)
CALCIUM: 77 mg
VITAMIN C: (41 mg)

PROTEIN: 4 g
SODIUM: 360 mg

FAT: 5 g
IRON: < 1 mg

◆ Chicken with Taro Leaves

YIELD: 50 portions
PORTION: 5–6 oz.

20 lb. taro leaves (see note)
3 qt. water
20 lb. chicken, boneless, cut into
  small pieces
2 T. garlic, minced

¾ c. oil
1 T. salt
1½ qt. water
1 gal. coconut milk

1. Wash taro leaves and remove stems and ribs. Simmer in water for 1 hour or until tender. Drain. Wring out leaves to remove excess water.
2. Sauté garlic and chicken in oil. Brown lightly. Add salt and water; simmer until tender. Remove chicken and drain.
3. Combine chicken with taro leaves. Add coconut milk and heat.

Note: Fresh spinach may be substituted for the taro leaves. Simmer for 20 minutes or until tender.

CALORIES: 462
CHOLESTEROL: 90 mg
VITAMIN A: 14768 IU

CARBOHYDRATE: 11 g
CALCIUM: 197 mg
VITAMIN C: 94 mg

PROTEIN: 40 g
SODIUM: 436 mg

FAT: 32 g
IRON: 8 mg

◆ *Pineapple Pickles*

MARINATE: 1–2
  weeks
YIELD: 50 portions
PORTION: 1½ T.

6 lb. pineapple, fresh
¾ qt. water
1¾ lb. sugar
¾ qt. cider vinegar

2 T. whole cloves
2 cinnamon sticks
3–5 chili peppers, red, dried
  (optional)

1. Peel and core pineapple. Cut into 1-inch cubes.
2. Combine water, sugar, and vinegar. Add cloves and cinnamon, tied in a
   piece of cheesecloth. Simmer for 15 minutes. Add pineapple, continue
   cooking over low heat until translucent, about 1½ hours. Pour into hot
   sterilized jars. Add one chili pepper to each jar. Let stand 1–2 weeks.

CALORIES: 75
CHOLESTEROL: 0 mg
VITAMIN A: 9 IU

CARBOHYDRATE: 19 g
CALCIUM: 6 mg
VITAMIN C: 6 mg

PROTEIN: <1 mg
SODIUM: 1 mg

FAT: <1 g
IRON: <1 mg

◆ *Haupia (Coconut Dessert)*

YIELD: 50 portions
PORTION: 4–5 1″ ×
  1″ × 2″ pieces

6 qt. coconut milk, canned
11 oz., 2 T. cornstarch

1 lb. sugar

Combine cornstarch and sugar. Add sufficient coconut milk to make a smooth
paste. Boil remaining milk and add cornstarch paste. Boil until mixture
thickens, stirring frequently. Pour into one 12″ × 20″ × 2″ pan and cool. Cut
into 1-inch squares.

CALORIES: 349
CHOLESTEROL: 0 mg
VITAMIN A: 0 IU

CARBOHYDRATE: 21 g
CALCIUM: 18 mg
VITAMIN C: 2 mg

PROTEIN: 4 g
SODIUM: <1 mg

FAT: 30 g
IRON: 2 mg

A Danish smörgåsbord with a selection of open-faced sandwiches and cauliflower and shrimp salad.

*T*he harsh climate and extensive seacoast of the Scandinavian countries, principally Norway, Sweden, Denmark, Finland, and Iceland, play a large part in determining the ingredients available to cooks of the region. Fish are the foundation of the cuisine, supplemented by an abundant use of dairy products. There are some similarities between the dishes of Scandinavia and those found in Germany and the Soviet Union. In the 19th century, bakers from Austria were brought to Denmark to fill the jobs of striking bakers there. They introduced the flaky, butter pastry that was the forerunner of the well-known "Danish," still known by the name *Weinerbrød* ("Vienna bread") in Denmark.

In earlier times, most of the fish, milk, and produce obtained during northern Scandinavia's short summers were preserved. Dried, fermented, pickled, salted, and smoked foods are still prevalent, and salty dishes are preferred. The diet is hearty and contains a substantial amount of fat, which was originally believed necessary to sustain people exposed to the cold climate. Today, there is a tendency for the food to be a little lighter. The cuisines of Norway, Sweden, and Denmark are all very similar. Finland's cooking has been influenced by the Soviet Union, which it borders to the south and west. Heavy soups and dumplings are characteristic dishes. Iceland, having at various times been ruled by both Denmark and Norway, has a cooking style that resembles the cuisine of both these countries.

Ingredients

MILK AND MILK PRODUCTS

Both cow's and goat's milk are widely available; in some areas, reindeer milk is consumed. Milk is consumed as a beverage and is also made into a variety of dairy products. Buttermilk, cream, and sour cream are used in numerous dishes. Cheese is also popular, specifically Danish blue cheese, semisoft

Havarti, Gjetost (a sweet cheese made from boiled cow's or goat's milk whey), Kuminost (flavored with caraway), and firm, nutty Tybo.

MEAT AND MEAT ALTERNATIVES

Cod, herring, and salmon are the most common types of fish consumed. Mackerel, pike, haddock, perch, eel, trout, turbot, and anchovies are but a few of the other fish eaten. Shellfish, including shrimp, lobster, crayfish, crab, mussels, and oysters, are also enjoyed. Caviar and the roe of salmon and other fish are considered delicacies.

Meat is eaten frequently, though usually not in large quantities. Pork, beef, veal, lamb, and mutton are consumed. More meat is consumed in Sweden than in other Scandinavian countries, but beef is not favored due to its poor quality. Pork is especially popular in Finland. Denmark is known for its ham. Lamb and mutton are frequently eaten in Norway, but lamb is a luxury in Denmark. In Iceland, smoked mutton is a specialty. Game meats such as hare, reindeer, and venison are used in some dishes. Ptarmigan, or arctic bird, and whale are sometimes consumed in Norway. Chicken is eaten frequently, as are duck, goose, partridge, and pheasant. Eggs are eaten often. Some dishes feature legumes, such as lentils and split peas.

FRUITS AND VEGETABLES

Apples are very popular. Cherries, pears, plums, rhubarb, and, in some areas, peaches and apricots, are available. Berries are commonly used, including blueberries, gooseberries, blackberries, lingonberries, strawberries, cranberries, and currants. Dried fruits, such as prunes and raisins, are called for in many recipes.

The most frequently used vegetables are potatoes, cabbage, beets, and onions. Potato flour is called for in many recipes. Cucumber, celery (both stalk and root), turnips, carrots, green beans, nettles, mushrooms, kohlrabi, spinach, asparagus, and sweet peppers are commonly available, although the Scandinavian diet does not rely heavily on vegetables, with the exception of potatoes. Wild mushrooms are picked, especially in Finland.

BREADS AND CEREALS

Whole grain products are eaten frequently. Rye is used in most breads, although wheat is used for some breads and for most pastries. Barley, oats, and rice are also consumed.

OTHER INGREDIENTS

A considerable amount of butter is used in Scandinavian cooking. Some dishes also use margarine, lard, or salt pork.

Almonds are the most popular nut. They are used extensively—whole, chopped, sliced, or ground—in desserts. Marzipan, a sweetened almond paste, is particularly popular. Chestnuts and walnuts are also used.

Coffee, tea, and hot chocolate are all consumed. Ale, beer, wine, and vodka are favored alcoholic drinks. The Scandinavian specialty is *aquavit* (meaning "water of life"), a liquor distilled from potatoes or grain, often flavored with herbs or spices, such as caraway. Imported wines tend to be expensive, but some fruit wines are made locally. Cordials such as the Danish Cherry Heering are popular.

Seasonings

Caraway, cardamom, and dill weed flavor many dishes. Other commonly used seasonings include thyme, tarragon, parsley, marjoram, bay leaves, and capers. Pungent spices, including garlic, horseradish, mustard, and pepper (black, white, and cayenne), are used, while vinegar and lemon juice provide tartness. Cinnamon, cloves, allspice, nutmeg, ginger, lemon and orange peel, and vanilla are found in sweet dishes. Chocolate is used frequently in Norway.

Preparation

Fresh fish is typically boiled, sautéed, or deep-fried, then served with a cream sauce. It is also combined with potatoes and cream in casseroles or with winter vegetables and sour cream in soups. Fish pudding is made from ground white fish combined with cream or milk and thickened with wheat or potato flour or cornstarch, then baked and topped with shrimp sauce. The process of preserving cod was developed in the region 1,000 years ago, and dried salt cod is used in many dishes today. *Lutefisk* is a Norwegian dish made from dried salt cod soaked for days in a mild lye solution, then boiled. Other Scandinavian preserved fish include salmon pressed with salt, pepper, sugar, and dill weed, called *gravlax*; smoked salmon known as *lox*; and many types of marinated herring.

Meat is frequently ground or finely chopped, then extended with other ingredients. Swedish-style meatballs are well known. Danish *frikadeller* is a patty made from ground pork and veal, bread crumbs or flour, onions, egg, and milk or soda water, fried in butter. Vegetables such as onions and cabbage are commonly stuffed with ground meat mixtures.

Sauces are prominent in Scandinavian cuisine. A hot or cold sauce is served with every dish, and most are rich, containing eggs and fresh or sour cream. Hollandaise sauce, sour cream with horseradish, melted butter, and mayonnaise mixed with anchovies or capers are a few examples.

Potatoes are included in almost every meal. It is not unusual to serve two or even three potato dishes at one time. The most popular way to cook potatoes is to boil them, then steam them until they are dry, but they may also be pan-fried or boiled and caramelized with sugar. Potato pancakes and dumplings are also common. Other vegetables, such as red cabbage and yellow or green peas are served as side dishes. Salads often feature cucumbers, celery, tomatoes, and other vegetables, apples and other fruit, as well as pickled fish and cured meats, usually mixed in a thick, plain dressing such as mayonnaise. A salad might also simply consist of pickled vegetables such as cucumbers or beets.

Scandinavian breads are frequently unleavened. *Lefser* is a popular Norwegian bread made with potato dough and fried on a griddle. Similar to a large, thin pancake, the lefser is folded with butter and sugar before being eaten. Flatbread, a very thin cracker, is also made in Norway. Traditionally, breads were dried to preserve them, and today many are still preferred crusty. Rusks are made from slices of wheat or rye bread toasted and dried in the oven.

Sweet baked goods are very popular. Doughnuts are common, especially the Danish fruit- or jam-filled puffs called *aebleskivers*. Pancakes are also well liked, although they are more often served as a dessert than for breakfast, with preserved fruit or jam. Cookies are a specialty, often flavored with cardamom, ginger, or cloves. In Norway, an almond paste confection called *kransekake* is the national cake. Soufflés, tiered cakes, napoleons, meringue tortes, almond paste cakes, and a great variety of other sweets are made for special occasions. Whipped cream is used extensively.

Meal Patterns

Breakfast in Denmark consists of coffee, dark and white breads with butter and jams, and perhaps an egg or cheese. In Norway, a more substantial breakfast is eaten, typically consisting of milk, a boiled egg, herring or other fish, oatmeal, cheese, bread with butter and jam, and coffee. A typical Scandinavian lunch is an open-faced sandwich and a glass of milk.

Appetizers are an important part of Scandinavian cuisine. Called *smörgåsbord* (meaning "sandwich table"), the selection of appetizers ranges from pickled herring, caviar, and oysters to stuffed vegetables and hard-boiled eggs, salads, cold cuts, croquettes, and hot dishes. Although the smörgåsbord started out as a prelude to a meal, it has expanded over time and today often constitutes the entire meal. Traditionally, the smörgåsbord is eaten in courses, beginning with herring dishes, progressing to cold fish and then meat and salad dishes, followed by hot dishes, and ending with desserts. Everything is washed down with aquavit, and coffee follows dessert.

For an ordinary meal at home, a small selection of simple appetizers is served, one meat or fish dish with potatoes, a salad or vegetable, and perhaps a dessert. In Norway, a soup may precede the meal; if there is no soup, dessert is usually served at the end of the meal. Fruit is often made into a hot or cold soup, which may serve as either the first course or the last. In Denmark, supper may be soup and pancakes; fish and boiled potatoes; or a minced-meat dish, boiled potatoes, and cucumber salad. Dessert is usually fruit porridge, pudding, fromage (a whipped cream and gelatin creation), or fruit.

In Denmark, supper is eaten at 6:00 P.M., after which people often go out for a glass of wine, beer and sandwiches, or cake and coffee. In Norway, dinner is served at 4:00 or 5:00, and a sandwich with tea or coffee is often eaten later, around 9:00 P.M.

M E N U

Scandinavian Dinner

Yellow Split-Pea Soup
Fried Trout with Sour Cream
and Lemon
Caramelized Potatoes
Peppernøtter
(pepper nut cookies),
Almond Cookies
and
Sour Cream Cookies

Serving suggestions: Offer buttered, parslied carrots and another potato dish (pan-fried or pancakes), if desired. Serve beer or apple juice.

M E N U

Smörgåsbord (Koldt Bord)

Open-faced Sandwiches
(bacon and mushroom,
cucumber and blue cheese,
egg and tomato,
pork and beet)
Sildesalat
(herring salad)
Pork-Stuffed Onion Rolls
Cauliflower and Shrimp Salad
Jansson's Temptation
(potato casserole)

Serving suggestions: The Scandinavian buffet table includes cold and hot dishes (such as roast beef, chicken salad, sardines, smoked salmon, and a selection of cheeses) as well as a dessert tray. Serve with dark rye, pumpernickel, and whole wheat breads and aquavit, beer, or apple juice.

Scandinavian Dinner

♦ *Yellow Split-Pea Soup*

YIELD: 50–60
portions
PORTION: 1 c.

9 lb. dried yellow split peas
3 gal. cold water
4 lb. onions, finely chopped
½ lb. whole onions, studded
  with cloves

8 lb. ham, cut into cubes
2½ T. marjoram
1½ T. thyme
salt to taste

Combine all ingredients. Bring to a boil and simmer until peas are tender, about 1 hour. Remove whole onions before serving.

CALORIES: 415	CARBOHYDRATE: 47 g	PROTEIN: 32 g	FAT: 18 g
CHOLESTEROL: 41 mg	CALCIUM: 39 mg	SODIUM: 856 mg	IRON: 4 mg
VITAMIN A: 99 IU	VITAMIN C: 3 mg		

♦ *Fried Trout with Sour Cream and Lemon*

YIELD: 50 portions
PORTION: 1 trout

50 (25 lb.) trout, fresh or frozen,
  and thawed
1 lb. flour
2 T. salt
2 tsp. pepper
4 oz. butter

½ c. vegetable oil
8 oz. butter
3 qt. sour cream
½ c. lemon juice
¾ c. parsley, chopped

1. Rinse fish in water, pat dry, and dredge in seasoned flour.
2. Pan-fry trout in butter and oil over medium heat until golden brown, approximately 5 minutes on each side, until fish flakes easily. Arrange fish in baking pan to keep warm in a 200°F oven.
3. Discard fat from skillet. Stir in fresh butter, melt, and mix with brown bits scraped from the bottom of the skillet. Add sour cream, heat gently (do not boil), and stir in lemon juice.
4. Pour sauce over hot fish and garnish with parsley.

CALORIES: 596	CARBOHYDRATE: 3 g	PROTEIN: 55 g	FAT: 61 g
CHOLESTEROL: 200 mg	CALCIUM: 136 mg	SODIUM: 163 mg	IRON: 3 mg
VITAMIN A: 1375 IU	VITAMIN C: 5 mg		

♦ *Caramelized Potatoes*

YIELD: 50
PORTION: 4 oz.

17 lb. small or new potatoes   1 lb. butter, melted
2 lb. sugar

1. Boil or steam potatoes until tender. Do not overcook. Peel.
2. In a large skillet, melt sugar over low heat, stirring constantly. When sugar turns light brown (do not overcook) stir in melted butter. Add potatoes (do not crowd pan) and shake or stir until they are coated. Remove potatoes and serve.

CALORIES: 218   CARBOHYDRATE: 37 g   PROTEIN: 2 g   FAT: 10 g
CHOLESTEROL: 21 mg   CALCIUM: 10 mg   SODIUM: 78 mg   IRON: < 1 mg
VITAMIN A: 278 IU   VITAMIN C: 17 mg

♦ *Peppernøtter (Pepper Nut Cookies)*

BAKE: 15 minutes
OVEN: 350°F
YIELD: 15 dozen
PORTION: 3–4
  cookies

1 lb. butter, softened   1 T. cloves, ground
1 lb., 11 oz. confectioner's sugar 1½ tsp. pepper
15 eggs, beaten   2 tsp. anise seed
½ c. lemon juice   2 tsp. allspice
2 T. lemon rind   1½ T. cardamom, ground
½ lb. candied orange peel, chopped 2 tsp. baking soda
½ lb. candied lemon peel, chopped   2 tsp. salt
4 lb. flour   1 tsp. vanilla flavoring
1 T. cinnamon powder   icing (recipe below)

1. Cream butter; add sugar and eggs. Stir in lemon juice, lemon rind, and candied fruit.
2. In a separate bowl, sift together dry ingredients. Add to butter mixture. Add vanilla flavoring and blend thoroughly.
3. Shape into 1-inch balls and chill at least 8 hours. Bake on greased cookie sheet until brown. Brush on icing while still warm.

Icing
¼ c. lemon juice   1 lb. confectioner's sugar

Combine lemon juice and sugar. Consistency should be thin enough so that it is easy to spread with a brush.

CALORIES: 344   CARBOHYDRATE: 60 g   PROTEIN: 6 g   FAT: 13 g
CHOLESTEROL: 99 mg   CALCIUM: < 1 mg   SODIUM: 241 mg   IRON: 2 mg
VITAMIN A: 371 IU   VITAMIN C: < 1 mg

Scandinavian cook-
ies: glazed pepper-
nøtter, crescent-
shaped almond
cookies, and sour
cream cookies.

◆ Almond Cookies

BAKE: 15 minutes
OVEN: 350°F
YIELD: 10 dozen
PORTION: 2–3
    cookies

2½ c. almonds, ground
1 lb. butter, unsalted
¾ lb. sugar
2 tsp. vanilla flavoring

1 tsp. salt
1 lb. flour, sifted
1 lb. confectioner's sugar

1. Cream butter and sugar until fluffy. Add almonds, vanilla, salt, and flour. Mix well. Refrigerate for at least 2 hours.
2. Shape dough into crescents, about 2 inches long and ½ inch wide. Bake on greased cookie sheet until very light brown. Do not overbake. Cool slightly; dust with confectioner's sugar.

CALORIES: 208
CHOLESTEROL: 20 mg
VITAMIN A: 277 IU

CARBOHYDRATE: 24 g
CALCIUM: 22 mg
VITAMIN C: 0 mg

PROTEIN: 2 g
SODIUM: 61 mg

FAT: 18 g
IRON: 1 mg

◆ Sour Cream Cookies

BAKE: 12 minutes
OVEN: 375°F
YIELD: 6 dozen
PORTION: 1–2
    cookies

1 lb. butter, unsalted
1½ lb. sugar
4 eggs
2 lb. flour
2 tsp. baking soda

2 tsp. baking powder
1½ tsp. salt
2 tsp. cardamom, ground
1 lb. sour cream
4 oz. confectioner's sugar

1. Cream butter and sugar until light and fluffy. Add eggs, one at a time, beating until creamy.
2. In a separate bowl, combine flour, baking soda, baking powder, salt, and cardamom.
3. Combine butter mixture, half the dry ingredients, and sour cream. Mix. Stir in remaining dry ingredients. Chill at least 8 hours.
4. Roll out dough ¼ inch thick. Cut into 3-inch circles and place on ungreased cookie sheet. Bake until golden brown. Dust with confectioner's sugar.

CALORIES: 218
CHOLESTEROL: 47 mg
VITAMIN A: 370 IU

CARBOHYDRATE: 30 g
CALCIUM: 18 mg
VITAMIN C: <1 mg

PROTEIN: 3 g
SODIUM: 183 mg

FAT: 13 g
IRON: 1 mg

Smörgåsbord (Koldt Bord)

◆ Open-faced Bacon and Mushroom Sandwiches

YIELD: 50 portions
PORTION: 2 half
    slices

50 slices wheat or rye bread
6 oz. butter
10–15 lb. bacon (100 strips)

1½ lb. mushrooms, sliced
6 oz. butter
½ oz. chives, chopped

1. Butter bread and slice in half.
2. Cook bacon until crisp. Drain.
3. Sauté mushrooms in butter. Top each piece of bread with one piece of bacon and a tablespoon of mushrooms. Garnish with chives.

CALORIES: 203   CARBOHYDRATE: 25 g   PROTEIN: 7 g   FAT: 18 g
CHOLESTEROL: 26 mg   CALCIUM: 31 mg   SODIUM: 441 mg   IRON: 1 mg
VITAMIN A: 228 IU   VITAMIN C: 5 mg

◆ Open-faced Cucumber and Blue Cheese Sandwiches

YIELD: 50 portions
PORTION: 2 half
    slices

50 slices white, wheat, or rye bread
6 oz. butter
4 lb. cucumbers, peeled and cored

1 lb. blue cheese
1 lb. cream cheese
¼ lb. salted peanuts, chopped

1. Butter bread and slice in half.
2. Whip cheeses together. Using a pastry bag, fill centers of cucumbers with cheese. Cover and chill. Slice cucumbers ¼ inch thick. Arrange on bread. Garnish with nuts.

CALORIES: 210   CARBOHYDRATE: 18 g   PROTEIN: 7 g   FAT: 18 g
CHOLESTEROL: 26 mg   CALCIUM: 101 mg   SODIUM: 357 mg   IRON: 2 mg
VITAMIN A: 341 IU   VITAMIN C: 1 mg

◆ Open-faced Pork and Beet Sandwiches

YIELD: 50 portions
PORTION: 2 half
    slices

50 slices dark rye or pumpernickel
    bread
6 oz. butter
3 lb. cooked roast pork, sliced thin

1½ lb. beets, julienned
2 white onions, sliced into rings
    and separated
1 lb. dill pickles, chopped

1. Butter bread and slice in half.
2. On each piece of bread arrange one slice of pork, a few strips of beets, and 1 or 2 onion rings. Garnish with dill pickles.

CALORIES: 208   CARBOHYDRATE: 18 g   PROTEIN: 10 g   FAT: 15 g
CHOLESTEROL: 35 mg   CALCIUM: 36 mg   SODIUM: 425 mg   IRON: 2 mg
VITAMIN A: 120 IU   VITAMIN C: 1 mg

◆ Open-faced Egg and Tomato Sandwiches

YIELD: 50 portions
PORTION: 2 half
    slices

50 slices whole-wheat or rye bread
6 oz. butter
30 hard-boiled eggs, sliced (10 slices
    per egg)

5 lb. medium tomatoes, sliced
3 oz. watercress or parsley, chopped

1. Butter bread and slice in half.
2. Arrange 3 slices of egg on each of 50 half-slices of bread. Arrange 2–3 slices of tomatoes on each of the other 50 slices. Garnish with watercress or parsley.

CALORIES: 161	CARBOHYDRATE: 20 g	PROTEIN: 10 g	FAT: 15 g
CHOLESTEROL: 166 mg	CALCIUM: 52 mg	SODIUM: 252 mg	IRON: 2 mg
VITAMIN A: 719 IU	VITAMIN C: 11 mg		

◆ Sildesalat (Herring Salad)

YIELD: 50 portions
PORTION: 3–4 oz.

3 lb. pickled herring, drained
    and chopped
3 lb. potatoes, boiled, chopped,
    and chilled
3 lb. beets, pickled and chopped
1 lb. apples, peeled and chopped
1 lb. onions, chopped
3 T. brown mustard

3 T. sugar
½ c. vinegar
1½ lb. sour cream
salt to taste
pepper to taste
½ oz. parsley, chopped
6 hard-boiled eggs, sliced

1. Combine herring, potatoes, beets, apples, onions, mustard, sugar, and vinegar.
2. Fold sour cream into salad, season with salt and pepper. Chill. Garnish with hard-boiled eggs and parsley.

CALORIES: 215	CARBOHYDRATE: 10 g	PROTEIN: 9 g	FAT: 22 g
CHOLESTEROL: 101 mg	CALCIUM: 81 mg	SODIUM: 300 mg	IRON: 2 mg
VITAMIN A: 556 IU	VITAMIN C: 8 mg		

◆ Pork-Stuffed Onion Rolls

BAKE: 30 minutes
OVEN: 400°F
YIELD: 50 portions
PORTION: 3 rolls

20 lb. large yellow onions, peeled
½ lb. onions, chopped
2 oz. butter
3 lb. potatoes, boiled and mashed
¼ lb. bread crumbs
5 lb. ground pork
2 c. light cream

1½ T. salt
2 tsp. pepper
5 eggs
¼ oz. dill, chopped
½ lb. butter, melted
½ lb. bread crumbs

1. Place whole onions in a pot with enough water to cover. Simmer, uncovered, for 40 minutes. Drain.
2. Sauté chopped onions in butter. Combine onions, mashed potatoes, bread crumbs, meat, cream, salt, pepper, eggs, and dill. Mix until well blended. Chill.
3. Pull off each layer of the boiled onions. Put a no. 40 scoop of meat filling inside each onion leaf. Fold edges over each other to enclose stuffing. Place onion rolls side by side with the seam down in greased 12″ × 20″ × 2″ baking pan. Brush well with butter. Bake 15 minutes. Baste with pan juices and sprinkle with bread crumbs. Bake until onions are light brown, about 15 minutes.

CALORIES: 252
CHOLESTEROL: 83 mg
VITAMIN A: 409 IU

CARBOHYDRATE: 19 g
CALCIUM: 74 mg
VITAMIN C: 16 mg

PROTEIN: 15 g
SODIUM: 403 mg

FAT: 19 g
IRON: 2 mg

◆ Cauliflower and Shrimp Salad

YIELD: 50 portions
PORTION: 3 oz.

20 lb. cauliflowerets, fresh or frozen
2 lb. mayonnaise
5 lb. small shrimp, shelled
   and cooked

3 T. capers
5 eggs, hard-boiled, sliced
1 oz. parsley, chopped
2 lb. lemon wedges

1. Steam cauliflower and cool.
2. Toss cauliflower, cold shrimp, and capers with mayonnaise. Garnish with hard-boiled eggs, parsley, and lemon wedges.

CALORIES: 217
CHOLESTEROL: 107 mg
VITAMIN A: 240 IU

CARBOHYDRATE: 5 g
CALCIUM: 191 mg
VITAMIN C: 103 mg

PROTEIN: 15 g
SODIUM: 207 mg

FAT: 29 g
IRON: 2 mg

◆ Jansson's Temptation (Potato Casserole)

BAKE: 45 minutes
OVEN: 400°F
YIELD: 50 portions
PORTION: 5 oz.

4 lb. onions, sliced
8 oz. butter
12 lb. potatoes, peeled, julienned
8 oz. anchovy fillets
1 T. pepper

8 oz. bread crumbs
2 oz. butter
3 qt. light cream
1 qt. milk, scalded

1. Sauté onions in 8 ounces butter until soft and translucent.
2. Layer onions, potatoes, and anchovies (ending with potatoes) in buttered 12″ × 20″ × 4″ baking pan. Season each layer with pepper.
3. Top with bread crumbs and dot with butter. Combine hot milk and cream and pour over potatoes. Bake until tender.

CALORIES: 363
CHOLESTEROL: 93 mg
VITAMIN A: 1053 IU

CARBOHYDRATE: 25 g
CALCIUM: 95 mg
VITAMIN C: 22 mg

PROTEIN: 6 g
SODIUM: 117 mg

FAT: 37 g
IRON: 1 mg

·18· COOKING FROM
·Spain and Portugal·

Portuguese garlic soup with chickpeas, garnished with mint and croutons.

*M*any ingredients typical of Spanish and Portuguese cooking originally came from other areas of the world. The settlers who first populated Spain and Portugal are believed to have come from Africa. Through the centuries, Phoenicians, Celts, Greeks, Carthaginians, and various Europeans came to Spain and Portugal, bringing with them such foods as chickpeas, olives, and grapes. The Arabs brought rice, almonds, sugar cane, and spices such as cinnamon, cloves, nutmeg, pepper, and saffron to the region in the 8th century.

Portuguese and Spanish explorers brought back rice and tea from Asia; coffee from Africa; and tomatoes, potatoes, corn, chili peppers, sweet peppers, vanilla, and pineapple from the New World.

It is often thought that Spanish cuisine, like Mexican, is hot and spicy. Although Mexico was once a colony of Spain, the foods frequently differ (for example, a *tortilla* in Spain is an omelet; in Mexico it is a fried flat bread). In fact, few spices are used in most Spanish foods; fresh, natural tastes are emphasized. Some regional dishes can be quite hot, however.

The mountain ranges crisscrossing Spain and Portugal tend to isolate the various regions. Indeed, at one time Spain was a collection of independent kingdoms. Today, a strong individuality is still evident, and regional differences are marked.

The central portion of Spain is known for its wild game and baby roasted meat. In fact, this region is notable for a lack of fish in its cuisine.

In the south is Andalusia, where the weather is hot and the food light. *Gazpacho*, a cold soup containing tomato, green pepper, cucumber, and garlic, is the best-known dish from this area. Little pork is eaten here due to the strong Islamic influence from Algeria and Morocco, countries to the south.

Spain's east coast is famous for its rice dishes, especially *paella*, which typically includes saffron-seasoned rice topped with chicken, mussels, shrimp, sausage, tomatoes, and peas. In the northeast is Catalonia, known for its *zarzuela* (meaning "operetta") of mixed seafood in a tomato sauce, and for its *romescu*, a sauce of ground almonds, garlic, tomatoes, paprika, vinegar, and olive oil. Nuts are also combined with seafood, as in lobster and chicken in hazelnut sauce.

The central part of northern Spain includes the Basque province. Basque cooking is known for its seafood dishes, such as stuffed crabs, baby eels with garlic, and squid in ink sauce.

The climate is cool and damp in the northwest provinces of Galicia and Asturias. Corn, chestnuts, and apples grow there. Cornbread is popular, and in Asturias, hard cider is drunk instead of wine. Northwest Spain is known for its *empanadas* (meat or fish pastries) and for its *fabada*, a bean stew. A specialty in Galicia is *caldo*, a thin soup made from aged salt pork, turnip greens, potatoes, and beans.

Portugal is set off from Spain by mountains, and the cuisine, while similar, has its own characteristic ingredients and techniques. As in Spain, olive oil, garlic, parsley, almonds, tomatoes, pork, beans, and eggs are regular ingredients. Fresh coriander is also used frequently. More fish and shellfish are used in Portugal and dried salt cod is a national specialty. Portuguese foods are generally more seasoned than those in Spain. More cream and butter are also used.

In the northern part of Portugal, cornbread, called *broa*, is also consumed. This region is known for its *caldo verde*, or kale soup, which is the national dish. Green wine is made from unripe grapes, and can be red or white in color. Rice is popular in this region, as it is throughout the country. Southern Portugal reflects a Muslim influence, much like Andalusia. There, figs, almonds, and olives abound. A wide variety of seafood is eaten and curried dishes are not uncommon. The Azores and the Madeiras, islands belonging to Portugal, provide pineapple and bananas.

Ingredients

MILK AND MILK PRODUCTS

Most of Iberia is not suitable for raising cattle; therefore, dairy products do not play a large part in the cuisine. Milk from cows, sheep, and goats is consumed and is used in some desserts. Sheep and goat cheeses are common as snacks or dessert, but are not often used in cooking.

MEAT AND MEAT ALTERNATIVES

The Spanish and Portuguese prefer young meat, such as suckling pig, baby lamb, kid (goat), and veal. All cuts of pork are used, and several types of sausages are made, including the paprika- and garlic-flavored *chorizo* (called *chouriço* in Portugal), *longanzino*, and the dry, spicy Portuguese *linguiça*. *Morcilla*, a blood sausage, and cured ham are popular. Pork, including variety cuts, is used in many dishes. Chicken is eaten, although game birds such as partridge and quail are nearly as common. Rabbit and other small game are eaten, too. Eggs are used extensively.

Fish, such as sole, bass, red mullet, sardines, trout, eel, and salmon are popular. Squid and shellfish, including lobsters, clams, crabs, crayfish, snails, langostinos, prawns, oysters, mussels, and scallops are frequently eaten. Dried salt cod, called *bacalhau*, is especially well liked in Portugal, where it is said there is a different dried salt cod dish for every day of the year. Garbanzo beans (chickpeas) are added to many entrées and are often served as side dishes, especially in Spain. Other legumes, such as fava, white, and lima beans, are also eaten.

FRUITS AND VEGETABLES

Grapes, lemons, and oranges are the most common fruits. Bananas and pineapples are popular in Portugal. Apples, peaches, apricots, figs, pomegranates, cherries, melons, and strawberries are available seasonally. Dried fruits and dates are also consumed.

More than a hundred kinds of olive are grown. Olives, chili and sweet peppers, potatoes, and tomatoes are the vegetables most often eaten. Cabbage, greens such as kale and spinach, and root vegetables, including carrots and turnips, are also favored. Artichokes, asparagus, eggplant, mushrooms, peas, and zucchini are featured in some dishes.

BREADS AND CEREALS

Wheat flour is used to make bread and pastries. Sweetened breads and rolls are particularly liked. Short-grain rice is common, especially along the east and west coasts of the Iberian peninsula. Cornbread is popular in northwestern Spain and in northern Portugal.

OTHER INGREDIENTS

Olive oil is used almost exclusively for cooking, even for deep-frying. Butter and lard are used occasionally. Nuts are added to many dishes. Almonds, pine nuts, hazelnuts, and walnuts are the most common. A paste made of sweetened ground almonds, called *marzipan* in Spain and *maçapão* in Portugal, is very popular.

Hot chocolate is a favorite beverage in Spain. Strong coffee is preferred by adults, while in Portugal both coffee and tea are consumed. Alcoholic beverages include beer and wine (both red and white). *Sangria*, red wine mixed with fresh fruit such as lemon and orange slices, is a Spanish specialty. Sherry is produced in Spain; Madeira and port are made in Portugal.

Seasonings

Garlic, tomatoes, and onions flavor many savory dishes in both Portugal and Spain. Parsley, mint, and fresh coriander are typically added to Portuguese dishes. Orange juice is also a popular flavoring agent. Sherry is used to flavor both main dishes and desserts in Spain; port and Madeira are used in Portugal. Saffron is added to rice in both countries. Cinnamon is common in sweets.

Preparation

Soups, stews, and one-dish entrées are popular in Spain. They often feature a variety of meats, vegetables, and seafood. A typical stew, *cocido*, is made from chickpeas, vegetables (such as cabbage, carrots, and potatoes) and meats (often chicken, beef, pork, and sausages), but the ingredients vary from region to region. These one-dish meals are served in three courses: the strained broth is eaten first, followed by a plate of the boiled vegetables, and finally a plate of the cooked meats. "Dry" soups, or *açordas*, which are usually thickened with day-old bread, are eaten almost daily in Portugal. Most often, they are made with fish or shellfish broth with vegetables and meat or fish added, and the soup is seasoned with garlic and fresh coriander. Raw eggs are stirred in at the last minute. In the Azore and Madeira Islands, *açorda d'azedo* is a dry soup eaten for breakfast that is made from cornbread, onions, garlic, vinegar, lard, and saffron, moistened with boiling water.

Although stewing is the most popular cooking method, many foods are fried, deep-fried, baked, or steamed. Sauces are important features of Spanish and Portuguese cuisine. *Alioli*, made from garlic pulverized with olive oil, salt, and a little lemon juice, is served with grilled or broiled meats and fish. Several sauces are based on tomatoes: *chilindrón*, made from tomatoes, onions, garlic, ham, and roast peppers, is typical. In Portugal, a sauce of very hot chili peppers steeped in oil, called *piri-piri*, is used. A characteristic of Iberian cooking is the combination of fruits or nuts with meat and poultry.

Beans, potatoes, and rice are staples of Portuguese cooking. In addition, bread is commonly eaten. At least two starch dishes are served with every meal—sometimes three or four. *Pan doce*, a sweet yeast bread, is a Portuguese specialty.

Desserts are often very rich, made with egg yolks, sugar, and almond paste. Custards, such as *flan*, are especially popular, and confections such as nougat paste, made of egg whites, honey, and almonds, are common.

Meal Patterns

By American standards, the Spanish and Portuguese appear to eat all day. They begin around 8 A.M. with a light breakfast *(desayano)* of coffee and bread with jam or pastries, such as the cylindrical doughnuts known as *churros*, followed by *almuerzo* or *las onces* at 11:00. This meal can consist of grilled sausage, an omelet, fried squid, or bread with tomato. A light snack, which usually includes the finger-foods known as *tapas*, is eaten around 1:00 P.M. as a prelude to the main meal, *comida*, which is eaten at 2:00 or 2:30. This is a three-course meal, consisting of a salad or soup as the first course, a fish or meat course, and dessert, which is usually fruit and cheese. Wine is served with the meal, and coffee follows dessert. Most businesses close between 1:00 and 4:00 to allow time for comida and a nap before the afternoon's work begins. *Merienda*, a snack of coffee or tea with pastries, is eaten at 5:00 or 6:00. Another round of tapas and a glass of sherry are often consumed at 8:00 or 9:00, before *cena*, or supper, which consists of three light courses, such as a soup, an omelet, and a dessert of fruit, eaten between 10:00 and midnight.

Meal patterns vary somewhat from region to region. In some areas, if a substantial number of tapas have been eaten earlier, dinner may be skipped. Meals are lighter in Andalusia; larger portions are eaten in northern areas. In Portugal, meals are usually earlier than in Spain, lunch being served at 1:30 or 2:00, and supper at 8:00 or 9:00.

M E N U
Spanish Dinner

Tapas:
Buñuelos de Chorizo
(sausage fritters)
Hígados al Jerez
(chicken livers in sherry sauce)
Gambas al Ajillo
(shrimp in garlic sauce)
Pork Chops with Sweet Peppers
Flan de Naranja
(orange custard)

Serving suggestions: Add a steamed seasonal vegetable tossed in olive oil and lemon juice; steamed rice; and sangria, sherry, or coffee.

M E N U
Portuguese Dinner

Garlic Soup with Chickpeas
Bolinhos de Bacalhau
(codfish balls)
Esparregado
(puréed greens)
Strawberries Macerated in Port

Serving suggestions: Crusty bread or corn bread may accompany the meal; for beverages, offer red wine or iced tea with lemon and mint.

Tapas, a selection of Spanish appetizers including buñuelos de chorizo (sausage fritters), gambas al ajillo (shrimp in garlic sauce), and higados al jerez (chicken livers in sherry sauce).

Spanish Dinner

◆ *Buñuelos de Chorizo (Sausage Fritters)*

FRY: 4–5 minutes
DEEP-FAT FRYER:
   370°F
YIELD: 50 portions
PORTION: 3 fritters

1½ lb. flour
12 egg yolks
¾ c. oil
2½ c. water

12 egg whites
2¼ lb. Spanish chorizo sausage,
   finely chopped (spicy Polish
   sausage can be substituted)

1. Place flour in bowl, make well in center. Add egg yolks, oil, and water. Mix.
2. Beat egg whites until stiff. Fold egg whites into batter. Let stand 15 minutes.
3. Stir sausage gently into batter.
4. Using a no. 60 scoop or heaping tablespoon, drop batter into hot oil. Fry until golden brown. Drain.

CALORIES: 281
CHOLESTEROL: 76 mg
VITAMIN A: 62 IU

CARBOHYDRATE: 11 g
CALCIUM: 18 mg
VITAMIN C: 5 mg

PROTEIN: 6 g
SODIUM: 234 mg

FAT: 41 g
IRON: 1 mg

◆ *Higados al Jerez (Chicken Livers in Sherry Sauce)*

YIELD: 50 portions
PORTION: 2 oz.

1 #10 can tomatoes, chopped
   (5½ lb. fresh, diced tomatoes
   can be substituted)
2 tsp. garlic, minced
2 c. sherry, dry

6½ lb. chicken livers
½ lb. flour
2½ T. salt or to taste
1 T. pepper
2 c. olive oil

1. Combine tomatoes, garlic, and sherry. Simmer until mixture has thickened, about 20 minutes.
2. Dredge chicken livers in seasoned flour.
3. Sauté livers in olive oil. Do not overcook. Livers should still be slightly pink in the center. Place livers in a 12″ × 20″ × 2″ pan. Smother with tomato sauce and gently toss.

CALORIES: 207
CHOLESTEROL: 372 mg
VITAMIN A: 10177 IU

CARBOHYDRATE: 7 g
CALCIUM: 17 mg
VITAMIN C: 19 mg

PROTEIN: 15 g
SODIUM: 454 mg

FAT: 28 g
IRON: 6 mg

♦ Gambas al Ajillo (Shrimp in Garlic Sauce)

YIELD: 50 portions
PORTION: 2 oz.
(6 medium
shrimp)

2 c. olive oil
½ lb. butter
6 lb. medium shrimp, raw, peeled,
and deveined
2 T. garlic, finely chopped or sliced
1 c. lemon juice

1 c. dry sherry
1 tsp. cayenne or to taste
1 T. salt or to taste
1 tsp. pepper or to taste
½ oz. parsley, chopped

1. Sauté shrimp and garlic in olive oil and butter until shrimp are pink, about
   3 minutes.
2. Combine lemon juice and sherry in small sauce pan and bring to a boil. Stir
   in seasonings. Add to shrimp and toss.
3. Garnish with parsley.

CALORIES: 165
CHOLESTEROL: 92 mg
VITAMIN A: 196 IU

CARBOHYDRATE: 2 g
CALCIUM: 40 mg
VITAMIN C: 4 mg

PROTEIN: 10 g
SODIUM: 126 mg

FAT: 21 g
IRON: 1 mg

♦ Pork Chops with Sweet Peppers

BAKE: 1½ hours
OVEN: 350°F
YIELD: 50 portions
PORTION: 5 oz.
(1 chop)

17 lb. pork chops (cut 3 to the
pound)
3 c. olive oil
4 lb. onions, chopped
3 T. garlic, minced
1 #10 can tomatoes, chopped and
drained

4 lb. green and red sweet peppers,
roasted (see paprikasaláta recipe,
page 46), peeled and sliced
3 T. salt or to taste
1½ T. pepper or to taste

1. Heat oil and brown chops. Remove chops from the oil and arrange in two
   12″ × 20″ × 2″ pans. Reserve oil.
2. Sauté onions and garlic in reserved oil.
3. Combine onion, garlic, tomatoes, sweet peppers, salt, and pepper. Spoon
   over pork chops. Cover and bake.

CALORIES: 602
CHOLESTEROL: 126 mg
VITAMIN A: 1300 mg

CARBOHYDRATE: 7 g
CALCIUM: 39 mg
VITAMIN C: 40 mg

PROTEIN: 37 g
SODIUM: 584 mg

FAT: 70 g
IRON: 3 mg

♦ *Flan de Naranja (Orange Custard)*

BAKE: 60 minutes
OVEN: 350°F
YIELD: 50 portions
PORTION: 4 oz.

2 lb. sugar
1 c. water
50 eggs

2 lb. sugar
3 qt. orange juice
3 T. orange rind, grated

1. Combine sugar and water in a heavy sauce pan. Cover and heat until sugar is melted. Remove cover and continue cooking until caramelized (golden brown).
2. Spoon 1 T. of caramelized sugar into custard cups.
3. Beat eggs well. Continue beating and add sugar, orange juice, and orange rind.
4. Pour 4 ounces into each custard cup. Place cups in baking pan. Pour hot water around cups and bake. Custard is done when knife inserted comes out clean. Cool. Unmold custard and scoop caramel over the top.

CALORIES: 221
CHOLESTEROL: 263 mg
VITAMIN A: 310 IU

CARBOHYDRATE: 37 g
CALCIUM: 34 mg
VITAMIN C: 25 mg

PROTEIN: 6 g
SODIUM: 61 mg

FAT: 8 mg
IRON: 1 mg

M E N U *Portuguese Dinner*

♦ *Garlic Soup with Chickpeas*

YIELD: 50 portions
PORTION: 1 c.

3 oz. garlic cloves
5 tsp. salt or to taste
2 c. olive oil
3 oz. fresh mint, chopped
3 oz. parsley, chopped

2½ gal. chicken stock
1 #10 can chickpeas, rinsed and drained
50 fresh mint sprigs
6 cups croutons

1. Purée garlic and salt to a fine paste in a food processor or blender.
2. Add olive oil slowly while continuing to blend. Add mint and parsley and blend 1 more minute.
3. Boil chicken stock and add chickpeas. Continue boiling for 5 minutes.
4. Immediately before serving, add garlic mixture and stir well. Garnish with mint and croutons.

CALORIES: 275
CHOLESTEROL: <1 mg
VITAMIN A: 515 IU

CARBOHYDRATE: 17 g
CALCIUM: 54 mg
VITAMIN C: 10 mg

PROTEIN: 8 g
SODIUM: 737 mg

FAT: 36 g
IRON: 2 mg

◆ Bolinhos de Bacalhau (Codfish Balls)

FRY: 3–4 minutes
DEEP-FAT FRY:
370°F
YIELD: 50 portions
PORTION: 4 balls

3½ lb. dried salt cod
4 lb. boiling potatoes, peeled and cubed
2 lb. onions, finely chopped
1 T. garlic, finely chopped
½ c. olive oil

½ oz. parsley, chopped
½ oz. fresh coriander, chopped
6 egg yolks
¾ tsp. cayenne
1 tsp. pepper
6 egg whites

1. Soak cod in a covered container in the refrigerator for 24 hours. Change water 4 to 6 times. Drain and rinse. Place in large pot. Add enough water to cover, and simmer, covered, until soft, about 20 minutes. Drain and flake finely.
2. Boil potatoes until tender. Drain. Mash potatoes together with cod.
3. Sauté garlic and onions in oil until onions are soft. Add to cod mixture. Add beaten egg yolks, parsley, coriander, cayenne, and pepper.
4. Beat egg whites until stiff. Fold into cod mixture. Use a no. 70 scoop to form balls. Fry until golden. Serve warm.

CALORIES: 258
CHOLESTEROL: 101 mg
VITAMIN A: 127 IU

CARBOHYDRATE: 7 g
CALCIUM: 34 mg
VITAMIN C: 9 mg

PROTEIN: 28 g
SODIUM: 2582 mg

FAT: 23 g
IRON: 1 mg

◆ Esparregado (Puréed Greens)

YIELD: 50 portions
PORTION: 4 oz.

24 lb. spinach, trimmed and washed
12 lb. young mustard or turnip greens, trimmed and washed
2½ c. olive oil
1 T. garlic, finely chopped
2½ lb. onions, finely chopped

1 tsp. nutmeg
3 T. salt
2½ T. pepper
25 tomatoes, cut in half and hollowed out, salted, and drained (optional)*

1. Steam or boil spinach and greens until wilted. Drain.
2. Heat oil in a large sauce pan. Sauté onions and garlic until golden brown. Add greens and nutmeg; cook over moderate heat 3 minutes. Toss with salt and pepper; adjust seasonings. Purée in a food processor or blender.
3. Puréed greens may be served in prepared tomatoes, baked 20 minutes in a 350°F oven.

CALORIES: 193
CHOLESTEROL: 10 mg
VITAMIN A: 24409 IU

CARBOHYDRATE: 17 g
CALCIUM: 446 mg
VITAMIN C: 177 mg

PROTEIN: 11 g
SODIUM: 671 mg

FAT: 19 g
IRON: 8 mg

*Not included in nutritional analysis.

◆ *Strawberries Macerated in Port*

YIELD: 50
PORTION: ½–¾ c.

10 qt. fresh strawberries
1 lb. sugar or to taste
2 c. port

½ c. orange juice
3 oz. fresh mint

1. Wash berries; hull and slice in half.
2. Toss berries with sugar, port, and orange juice. Cover and refrigerate 2–3 hours. Garnish with mint sprigs.

CALORIES: 85
CHOLESTEROL: 0 mg
VITAMIN A: 33 IU

CARBOHYDRATE: 18 g
CALCIUM: 18 mg
VITAMIN C: 68 mg

PROTEIN: <1 g
SODIUM: 3 mg

FAT: <1 g
IRON: <1 mg

Pho, Vietnamese beef soup topped with bean sprouts, fresh coriander, and onion rings.

*D*espite *China's conquest and occupation of Vietnam* for over a thousand years, Vietnam has managed to retain its own distinct language, culture, and cuisine. Still, many features of Vietnamese cooking can be traced back to Chinese roots. The use of chopsticks, serving rice as a separate dish rather than as a component of other dishes, and stir-frying are practices more akin to Chinese than to other Southeast Asian cuisines. However, there are many differences as well. Vietnamese dishes use less oil and cornstarch than do Chinese dishes. The French rule of Vietnam during the 19th century brought French bread, pâtés, and a few French vegetables, which have become common ingredients in the Vietnamese diet.

A narrow band stretching over 1,000 miles, geographically Vietnam comprises low-lying, fertile areas in the north and south, separated by a mountainous region in the center of the country. In the north, foods are less spicy hot, though black pepper is widely used. Fewer ingredients and spices are available. Crab is a favorite food. Cooked rather than raw vegetables are generally preferred.

In the central part of the country, once the home of kings, emphasis is still placed on decorative presentation of food. Foods are often very spicy, with chili peppers and shrimp paste being two of the most frequently used seasonings. Meals tend to be made up of small portions of many dishes. Southern Vietnam is hot and humid, with a great variety of vegetables and fruits available. Several raw fruits and vegetables are consumed, especially in salads and garnishes. Coconut is often used in the recipes from this region. Food is spicier than in the north, and an Asian Indian influence can be seen in the use of curries.

Ingredients

MILK AND MILK PRODUCTS

Sweetened condensed milk is frequently used in beverages, especially coffee. Cream is used in some French-influenced dishes.

MEAT AND MEAT ALTERNATIVES

Fish and shellfish provide most of the protein in the Vietnamese diet. Numerous freshwater and saltwater varieties are available: carp, catfish, trout, sea bass, shrimp, crab, jellyfish, and squid are especially popular. Several types are dried before use, particularly shrimp, squid, and jellyfish (which is said to give a crunchy texture when added to foods). Many people prefer river fish to sea fish. Sauces are frequently made from fish, oysters, and shrimp. Shrimp chips, made from shrimp, tapioca starch, and egg white, are light, fried, crisp chips that have become a popular snack.

Pork is the most frequently eaten meat. Chicken and duck are also popular. Beef is well liked but is expensive. Sausages are made by people of Chinese descent. Eggs are added to many dishes. Legumes and their products, notably bean curd, yellow (skinned) mung beans, and cellophane noodles made from mung beans, are frequently used.

FRUITS AND VEGETABLES

Bananas and plantains, pineapple, papaya, limes and mangoes are common fruits in Vietnam. Soursop, star fruit (a star-shaped fruit with a tart flavor), custard apple (with a creamy pulp), *tamarind* (a pod with a tart pulp), jackfruit, and *durian* (known for its overpowering odor and delicious taste) are used frequently. Sugar cane is also eaten like a fruit.

Fresh and preserved vegetables are used frequently in Vietnamese cooking. Bamboo shoots, bean sprouts, cabbage (including Chinese bok choy), white radish, winter melon, lily buds, lotus root, and snow peas are cultivated. Dried Chinese black mushrooms, straw mushrooms, and cloud ears are also used. Broccoli, celery, tomatoes, carrots, lettuce, cucumbers, green beans (including Chinese long beans), leeks, scallions, and squashes are often eaten. The French introduced asparagus, white potatoes, and shallots, which are eaten frequently. Mustard greens and Chinese cabbage are often preserved.

BREADS AND CEREALS

Rice is used more often than any other grain. Both long-grain and glutinous types are common, as are rice noodles, which come in three forms: flat noodles called rice sticks, round noodles, and very thin noodles called vermicelli. Rice paper, a very thin sheet of rice dough used to wrap foods, is similar to Chinese egg roll wrappers. There is an art to making rice paper at home, one that every bride was traditionally expected to know. Today, rice wrappers are usually made commercially. Roasted rice flour is called for in many dishes. Wheat is used to make the Japanese-style noodles known as *somen* and for French bread, pastries, and cakes.

OTHER INGREDIENTS

Lard was used for cooking until vegetable oils were introduced. Now these lighter oils, particularly corn, peanut, and soybean oils, are preferred. Peanut oil is thought best for deep-frying. Many nuts and seeds are added to dishes. Peanuts, coconut, and sesame seeds are the most common, though other kinds such as cashews, almonds, pumpkin seeds, macadamia nuts, and pili nuts are also used.

Tea is the universal beverage of Vietnam. It is served both before and after, but not during, meals. Tea is often blended with flowers such as rose petals, jasmine blossoms, chrysanthemums, and lotus blossoms; the latter are especially popular. Coffee is also frequently consumed for breakfast, with snacks, and after meals. Soup is the traditional beverage during meals, but increasingly, soft drinks are served to women and children, and beer to men. Sweetened soybean milk and other bean drinks, as well as a variety of fruit drinks are also common. Rice wine may be served at special occasions.

Seasonings

Fresh herbs flavor most Vietnamese dishes. Fresh coriander, mint, and basil are used most often, although the varieties of mint and basil are different from those used in Western countries. Lemon grass, which resembles scallions, has a strong citrus flavor. Garlic, ginger root, and chili peppers are also commonly added to dishes. Black pepper is used extensively, especially in northern Vietnam, and peppercorns are also picked green and pickled. Chinese five-spice powder is sometimes used, as are cinnamon and star anise. Coconut milk, lime juice, scallions, and shallots flavor many foods.

Sauces made from fermented fish are essential to Vietnamese cuisine. *Nuoc mam* is made from salted fish, some of them so tiny they are called rice fish because they resemble grains of rice. Properly used, nuoc mam provides saltiness, but does not overwhelm dishes. Flavoring sauces are also made from oysters, anchovies, and shrimp. Tomato paste, tamarind, and soy sauce are imports that are used occasionally. Rice flour, cornstarch, potato starch, and tapioca starch are used to thicken foods. Agar-agar, a seaweed extract, is used like gelatin to make aspics and other jellied foods. Alum, a sour compound, is used to keep foods crisp.

Preparation

Simmering is the cooking method most often employed in Vietnam, although stir-frying, pan-frying, deep-frying, steaming, and grilling are done often. Traditionally, a small clay stove on the kitchen floor was used for most of the cooking, with smaller charcoal stoves available at the table. Today, gas and electric appliances, including electric rice cookers, are popular. Chopsticks are the primary cooking utensils.

Soup is served at nearly every meal, including breakfast. An especially popular soup for breakfast and at other times is *pho bo ha noi*, a beef soup from Hanoi. The broth for this soup contains beef bones, onions, ginger root, and cinnamon, and is traditionally simmered at least 12 hours. Rice noodles are added at the last minute, along with thin slices of raw beef, raw vegetables, and bean sprouts, then heated until they are barely cooked. Fresh coriander and nuoc mam are individually added when the soup is served. Other favorites include Saigon soup, made with chicken, pork, beef, and seafood, and asparagus crab soup. Most Vietnamese soups are hearty, and many are served over rice or noodles.

Nuoc cham is a condiment made from nuoc mam, chili peppers, vinegar, sugar, garlic, and lime juice; the exact composition depends on the dish it accompanies. Nuoc cham is on the table at every meal, and it is used as a dipping sauce for snack foods such as *cha gio*, little rolls of minced pork, crab, mushrooms, and vegetables wrapped in rice paper and deep-fried. When they are eaten, cha gio are commonly wrapped in a leaf of lettuce with coriander and basil and dipped in nuoc cham.

Meat and shrimp can be pounded with a mortar and pestle to make French-inspired pâtés (now often commercially made), which are chilled and served as an appetizer or made into sandwiches with French bread or rice cakes. The mortar and pestle is also used for mashing garlic and other seasonings for sauces.

Banana leaves are used for wrapping foods while they cook. Cakes are made from ground beans, glutinous rice, or arrowroot paste sweetened with sugar and flavored. The mixture is wrapped in banana leaves and steamed. The most popular are the rice cakes called *banh chung*.

Salads are popular. *Goi go* consists of cooked chicken and shredded cabbage, with chopped mint and coriander; nuoc cham is used as dressing. With many meals, a plate of lettuce, chopped coriander and mint, and other herbs or raw vegetables is on the table; each diner can select some of these to combine with other food. Lime and chopped peanuts are also used as garnishes.

Meal Patterns

Two or three simple meals are eaten daily, as well as between-meal snacks. Breakfast usually consists of a noodle soup served with abundant fresh coriander. Rice, accompanied by meat, poultry, or fish, is the basis of other meals. A typical lunch or supper consists of soup, a simmered meat or fish dish or possibly two (one stir-fried, perhaps), a raw vegetable and herb plate, and rice. The usual condiments are chili peppers and nuoc cham. All the food is served at once, and the soup is often poured over the rice. No dessert is served with meals.

Each diner receives a bowl for rice with chopsticks on the right and a metal or porcelain soup spoon on the left. A plate for bones, shells, and so on may be included. Small bowls of dipping sauces may also be placed on the plate. More rice is added to the bowl as desired, and small amounts of the other dishes are taken from the serving bowl to top the rice.

Special meals for guests or holidays feature more elaborate foods and are served in courses. Tea is offered first, then appetizers with wine or soft drinks, followed by soup, then the main dishes, and finally dessert, which is usually fruit.

Street vendors offer the beef soup pho bo ha noi (usually called just pho), rice, dried fish, bananas, and tea. French bread with pâté may take the place of either lunch or supper. Sweets and cakes (especially French-style pastries) are eaten as between-meal snacks and are offered to guests. The diet of the poor consists largely of rice, nuoc mam, some fish, and tea.

M E N U

Vietnamese Dinner

Pho (beef soup)
or
Crab and Asparagus Soup
Goi Go
(chicken salad)
Pork with Lemon Grass
Fried Bean Curd with Vegetables

Serving suggestions: Offer pork and bean curd with steamed long-grain rice and beer, fruit juice, or tea; serve a French-style pastry for dessert with strong coffee.

Vietnamese Dinner

◆ *Pho (Beef Soup)*

YIELD: 50 portions
PORTION: 1 c.

3 gal. beef stock
5 lb. beef chuck, cubed
5 pieces fresh ginger root, cut into
  2″ pieces
15 shallots
10 star anise
5 cinnamon sticks
10 oz. nuoc mam (fish sauce)
1 T. salt or to taste
2½ lb. roast beef, cooked and cut
  into 3″ × 4″ pieces, sliced thin

2 oz. fresh coriander, chopped
1 lb. scallions, chopped
2 lb. onions, thinly sliced
1¼ lb. bean sprouts, blanched
2½ lb. rice sticks, boiled 5 minutes,
  drained, rinsed with cold water
3 lb. lime wedges
5 hot chili peppers, sliced into thin
  rings

1. Combine beef stock and chuck.
2. Char ginger and shallots over an open flame. Add ginger, shallots, anise, and cinnamon to stock and simmer for 1½ hours.
3. When chuck is tender, remove from soup. Cut into bite-size pieces. Reserve.
4. Add fish sauce and salt to soup.
5. To assemble soup, distribute rice sticks, roast beef, cooked meat, coriander, scallions, half the onions, and a few bean sprouts in individual soup bowls. Just before serving, pour in the hot soup.
6. Serve with limes, hot chili peppers, and remaining bean sprouts and onions.

CALORIES: 300   CARBOHYDRATE: 25 g   PROTEIN: 25 g   FAT: 12 g
CHOLESTEROL: 59 mg   CALCIUM: 43 mg   SODIUM: (200 mg)   IRON: 4 mg
VITAMIN A: (400 IU)   VITAMIN C: (17 mg)

◆ *Goi Go (Chicken Salad)*

YIELD: 50 portions
PORTION: ½ c.

6 lb. cabbage, shredded
3 lb. carrots, shredded
6 lb. cooked chicken, shredded
1 qt. nuoc mam (fish sauce)
1¼ c. vinegar or lemon juice

1½ qt. water
1 lb. sugar
2½ tsp. garlic, chopped
2½ tsp. chili peppers, chopped
  (optional)

1. Mix together cabbage, carrots, and chicken.
2. Mix remaining ingredients and pour on top of salad.

CALORIES: 200   CARBOHYDRATE: 20 g   PROTEIN: 20 g   FAT: 7 g
CHOLESTEROL: 46 mg   CALCIUM: 41 mg   SODIUM: NA   IRON: 1 mg
VITAMIN A: 7776 IU   VITAMIN C: 30 mg

♦ *Asparagus and Crab Soup*

YIELD: 50 portions
PORTION: 1 c.

2½ gal. chicken stock
2 oz. nuoc mam (fish sauce)
1⅓ c. vegetable oil
1½ t. garlic, chopped
1 oz. scallions, white part only,
  chopped (save greens)
2 lb. crabmeat
½ tsp. pepper

2⅔ T. cornstarch, dissolved in
  ½ c. water
4 eggs, lightly beaten
4 lb. asparagus, cooked, cut into
  bite-size pieces
½ tsp. pepper
1 oz. fresh coriander, chopped

1. Combine chicken stock and fish sauce.
2. Sauté garlic and scallions in oil.
3. Add crabmeat and fry for 5 minutes. Stir in pepper. Combine crabmeat mixture and soup stock; bring to a boil.
4. Stir in cornstarch-water mixture. Continue boiling 1–2 minutes.
5. Stir eggs into boiling soup, stirring continuously for 2 minutes.
6. Add asparagus and pepper. Cook until asparagus is heated.
7. Garnish with coriander and chopped green part of scallions before serving.

CALORIES: 117
CHOLESTEROL: 33 mg
VITAMIN A: 350 IU

CARBOHYDRATE: 3 g
CALCIUM: 27 mg
VITAMIN C: 8 mg

PROTEIN: 9 g
SODIUM: 681 mg

FAT: 8 g
IRON: < 1 mg

◆ *Pork with Lemon Grass*

YIELD: 50 portions
PORTION: 6 oz.

2 gal. water, boiling
15 lb. pork hocks, thickly sliced
10 stalks fresh lemon grass,* or
    ¾ cup dried
8 garlic cloves, peeled

1¾ lb. roasted peanuts, unsalted
2½ T. curry powder
3 T. salt
10 oz. sugar
2 tsp. pepper

1. Bring water to boil and add pork hocks, lemon grass, and garlic. Return to a boil. Skim off brown foam. Cover and simmer 1½ hours.
2. Add peanuts and seasoning to simmering pork hocks. Mix well and continue to simmer, uncovered. Cook for another 30 minutes or until most of the liquid has evaporated.

CALORIES: 380
CHOLESTEROL: 136 mg
VITAMIN A: 3 IU

CARBOHYDRATE: 10 g
CALCIUM: 77 mg
VITAMIN C: <1 mg

PROTEIN: 30 g
SODIUM: 387 mg

FAT: 25 g
IRON: <1 mg

*If using fresh lemon grass, discard outer leaves and upper two-thirds of stalk. If using dried, it must be soaked in warm water for 2 hours, then drained.

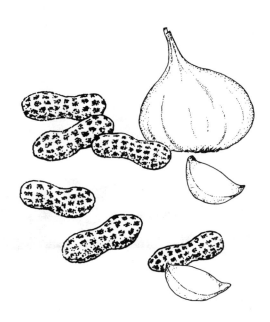

♦ *Fried Bean Curd with Vegetables*

YIELD: 50 portions
PORTION: 5 oz.

8 lb. bean curd, cut into 1" cubes
1 qt. vegetable oil
1 lb. scallions, white part only, sliced
1 lb. cauliflowerets
3 lb. string beans, cut in half

1 lb. carrots, peeled and sliced diagonally
2 qt. coconut milk
1 qt. water
2 T. salt or to taste
½ c. soy sauce
2½ T. sugar

1. Fry bean curd in oil until completely browned on all sides. Remove and drain. Reserve ⅓ cup oil in pan.
2. Stir-fry scallions in oil until they start to turn brown. Add cauliflower, string beans, and carrots; coat with oil. Add fried bean curd; stir for an additional minute.
3. Mix in remaining ingredients. Cover and simmer until vegetables are tender, approximately 10 minutes.

CALORIES: 244
CHOLESTEROL: 0 mg
VITAMIN A: 1294 IU

CARBOHYDRATE: 8 g
CALCIUM: 123 mg
VITAMIN C: 10 mg

PROTEIN: 8 g
SODIUM: 462 mg

FAT: 31 g
IRON: 3 mg

·20· COOKING FROM
· West Africa ·

A West African
menu featuring
chicken smothered
in peanut sauce,
rice balls, and adalu
(mashed
vegetables).

Before West Africa was visited by the Europeans, the native diet consisted largely of grains and yams, supplemented by small amounts of meat, vegetables, and fruit. The French, Dutch, British, Portuguese, and Germans have all, at various times, controlled parts of West Africa. Senegal, Guinea, the Ivory Coast, and Benin were all taken over by the French; Gambia, Sierra Leone, Ghana, and Nigeria were controlled by the British; Cameroon and Togo fell under German influence; and Guinea-Bissau belonged to the Portuguese. Despite West Africa's subsequent independence, the colonial history of these nations continues to influence their cuisine.

In Senegal, the French influence can be seen in the use of white potatoes. However, rice and couscous are also frequently eaten. Peanuts are a major crop. Since there are many Muslims in Senegal, pork is rarely eaten.

In British-influenced Ghana, tea has replaced the traditional beverages. A typical main dish is a stew of meat, beans, onions, tomato, okra, eggplant, and chili peppers.

In Liberia, founded by freed American slaves, sweet desserts and American pastries are popular. Bacon, pig's feet, and other forms of pork are eaten, and a national favorite is goat soup. Rice is a staple, often eaten twice a day.

Away from the coast, the diet is still much the same as it was in precolonial times. Grains and dishes of green vegetables with peas, beans and cereals form the main part of the diet, supplemented by starchy roots and a variety of native fruits. Cassava and corn, brought to the region from America, have been integrated into the diet.

Today, traditional ingredients are being used in new ways by innovative West African chefs. Yams are being turned into croquettes and thin crispy chips, for example. Bananas are being used in many ways: in salads and cakes, fermented into wine, and fried for dessert with cinnamon and orange slices or with a chocolate topping.

Ingredients

MILK AND MILK PRODUCTS

Few milk products are used in traditional West African cooking. Desert nomads drink camel's milk and use goat cheese and yogurt when available.

MEAT AND MEAT ALTERNATIVES

Fish—fresh, dried, salt-cured, or smoked—is eaten often, especially in coastal areas. Carp, cod, red snapper, and tilapia are representative types. Crab, oysters, and shrimp are gathered from the sea, and forest snails are found in the woods. Mutton, goat, and beef are popular, though scarce in many areas. Chicken is well-liked, and eggs are eaten frequently.

Legumes are an important ingredient. Beans, such as black beans, red beans, and black-eyed peas, are added to many dishes. A versatile bean purée is made with coconut milk; when sugar is added it can be eaten as a sweet, or it can be thinned and drunk as a beverage. Peanuts, also called groundnuts, and a related legume called the Bambara groundnut, are commonly used as an ingredient in soups and stews and as the basis for a sauce served with grilled food.

FRUITS AND VEGETABLES

Many tropical fruits are available, but few are widely eaten. Bananas and plantains are the most popular. Oranges, watermelon, pineapple, papaya, guavas, and dates are some of the other fruits commonly consumed. Root vegetables play an important part in the West African diet. Cassava is used in numerous ways. White yams, taro, and sweet potatoes are staples in many regions. Leaves of root vegetables, sometimes called *callaloo* or *cocoyam*, are also eaten. Tomatoes, avocados, onions, okra, squash, pumpkin, and peppers, both hot and sweet, are the most frequently eaten nonstarchy vegetables. Several types of eggplant are eaten.

BREADS AND CEREALS

Millet, wheat, rice, and corn are eaten in some regions, most often as porridge.

OTHER INGREDIENTS

Palm oil is used to cook many foods, giving them a distinctive red color. Coconut and peanut oils are common, and other fats, such as shea butter (made from the nut of a tree), are also used.

Coconut meat is used in many dishes, as are the seeds of squash, pumpkins, and melons. Watermelon seeds (called *egusi*) are dried and ground into flour. Sesame seeds, kola nuts, and cashews are also used, and nuts of palm trees are an ingredient in many dishes.

Palm wine, ginger beer, corn beer, and coconut milk are traditional beverages. Beer, fruit juices, coffee, and tea are also favored.

Seasonings

Most foods are preferred very spicy. Garlic, fresh ginger root, lemon juice, and onion are the most frequently used seasonings. Several types of chili pepper are used, including one called *pili-pili*, which is said to be hotter than cayenne pepper. Sweet peppers are also added to many dishes. Cinnamon, nutmeg, cloves, vanilla, thyme, bay leaves, and cumin are called for in some recipes. Some unusual flavorings, such as ground baobab seeds and malagueta pepper, are used in certain areas. Coconut milk and cream flavor many foods. Both honey and sugar are used as sweeteners. Chocolate, which is produced in raw form in large quantities by some West African countries, is used only occasionally.

Preparation

West African foods are usually simmered or fried, though grilling and baking are common in some areas. Many dishes are still cooked over three-stone hearths, which are found throughout the area. Dishes are often one-pot meals, and stews are particularly popular. Fish and meat are often cooked together. Typically meat and/or fish is simmered with vegetables and spices, including tomatoes, onions, and chili peppers. Stews are preferred "sticky" and thickened with mashed yam, sweet potato, plantain, bean purée, okra, or grated coconut. An example is *jollof rice* (versions of the dish are prepared throughout the region), which features a mixture of rice with meat, chicken, and/or shrimp cooked with tomatoes and other vegetables such as eggplant, peas, pumpkin, and spinach. Peanut stews combine chicken, fish, or meat with peanut butter, tomatoes, and chili peppers.

A starchy food usually accompanies a stew and may be plain boiled rice (sometimes formed into cakes or balls); corn cakes; a porridge of corn, millet, or *gari* (slightly fermented cassava flour); or *fufu*, which is made from pounded cassava, yams, or plantains. Balls of mashed yam can be used as dumplings. Rice cooked with coconut cream is used as a side dish with shellfish. Stews are also frequently served with a tray of garnishes, often including grated coconut, chopped egg, peanuts, cubed avocado, spiced okra, diced papaya, tiny eggplants, fried plantains, chunks of pineapple, and chopped onion.

Fish may be eaten raw after being salted and "cooked" in a marinade of lemon juice, then rinsed and dressed with oil, chili peppers, thyme, parsley, and grated coconut.

Marinades with a lemon juice base are used often, and help to tenderize tough meat and chicken. Meat, fish, and poultry prepared this way is called *yassa* in Senegal. Another tenderizing technique is wrapping meat in papaya leaves (which contain an enzyme that acts on the meat) and then letting it stand overnight.

Meal Patterns

Two or three meals a day are typically eaten in West Africa, and snacking is common. Typical breakfast or brunch dishes are millet porridge with dark brown vanilla-flavored sugar, eggs baked on a layer of mashed yam, or *gari foto*: eggs scrambled with cassava meal, tomatoes, and onions, with red beans as a side dish.

The main meal usually consists of a stewlike dish, a starch dish, and garnishes. In some areas a large variety of different dishes is served at once. Fresh fruit is most often eaten for dessert. For a special occasion, appetizers and a fancy dessert can be included, and the meal may be served in courses. Dessert omelets and fritters containing fruit are made in restaurants. In many areas, food is eaten with the fingers.

Southern Cooking

West African blacks brought many of their native foods, such as black-eyed peas, okra, sesame seeds, and watermelon, to America when they were taken as slaves. Even peanuts, which are from South America, came to the United States via West Africa. When African ingredients were unavailable, traditional dishes were prepared with whatever foods were provided by slave owners. As cooks for wealthy households, blacks were exposed to the foods of other cultural groups in the area, including British, French, and Spanish. Many blacks also became familiar with Native American dishes. The blending of these foods and cooking methods resulted in the distinctive cuisine for which the South is famous.

Boiling and frying were the most popular cooking methods during the slave period, and they continue to be used today. Many foods are still preferred spicy hot and thick or sticky in consistency. Dishes are sometimes seasoned with hot sauce (which replaced the chilis used in Africa), onions, lemons, tomatoes, and sweet peppers. Although okra is often added to thicken stews, sassafras (a native herb introduced to the slaves by the Native Americans) is commonly used to thicken dishes as well. The Southern specialty *gumbo z'herbes* is very similar to West African stew. Southern fried foods, such as chicken and catfish, were also developed by the slaves, using available ingredients such as cornmeal for the coating.

Pork and pork variety cuts, such as maw, head, hocks, feet, and chitterlings (intestines, pronounced "chitlins") replaced almost all other West African meats in the diet of the slaves, who made good use of any parts of the pig that were discarded by their masters. Salt pork was also usually available. These cuts are often featured in Southern dishes today. Favorites include ham, fried or boiled chitterlings, pickled pig's feet, sausages such as head cheese, and barbecued ribs.

Chicken has retained its popularity from the slave period through today. Small game, such as opossum, rabbit, squirrel, raccoon, muskrat, frogs, and freshwater fish (such as catfish) were caught to supplement the slave diet, and these foods are still occasionally used. Legumes, especially beans and peas, remain an important ingredient in Southern cuisine.

Corn was commonly available, and it was eaten most often as cornmeal, hominy, or grits. Corn products are prepared as cereals, side dishes, and puddings, and they are baked into biscuits, breads, and fried cakes, such as corn pone and hush puppies. Wheat flour biscuits are also common.

Greens and sweet potatoes were also provided by slave owners. Some slaves grew their own vegetables, including black-eyed peas, cabbage, collards, mustard greens, okra, squashes, and turnips. Many of these have remained popular. Greens are cooked in a manner that reflects a West African influence. They are boiled well, flavored with hot sauce, onions and/or sweet peppers, and lemon juice or vinegar. A small amount of salt pork, bacon, or ham is added for flavor. The cooking liquid from the greens, called *pot likker*, is also served as a hot beverage.

Desserts are usually baked or stewed. Apples, bananas, all types of berries, melons (including watermelon), peaches, and pumpkin are often used in these dishes, as are nuts and seeds, such as peanuts, pecans, and sesame seeds. Molasses, originally provided by slave owners, is still used in many desserts. Puddings (including bread pudding and rice pudding), pies (including squash and sweet potato), cakes, cookies, candies (such as the Southern specialty known as pralines), and fruit cobblers are popular.

Traditional Southern meal patterns developed after the slave period, when food became more readily available for both blacks and whites. Breakfast was typically large and might include eggs, bacon or ham, grits, biscuits, and fried sweet potatoes. Lunch was the main meal of the day, eaten in the midafternoon. The entrée was usually boiled, featuring beans or greens with pork, often in a stew. Potatoes, other vegetables, and bread or biscuits were also served. Supper often included meat, potatoes, and a vegetable. Some type of dessert always concluded the meal.

Traditional Southern foods are still popular today with both blacks and whites. However, modern Southern meal patterns are as varied as they are in any other region of the United States. Few blacks continue to eat traditional Southern meals in full, even if they reside in the South. West African dishes are eaten even less often. A complete Southern breakfast might be served only on weekends, for example. West African food might be prepared to celebrate a holiday such as *Kwanzaa*, the African-American New Year. Many Southern American dishes, such as barbecued ribs and sweet potato pie, have been dubbed "soul food" and have been adopted by blacks as a symbol of cultural solidarity.

M E N U **West African Dinner**

◆ Coconut Soup

YIELD: 50 portions
PORTION: 1 c.

1½ gal. beef stock
1 gal. coconut milk
3 lb. eggplant, peeled and diced
½ c. lemon juice

1½ T. salt
2 tsp. ginger
1 oz. parsley, chopped

1. Combine beef stock and coconut milk; bring to a boil. Add eggplant and lemon juice. Simmer, covered, until mixture is well cooked, about 50 minutes. Purée soup.
2. Add salt and ginger. Heat before serving. Garnish with parsley.

CALORIES: 207
CHOLESTEROL: 2 mg
VITAMIN A: 51 IU

CARBOHYDRATE: 5 g
CALCIUM: 25 mg
VITAMIN C: 4 mg

PROTEIN: 4 g
SODIUM: 574 mg

FAT: 21 g
IRON: 2 mg

♦ Chicken in Peanut Sauce

BAKE: 1 hour
OVEN: 350°F
YIELD: 50 portions
PORTION: 5 oz.

20 lb. boneless chicken, cut into bite-size pieces
1½ c. vegetable oil
2½ lb. onions, chopped
1 #10 can tomatoes, peeled, chopped, and drained
4 lb. sweet peppers, seeded and sliced thin

1½ T. thyme
6 T. bay leaves, crumbled
1½ T. salt
½ T. cayenne
6 lb. whole okra, frozen
2 qt. peanut butter
2 qt. chicken stock

1. Brown chicken in oil over high heat. Reserve oil, place chicken in two 12″ × 20″ × 2″ baking pans.
2. Add onions, tomatoes, and sweet peppers to oil and sauté until soft. Add to the chicken. Sprinkle with thyme, bay leaves, salt, cayenne, and okra.
3. Combine peanut butter and chicken stock. Pour over chicken mixture. Cover and bake for 1 hour. Check liquid after half an hour and add more liquid if needed.

CALORIES: 597
CHOLESTEROL: 113 mg
VITAMIN A: 971 IU

CARBOHYDRATE: 17 g
CALCIUM: 106 mg
VITAMIN C: 44 mg

PROTEIN: 51 g
SODIUM: 577 mg

FAT: 64 g
IRON: 3 mg

♦ Rice Balls

YIELD: 50 portions
PORTION: 2 balls

4 lb. short-grain rice
2 gal. water

2 T. salt

1. Combine all ingredients in a pot and bring to a boil. Cover and cook over low heat 20–25 minutes, until rice mashes easily against the side of the pot. Mash rice. Grains should be partially broken; rice will stick together. Cool.
2. Using a no. 16 scoop, rinsed with water, scoop rice balls into a greased serving pan. Rice balls may be eaten cold or steamed to reheat.

CALORIES: 131
CHOLESTEROL: 0 mg
VITAMIN A: 0 IU

CARBOHYDRATE: 30 g
CALCIUM: 7 mg
VITAMIN C: 0 mg

PROTEIN: 2 g
SODIUM: 266 mg

FAT: <1 g
IRON: <1 mg

Adalu (Mashed Vegetables)

YIELD: 50 portions
PORTION: 4–5 oz.

12 lb. cooked kidney beans
12 lb. cooked corn or yams, or
  uncooked bananas
½ T. cayenne

1 T. salt
1½ lb. onions, finely chopped
1½ c. palm oil

1. Mash beans and vegetables together and season with cayenne and salt.
2. Sauté onions in oil. Add to above mixture and thoroughly combine.

YAMS:	CALORIES: 330 CHOLESTEROL: 0 mg VITAMIN A: 25 IU	CARBOHYDRATE: 59 g CALCIUM: 43 mg VITAMIN C: 7 mg	PROTEIN: 11 g SODIUM: 197 mg	FAT: 13 g IRON: 5 mg
CORN:	CALORIES: 286 CHOLESTEROL: 0 mg VITAMIN A: 394 IU	CARBOHYDRATE: 47 g CALCIUM: 40 mg VITAMIN C: 7 mg	PROTEIN: 12 g SODIUM: 140 mg	FAT: 14 g IRON: 5 mg
BANANAS:	CALORIES: 301 CHOLESTEROL: 0 mg VITAMIN A: 100 IU	CARBOHYDRATE: 52 g CALCIUM: 44 mg VITAMIN C: 11 mg	PROTEIN: 10 g SODIUM: 137 mg	FAT: 13 g IRON: 4 mg

Ginger Beer

YIELD: 3 gal.
PORTION: 1 c.

1½ lb. ginger root, peeled and
  grated
3 qt. boiling water
2½ gal. cold water

2½ c. lemon juice
1 T. whole cloves
6 cinnamon sticks
2½ lb. sugar

1. In a food processor or blender purée ginger with 2 cups of boiling water. Empty into a large nonmetallic bowl or tub and add remaining water. Let stand for 2 hours. Strain through several layers of cheesecloth. Squeeze plup to remove all of the liquid.
2. Add cold water, lemon juice, and spices. Stir and let stand for an hour or two. Let sediment settle. Carefully decant the clearer liquid. Discard sediment.
3. Add sugar and stir until dissolved. Chill. This strong ginger beer may be diluted with water to taste.

CALORIES: 102
CHOLESTEROL: 0
VITAMIN A: 3 IU
CARBOHYDRATE: 27 g
CALCIUM: 8 mg
VITAMIN C: 4 mg
PROTEIN: <1 g
SODIUM: 5 mg
FAT: <1 g
IRON: <1 mg

Traditional Southern Supper

◆ *Corn Soup*

YIELD: 50 portions
PORTION: 1 c.

2 lb. bacon, sliced and chopped
2 lb. onions, finely chopped
1 lb. celery, coarsely chopped, with
stalks and leaves
8 lb. potatoes, peeled and diced
2 gal. water

1 tsp. nutmeg
3 T. salt
1 tsp. white pepper
1 gal. milk
1 gal. half-and-half
1 #10 can whole kernel corn,
drained

1. Fry bacon till crisp. Reserve bacon and fat.
2. Sauté onions and celery in bacon fat until softened.
3. Combine potatoes, water, nutmeg, salt, pepper, onions, celery, and bacon. Simmer, covered, until potatoes are soft, about 10 minutes.
4. Stir in milk, half-and-half, and corn. Cover and simmer until soup is heated through. Adjust seasonings.

CALORIES: 179   CARBOHYDRATE: 25 g   PROTEIN: 8 g   FAT: 11 g
CHOLESTEROL: 22 mg   CALCIUM: 165 mg   SODIUM: 667 mg   IRON: 1 mg
VITAMIN A: 319 IU   VITAMIN C: 15 mg

◆ *Ham Hocks with Black-eyed Peas*

YIELD: 50 portions
PORTION: 1 c.

12 lb. smoked ham hocks
6 lb. dried black-eyed peas
2 lb. onions, chopped
1 lb. celery, chopped

4 oz. can green chiles, drained and
chopped, or to taste
1 tsp. pepper or to taste

Place ham hocks in enough water to cover. Bring to a boil and simmer, partially covered, until hocks are tender, about 2 hours. Mix in the remaining ingredients. Simmer, partially covered, until peas are tender. Add more water if necessary. Adjust seasoning.

CALORIES: 304   CARBOHYDRATE: 36 g   PROTEIN: 22 g   FAT: 13 g
CHOLESTEROL: 28 mg   CALCIUM: 51 mg   SODIUM: 559 mg   IRON: 5 mg
VITAMIN A: 61 IU   VITAMIN C: 8 mg

♦ Greens

YIELD: 50 portions
PORTION: ½ c.

25 lb. turnip or mustard greens,
    stripped from stem
12 lb. salt pork, cut into 1" cubes
2½ qt. water
4 lb. onions, chopped

3 T. sugar
1 T. salt or to taste
½ tsp. pepper or to taste
2 T. lemon juice or to taste
½ tsp. Tabasco or to taste

1. Fry salt pork over moderate heat until pork is crispy. Reserve pork and fat. Pour water into pan and bring to a boil. Scrape bottom of pan to dissolve brown bits. Reserve liquid.
2. Cook greens, stirring frequently, over high heat until wilted. Add pork, fat, reserve liquid, onions, and sugar. Stir and cover pot. Simmer until greens are tender, about 45 minutes. Season with salt, pepper, lemon juice, and Tabasco.

CALORIES: 343
CHOLESTEROL: 153 mg
VITAMIN A: 13057 IU

CARBOHYDRATE: 14 g
CALCIUM: 374 mg
VITAMIN C: 131 mg

PROTEIN: 24 g
SODIUM: 1616 mg

FAT: 39 g
IRON: 4 mg

♦ Sweet Potato Pone

BAKE: 1 hour
OVEN: 350°F
YIELD: 50 portions
PORTION: 4 oz.

14 lb. sweet potatoes, peeled,
    cooked, and mashed
1 lb. butter or margarine, melted
1 lb., 12 oz. sugar
3½ c. dark corn syrup
3½ c. milk
16 eggs, well beaten

1 T. allspice
2 tsp. cloves, ground
2 tsp. ginger, powdered
1 T. cinnamon
2 T. vanilla flavoring
1 lb. pecans, chopped

Combine ingredients and mix well. Pour into three greased 2″ × 12″ × 18″ pans. Bake. Pone may be served cold or at room temperature.

CALORIES: 374
CHOLESTEROL: 107 mg
VITAMIN A: 8835 IU

CARBOHYDRATE: 51 g
CALCIUM: 95 mg
VITAMIN C: 16 mg

PROTEIN: 6 g
SODIUM: 155 mg

FAT: 25 g
IRON: 2 mg

Ham hocks, black-eyed peas, boiled greens, and corn bread are a traditional Southern meal.

◆ Glossary of Ethnic Ingredients ◆

Abalone: Large, flat mollusk with finely textured, sweet flesh in the broad, muscular foot that holds it to rocks (must be pounded before use). It is common in the waters off Asia, California, Mexico, and New Zealand. Available fresh, frozen, canned, and dried. Substitutes—pounded squid meat may be used, although flavor and texture differ slightly.

Achiote: See *annatto.*

Ackee (akee, achee): Red fruit with three segments containing large inedible seeds and flesh that looks like scrambled eggs. Available canned. Substitutes—none.

Adzuki Bean (aduki, azuki): Very small, dark red bean used primarily in Japanese cooking. Substitutes—none.

Ajowan (ajwain, carom seeds): Similar to celery seeds in appearance and to thyme in flavor. Used in Asian Indian and Middle Eastern cooking. Substitutes—none.

Almond Paste: Arab confection of ground almonds kneaded with sugar or cooked sugar syrup (some brands also contain egg white) used in many European and Middle Eastern desserts. Marzipan is a type of almond paste made with finely ground blanched almonds. Substitutes—none.

Amchoor: Dried, unripe mango slices or powder, with a sour flavor. Substitutes—lemon juice, 2 tablespoons for each teaspoon of amchoor powder.

Angelica: Herb with a licorice flavor commonly used in European dishes. Usually available candied. Substitutes—none.

Annatto (achiote, atchuete): Seeds of the annatto tree used to color foods red or golden yellow. Used in Latin America, India, Spain, and the Philippines. In the United States, annatto is added to some Cheddar-style cheeses, margarines, and butter for color. May be cooked whole in oil or lard to produce the right hue or used as a ground spice. Substitutes—paprika, turmeric, or saffron will produce a similar color.

Artichoke: Globelike vegetable member of the thistle family, with multiple, edible bracts ("leaves") crowning the undeveloped, edible flower (the

237

"heart"). The flavor is slightly sweet. Popular in Middle Eastern and southern European dishes. Available fresh, frozen, and marinated in oil. Substitutes—none.

Asafetida: Dried resin with a pungent odor reminiscent of burnt rubber, which nonetheless imparts a delicate onionlike flavor. It is available as lump or powder and is commonly used in Asian Indian dishes. Substitutes—none.

Asian Pear (apple pear): Round, yellow fruit from Asia with the crispness of an apple and the flavor of a pear. Substitutes—a firm, fresh d'anjou pear or golden delicious apple (flavor will differ slightly).

Avocado (alligator pear): Pear-shaped to round fruit with leathery skin (green to black) and light green, buttery flesh. Native to Central America. Three varieties are often available. Eaten mostly as a vegetable, though considered a fruit in some cuisines. Substitutes—none.

Bacalao (bacalhau, baccala): Cod preserved by drying and salting. Must be soaked, drained, and boiled before use. Substitutes—none.

Bagoong: See *fish paste*.

Bagoong-Alamang: See *shrimp paste*.

Bambara Groundnut: Legume very similar to peanuts, native to Africa. Substitutes—peanuts.

Bamboo Shoot: Crisp, cream-colored, conical shoot of the bamboo plant. Used fresh (stored in water) or available canned in brine (whole or sliced). Substitutes—celery heart or sliced kohlrabi can be used, with a slight difference in flavor.

Bangus: See *milkfish*.

Baobab Seeds (monkey bread, lalu powder): Slightly sweet seeds from the large fruit of the native African baobab tree. Used roasted or ground. Substitutes—none.

Basmati Rice: See *rice*.

Bean Curd (tofu): Custardlike, slightly rubbery, white curd with a bland flavor made from soybean milk. Japanese bean curd (called tofu) tends to be softer than Chinese, which is preferred for stir-fried dishes. Substitutes—none.

Bean Sprouts: The young sprouts of mung beans or soybeans popular in Asian cooking (sprouts may also be grown from the tiny seeds of alfalfa, also a legume). The crisp 1- to 2-inch sprouts are eaten fresh or added to stir-fried dishes. Substitutes—the sprouts may be used interchangeably, although alfalfa sprouts are much smaller and soften completely when cooked and are best used raw. Sliced celery or cucumber will provide a similar texture, but a different flavor.

Beans: See each type.

Betel: The heart-shaped leaves of the betel vine (related to black pepper) are used to wrap betel, or areca, nuts (from the Areca palm) and spices for paan in India. Betel nuts and leaves are chewed together in many Southeast Asian countries and in India to promote digestion. May stain the teeth red. Substitutes—none.

Bitter Almond: An almond variety with an especially strong almond flavor, often used to make extracts, syrups, and liqueurs. Grown in the Mediterranean region, bitter almonds are used in European dishes. They contain prussic acid and are toxic when raw (they become edible when cooked) and are unavailable in the United States. Substitutes—almond extract used in small amounts will approximate the taste.

Bitter Melon (bitter gourd): Bumpy-skinned Asian fruit similar in shape to a cucumber that is green when ripe, turning yellow or orange as it becomes overripe. The flesh has melonlike seeds and an acrid taste (the flavor and odor become stronger the longer it ripens). Substitutes—none.

Black Bean (turtle bean): Small (less than one-half inch) black bean (dried) used extensively in Central American, South American, and Caribbean cooking. Substitutes—none.

Black Beans, Fermented: Black soybeans salted and fermented to produce a piquant condiment. Used in Chinese cooking as a seasoning or combined with garlic, ginger, rice wine, and other ingredients to make black bean sauce. Substitutes—none.

Black Mushrooms: See *mushrooms.*

Black-Eyed Pea (cow pea): Small legume (technically neither a pea nor a bean), white with a black spot, native to Africa and southern Asia. Substitutes—may be used interchangeably with pigeon peas.

Bok Choy (Chinese chard): Vegetable of the cabbage family with long, white leaf stalks and smooth, dark green leaves. Substitutes—napa cabbage or romaine lettuce.

Breadfruit: Large, round tropical fruit with warty, green skin and starchy, white flesh. It must be cooked and is usually served as a vegetable. Available canned. Substitutes—potatoes or cassava.

Buckwheat (kasha): Nutty-flavored cereal native to the Soviet Union (where it is called kasha), sold as whole seeds (groats) and ground seeds (grits if coarsely ground, flour if finely ground). It is common in Soviet and Eastern European cooking. Substitutes—none.

Buffalo Berry: Scarlet berry of the *Sheperdia* genus, so-called because it was usually eaten with buffalo meat by the Native Americans. Substitutes—none.

Bulgur (bulghur, burghul): Nutty-flavored cracked grains of whole wheat that have been precooked with steam. Available in coarse, medium, and fine grades. Substitutes—cracked wheat, although the flavor is not identical, and preparation differs because the cracked wheat must be cooked (not just soaked) before use.

Burdock Root (gobo): Long, thin root with crisp, white flesh and thin, brown skin with an earthy, sweet flavor. Popular in Asian cooking. Substitutes—none.

Cactus: The paddles (nopales and nopalitos) and the juicy, reddish fruit (tuna) of the prickly pear cactus, eaten in the American Southwest and

Mexico. The paddles are used fresh, cooked, or pickled. Available canned. Substitutes—none.

Calabash: Gourdlike fruit of a tropical tree native to the New World. Substitutes—butternut or Hubbard squash.

Calabaza: Round or oblong winter squash with yellow flesh and a flavor similar to pumpkin. Substitutes—butternut or Hubbard squash.

Calamansi: Small, sour lime used to flavor foods in Filipino cooking. Substitutes—limes.

Callaloo (cocoyam): Edible leaves of root vegetables, especially malanga and taro. Callaloo is sometimes the name of a dish made from these leaves. Substitutes—spinach or chard.

Candlenut (kukui nut): Oily tropical nut sold only in roasted form (it is toxic when raw). Popular in Malaysia, Polynesia, and Southeast Asia. Substitutes—blanched almonds or macadamia nuts.

Cannellini: See *kidney bean.*

Capers: Small, gray-green flower buds from a bush native to the Mediterranean. They are commonly pickled. Substitutes—none.

Carambola: See *star fruit.*

Cardoon: Member of the artichoke family that looks like a spiny celery plant, popular in Italian cooking. Substitutes—celery or celeriac, although the flavor is not similar.

Cashew Apple: The fleshy "false fruit" to which the cashew nut is attached. Native to Brazil, it is eaten in the Caribbean and India as well. Substitutes—none.

Cassarep: Caribbean sauce made from the juice of the bitter variety of cassava cooked with raw sugar. Substitutes—none.

Cassava (manioc, yuca): Tropical Latin American tuber (now eaten in most tropical areas of the world) with rough, brown skin and mild, white flesh. Two types exist: bitter (poisonous unless leached and cooked) and sweet. Cassava starch is used to make the thickening agent tapioca. Substitutes—taro root.

Caviar: Fish roe classified by source and quality. Black or gray beluga caviar is harvested from large sturgeons and is considered best; sevruga and osetra caviar are obtained from smaller sturgeon and are therefore smaller and often darker colored. The large red eggs of salmon are commonly called red caviar. The choicest caviar is lightly salted and carefully sieved by hand. The poorer quality caviar is heavily salted and pressed into blocks. Substitutes—none.

Celeriac (celery root): Gnarled, bulbous root of one type of celery, with brownish skin, tannish flesh, and nutty flavor. Substitutes—none.

Cèpes: See *mushrooms.*

Chanterelles: See *mushrooms.*

Chayote (christophine, chocho, mirliton, vegetable pear): Thin-skinned, green (light or dark), pear-shaped squash. Native to Mexico, it is now common in

Central America, the Caribbean, southern United States, and parts of Asia as well. Substitutes—yellow summer squash or pattypan squash.

Cherimoya (custard apple): Large, dimpled, light green fruit native to South America. White flesh is creamy in texture and similar to fruit salad in taste. Substitutes—none.

Chicharrónes: Deep-fried pork skin, fried twice to produce puffy strips. Substitutes—none.

Chickpea (garbanzo bean): Pale yellow, round legume popular in Middle Eastern, Spanish, Portuguese, and Latin American cooking. Can be purchased canned or dried. Substitutes—none.

Chicory: Bitter, roasted root of the chicory plant used as a substitute for coffee. Often added to dark coffee in Creole cooking.

Chili Pepper (chile): Although chili peppers, or chiles, are often called hot peppers, the fruits are not related to Asian pepper (such as black pepper) but are pods of capsicum plants, native to Central and South America. Over 100 varieties are available, from less than 1 inch in length to over 8 inches long. They may be fresh or dried. The alkaloid capsaicin, found mostly in the ribs of the pods, is what makes chili peppers hot. In general, the smaller the chile, the hotter it is. Common types include mild Anaheim (also called California or New Mexico chili); cayenne (used mostly dried and powdered as the spice cayenne); dark green, medium hot jalapeño (often available canned); spicy, rich green poblano (used fresh or ripened and dried, when it is called ancho); hot serrano (small, bright green or red); and very hot chili de arbol, japones, péquin, and tabasco (all small, red chiles, often used dried). Substitutes—some chili peppers can be used interchangeably, such as jalapeños and serranos. Powdered cayenne to taste can be used in place of the hotter, dried chili peppers.

Chinese Date (jujube): Small Asian fruit (not actually belonging to the date family) usually sold dried. Red dates are the most popular, but black and white are also available. Substitutes—prunes, although the flavor is slightly different.

Chinese Parsley: See *coriander*.

Chitterlings (chitlins): Pork small intestines, prepared by boiling or frying. Substitutes—none.

Chokecherry: Tart, reddish black native American cherry (*Prunus virginiana*). Substitutes—any sour cherry.

Chrysanthemum Greens: Spicy leaves of a variety of chrysanthemum (not the American garden flower), popular in Asian stir-fried dishes. Substitutes—spinach, especially the more bitter varieties.

Cilantro: See *coriander*.

Citron: Candied peel of a yellow-green, apple-sized citrus fruit. Available crystallized and as preserves. Substitutes—crystallized lemon peel can be used in recipes with a mixture of candied fruits.

Clotted Cream (Cornish cream, Devonshire cream): Very thick cream made by allowing cream to separate from milk, then heating it and cooling it so that it ferments slightly. Finally the cream is skimmed from the milk (although Cornish cream is skimmed before heating and cooling). It is popular in southwest England where it is spread on bread or used as a topping for desserts. Substitutes—cream cheese or sweet butter, depending on use.

Cloud Ears: See *mushrooms.*

Coconut Cream: High-fat cream extracted from fresh grated coconut. Substitutes—cream, but the flavor is not similar.

Coconut Milk: Liquid extracted with water from fresh grated coconut. Substitutes—whole milk, but the flavor is not similar.

Cocoyam: See *callaloo.*

Coriander (cilantro, Chinese parsley): Fresh leaves of the coriander plant with a distinctive, aromatic flavor common in Asian, Middle Eastern, Indian, and Latin American cooking. Substitutes—flat-leaf parsley looks similar and may be used as a garnish, although the flavor is not similar.

Couscous (cuscus): Small granules of semolina flour, used as a grain in African, Italian, and Middle Eastern dishes. Substitutes—none.

Cow Pea: See *black-eyed pea.*

Cracked Wheat: Cracked raw kernels of whole wheat used in Middle Eastern cooking. Substitutes—bulgur is similar, but is precooked.

Crayfish (crawdad, crawfish): Small, freshwater crustacean, 4 to 6 inches long, that looks and tastes something like lobster. Different species are found in Europe and the United States (California, Louisiana, Michigan, and the Pacific Northwest). The names crayfish and crawfish are also applied to the langostino, a saltwater crustacean that lacks large front claws. Substitutes—large prawns, although the flavor is different.

Crème Fraîche: Slightly thickened, slightly fermented cream popular in France. Substitutes—1 tablespoon buttermilk added to 1 cup heavy cream fermented at room temperature overnight, then refrigerated (this substitute will thin out and separate during cooking, unlike real crème fraîche).

Curry Powder: The Western version of the fresh Asian Indian spice mixture (garam masala) used to flavor curried dishes. Up to 20 spices are ground, then roasted, usually including black pepper, cayenne, cinnamon, coriander, cumin, fenugreek, ginger, cardamom, and turmeric for color. Substitutes—none.

Cuttlefish (inkfish): A mollusk that is similar to squid, but smaller. Available fresh or dried. Substitutes—none for dried fish; for fresh fish, use an equal amount of squid.

Daikon (icicle radish, white radish): Relatively mild, white radish common in Asian cooking. The Japanese variety is the largest, often 12 inches long, shaped like an icicle. The Chinese variety tends to be smaller. All varieties are interchangeable. Substitutes—any white radish (including European types).

Dals: Asian Indian term for split lentils and chickpeas. Many types are available. Substitutes—different lentils are interchangeable.

Dilis (daing): Small, silvery fish related to anchovies, dried and salted. Used in Filipino dishes. Substitutes—none.

Durian: Cantaloupe-sized, spiked fruit native to Malaysia with a strong odor and sweet, creamy flesh. Substitutes—none.

Eggplant: Pear-shaped to round member of the nightshade family with smooth, thin skin (white or deep purple in color) and spongy, off-white flesh. Native to India, it has a mildly bitter flavor. Two types widely available are the small, thin variety known as Japanese or Chinese eggplant and the more common larger, rounder variety. Substitutes—none.

Egusi: Seeds from an African watermelon similar to a pumpkin or gourd, often ground or pounded into a paste. Substitutes—pumpkin seeds (if whole required), mashed beans, or eggplant (if paste required).

Enoki: See *mushrooms*.

Epazote (Mexican tea): Pungent herb (*Chenopodium ambrosioides*) related to pigweed or goosefoot (and sometimes called by these names). Found in Mexico and parts of the United States. Often added to bean dishes to reduce gas. Substitutes—none.

Fava Bean (broad bean, horse bean, Windsor bean): Large, green, meaty bean sold fresh in the pod. Smaller, white or tan fava beans are dried or canned and cannot be used interchangeably with the fresh beans. Common in Italian and Middle Eastern cooking. Substitutes—none.

Fennel: Light green plant with slightly bulbous end and stalks with feathery, dark green leaves, a little like celery. Used like a root vegetable. Delicate licorice or anise flavor. Substitutes—none.

Fenugreek: Tan seeds of the fenugreek plant, with a flavor similar to artificial maple flavoring. Essential in the preparation of Asian Indian spice mixtures (called curry powder in the United States). Substitutes—none.

Filé Powder: See *sassafras*.

Fish Paste (bagoong): Thick, fermented paste made from fish, used as a condiment and seasoning in the Philippines. Substitutes—none.

Fish Sauce (nuoc mam, patis): Thin, salty, brown sauce made from fish fermented for several days. Asian fish sauces vary in taste from mild to very strong, depending on the country and the grade of sauce. Filipino patis is the mildest, Vietnamese nuoc mam is among the most flavorful. Nuoc cham is a sauce made from nuoc mam by the addition of garlic and chili peppers. Substitutes—none.

Five-Spice Powder: A pungent Chinese spice mixture of anise, cinnamon, cloves, fennel seeds, and Szechuan pepper. Substitutes—none.

Garbanzo Bean: See *chickpea*.

Gari: Flour made from cassava (plain, toasted, or fermented). Substitutes—cornmeal, but the flavor is not similar.

Ghee: Clarified butter used in India. The term is also used for vegetable shortening. Substitutes—vegetable shortening.

Ginger Root: Knobby, brown-skinned root with fibrous, yellow-white pulp and a tangy flavor. Used sliced or grated in Asian dishes. Also available dried, ground, or candied. Substitutes—none. Powdered ginger cannot be used in place of fresh ginger root, as the flavor is very different.

Ginkgo Nut: Small pit of the fruit of the ginkgo tree (ancient species related to the pine tree), dried or preserved in brine, common in Japan. Substitutes—none.

Ginseng: Aromatic, forked root with bitter, yellowish flesh, used in some Asian dishes and beverages. Substitutes—none.

Glutinous Rice: See *rice.*

Granadilla: See *passion fruit.*

Grape Leaves: Large leaves of grape vines preserved in brine, common in Middle Eastern cooking. Substitutes—none.

Greens: Any of numerous cultivated or wild leaves, such as chard, collard greens, dandelion greens, kale, milkweed, mustard greens, pokeweed, purslane, and spinach. Substitutes—greens may be used interchangeably, with slight changes in flavor.

Grits: Coarsely ground grain, especially hominy, which is typically boiled into a thick porridge or fried as a side dish. Served often in the southern United States. Substitutes—none.

Guava: Small, sweet fruit with an intense floral aroma, native to Brazil. Skin is yellow-green or yellow, and the grainy flesh ranges from white or yellow to pink and red. Many varieties are available, including strawberry guava and pineapple guava. Guava is popular as jelly, juice, or paste. Substitutes—strawberries.

Head Cheese: Loaf of seasoned meat made from the hog's head, sometimes also feet and organs. Substitutes—none.

Heart of Palm: White or light green interior of the palm tree. Available canned. Substitutes—none.

Hog Peanut: A high-protein underground fruit that grows on the root of the vine *Falcata comosa* in the central and southern United States. The peanut has a leathery shell that can be removed by boiling or soaking. The nut meat can be eaten raw or cooked. Substitutes—unroasted peanuts.

Hoisin Sauce: Popular Chinese paste or sauce, reddish brown in color, with a spicy sweet flavor. It is made from fermented soybeans, rice, sugar, garlic, ginger, and other spices. Substitutes—none.

Hominy (pozole): Lime-soaked hulled corn kernels with the bran and germ removed. Substitutes—none.

Hot Pepper: See *chili pepper.*

Hot Sauce: Sauce made from fermented chili peppers, vinegar, and salt (Tabasco sauce is the best-known U.S. brand). Substitutes—dried red pepper flakes or cayenne provide a similar flavor.

Indian Breadroot: Large white starchy root (*Psoralea esculenta*) indigenous to the western United States. It can be eaten raw, peeled and roasted, boiled, or dried and ground into a flour. Substitutes—turnips.

Jackfruit: Large (up to 100 pounds) fruit of the jack tree, related to breadfruit and figs, native to India. Two varieties are widely eaten, one sweeter than the other. Available canned. Substitutes—none.

Java Plum (rose apple, jambo, jaman): *Eugenia jambolana*, a small sour fruit grown in the Philippines.

Jerusalem Artichoke (sunchoke, sunroot): Small, nubby-skinned tuber that is the root of a native American sunflower. It is neither from Jerusalem nor related to the artichoke, although the flavor when cooked is similar. It is used both raw and cooked. Substitutes—jícama if uncooked, turnip if cooked, although the flavor will be different in both substitutions.

Jicama: Medium to large tuber with light brown skin and crisp, white flesh. Used raw in Mexican dishes, it has a sweet, bland flavor similar to peas or water chestnuts. Substitutes—equal amounts of sliced water chestnuts.

Juniper Berry: Distinctively flavored dark blue berry of the juniper evergreen bush, native to Europe. Used to flavor gin. Substitutes—small amounts of gin added before cooking will approximate the flavor.

Kamias: Sour, cucumberlike fruit native to the Philippines. Used to achieve a sour, cool flavor in Filipino cooking. Substitutes—none.

Kasha: See *buckwheat*.

Kidney Bean: Medium-sized, kidney-shaped bean light to dark red in color (a white variety is popular in Europe, especially Italy, where they are known as cannellini). The flavorful beans are common in Europe, Latin America, and the United States. Substitutes—red beans or pinto beans can be used in place of red kidney beans, although they are not as meaty. Great northern beans or navy beans can be used instead of cannellini.

Kohlrabi: Light green or purple, round vegetable that grows above the soil and produces stems bearing leaves on the upper part of it. A member of the cabbage family, it can be eaten raw or cooked. Substitutes—turnips for both raw and cooked dishes.

Kola Nut: Bitter nut of the African kola tree (extracts from this nut were used in the original recipe for Coca-Cola). Substitutes—none.

Kukui Nut: See *candlenut*.

Kumquat: Small, bright orange, oval fruit with a spicy citrus flavor common in China and Japan. Also available in syrup and candied. Substitutes—none.

Lemon Grass (citronella root): Large, dull green grass with lemony flavor common in Southeast Asian dishes. Available fresh, dried or powdered. Substitutes—1 teaspoon of grated lemon rind for each stalk of lemon grass.

Lily Buds (golden needles): The dehydrated buds of lily flowers used in the cooking of China. Substitutes—none.

Lingonberry: Small, wild variety of the cranberry found in Canada and northern Europe. Usually available as preserves. Substitutes—cranberries can be used to replace fresh lingonberries.

Litchi (lychee): Small Chinese fruit with translucent white flesh and a thin brown hull and single pit. The flavor is grapelike but less sweet. Available fresh and canned. Dried litchis, also called litchi nuts, have an entirely different flavor and texture. Substitutes—none.

Long Bean (Chinese green bean, yard-long bean): Roundish Asian bean, 12 to 30 inches long. Similar in taste to string beans, long beans are more soft and chewy, less juicy and crunchy than string beans. Substitutes—string beans.

Long-Grain Rice: See *rice.*

Loquat: Slightly fuzzy, yellow Asian fruit about 2 inches across, with a slightly tart peach flavor. Available dried and in syrup. Substitutes—none.

Lotus Root (water lily root): Tubular vegetable (holes, as in Swiss cheese, run the length of the root, producing a flowerlike pattern when the root is sliced) with brownish skin and crisp, sweet, white flesh. Becomes starchy when overcooked or canned. Substitutes—baking potatoes, but the flavor is not similar.

Macadamia Nut: Round, creamy nut native to Australia, now grown in Africa, South America, and Hawaii. Substitutes—blanched almonds.

Mahimahi (dolphinfish): A saltwater finfish found off the coasts of Florida and Hawaii. Substitutes—halibut, sea bass, or swordfish.

Mahlab: Middle Eastern spice made from ground black cherry kernels, which impart a fruity flavor to foods.

Malagueta Pepper (guinea pepper): Small West African berries related to cardamom, with a hot, peppery flavor. Substitutes—black pepper.

Malanga (yautia): Caribbean tuber with cream-colored, yellow, or pinkish flesh, dark brown skin, and nutty flavor. Substitutes—cassava or taro root.

Mamey: Medium-sized, egg-shaped fruit with brown skin and soft flesh ranging in color from orange to yellowish to reddish. It has a flavor similar to pumpkin. Substitutes—none.

Mango: Fruit native to India, yellow to red when ripe, averaging 1 pound in weight. The flesh is pale and sour when the fruit is unripe, bright orange and very sweet when it is ripe. Used unripe for pickles and chutneys, ripe as a fresh fruit. Substitutes—none.

Manioc: See *cassava.*

Marzipan: See *almond paste.*

Masa: Dough used to make tortillas and tamales. Usually made fresh from dried corn kernels soaked in a lime solution, or from one of two instant "flours" available: masa harina (tortilla mix made from dehydrated fresh masa) or masa trigo (wheat flour tortilla mix). Substitutes—none (corn-meal cannot be used to make masa).

Mastic: Resin from the lentisk bush that has a slightly piney flavor, used to flavor Middle Eastern foods. Available in crystal form. Substitutes—none.

Milkfish (bangus): Silvery, bony fish with oily flesh popular in Filipino cooking. Substitutes—none.

Millet: Cereal native to Africa, known for its high-protein, low-gluten content and ability to grow in arid areas. Substitutes—sorghum (needs nearly 4 times as much water to prepare, however).

Mirin: Sweet rice wine used in Japanese dishes. Substitutes—sweet sherry (although the flavor is slightly different) or 1 part sugar for every 3 parts mirin called for.

Miso: Fermented soybean paste, white (mild flavored) or red (strongly flavored), common in Japanese cooking. Substitutes—none.

Morels: See *mushrooms*.

Mullet: Finfish of two families that can be black, gray, or red. The flesh is a mix of dark, oily meat and light, nutty-tasting meat. The texture is firm, but tender when cooked. Substitutes—none.

Mung Bean: Yellow-fleshed bean with olive or tan skin common in the cooking of China and India. Substitutes—dried yellow peas can be used in cooked dishes.

Mushrooms: Fresh or dried fungus used to flavor dishes throughout the world. Common Asian types include enoki (tiny yellow mushrooms with roundish caps), oyster mushrooms (large, delicately flavored gray-beige caps that grow on trees), shiitake (dark brown with wide flat caps, available dried as Chinese black mushrooms), straw mushrooms (creamy colored with bell-like caps), and cloud ears or wood ears (a large flat fungus with ruffled edges, available dried). Those popular in Europe, available both fresh and dried, include chanterelles (a golden mushroom with an inverted cap), morels (a delicately flavored mushroom with a dark brown wrinkled cap), and porcini or cèpes (large, brown mushrooms with caps that are spongy underneath, also called boletus). Substitutes—commercial hot-house mushrooms can be used in place of fresh Asian or European mushrooms, but the flavor will not be as intense; they are not recommended as substitutes for dried mushrooms. Dried mushrooms can be used interchangeably, although the color or flavor may change slightly.

Nance: Small, yellow tropical fruit similar to cherries with a slightly tart flavor. Two varieties are available. Substitutes—fresh sour cherries, although the flavor will differ slightly.

Napa Cabbage (celery cabbage, Chinese cabbage): Bland, crunchy vegetable with broad, white or light green stalks with ruffled leaves around the edges. Several types are available, similar in taste (do not confuse with bok choy, however, which is a different variety of this species). Substitutes—savoy cabbage.

Nopales (nopalitos): See *cactus*.

Nuoc Cham: See *fish sauce*.

Nuoc Mam: See *fish sauce.*

Okra: Small, green, torpedo-shaped pod with angular sides. A tropical African plant valued for the carbohydrates in it that are sticky and mucilaginous. It is used as a vegetable and to thicken soups and stews. Substitutes — green beans, if thickening is not a consideration.

Olive: Fruit of a tree native to the Mediterranean. Green olives are preserved unripe, and include the large, soft Greek olives. Kalamata olives are a medium-sized, purplish Greek olive. Dark olives are picked in autumn, often cured in salt, with a tannic flavor. Ripe, black olives are smooth-skinned and mild-flavored or wrinkled with a strong tannic flavor. Substitutes — olives differ greatly in taste and are not interchangeable.

Ostiones: Oyster native to the Caribbean that grows on the roots of mangrove trees. Substitutes — other fresh oysters.

Oyster Mushrooms: See *mushrooms.*

Oyster Sauce: Thick, brown Chinese sauce made with soy sauce, oysters, and cornstarch. Substitutes — 1 teaspoon of other Asian fish sauce and 1 teaspoon of water mixed with 1 teaspoon of cornstarch can be used for each tablespoon of oyster sauce, although the flavor will differ slightly.

Pacaya Bud: The bitter flower stalk of the pacaya palm found in Central America. The edible stalk is about 10 inches long and is encased in a tough, green skin, which must be removed before cooking. Substitutes — canned hearts of palm.

Palm Oil (dendê oil): Oil from the African palm, unique for its red-orange color. Substitutes — coconut or other vegetable oil colored with a few drops of food coloring or 1 tablespoon of paprika to each cup of oil (steep for one-half hour, then strain).

Papaya: Thin-skinned, green (underripe), yellow, or orange fruit with sweet flesh colored gold to light orange to pink. Mexican (large and round) and Hawaiian (smaller and pear shaped) varieties are available. The shiny, round black seeds are edible. Unripe papaya is used in pickles; the ripe fruit is eaten fresh. Substitutes — canteloupe can be used in recipes calling for ripe papaya, although the flavor will differ.

Paprika: Powdered red peppers especially popular in Hungarian cooking. Paprika is made from several types of *Capsicum annum*, related to bell and chili peppers. Paprika is usually designated "sweet" or "hot." Spanish paprika, used in Spanish and Middle Eastern dishes is more flavorful. Substitutes — none.

Passion Fruit (granadilla): Small, oval fruit with very sweet, gelatinous pulp. Yellow- and purple-skinned varieties are available. Passion fruit is often made into juice. Substitutes — none.

Patis: See *fish sauce.*

Pawpaw (tree melon): Light orange fruit that tastes like a cross between a banana and a melon. Native to the Americas, it is approximately 6 inches long. Substitutes — none.

Pepitas: Pumpkin or squash seeds common in Latin American cooking. May be hulled or unhulled, raw or roasted, salted or unsalted. Substitutes — sunflower seeds can be used, but these are more flavorful than pepitas.

Peppers: Misnamed pods of the capsicum plants native to South and Central America (not actually related to Asian pepper plants, which produce black pepper). Peppers are divided into sweet and hot types (see *chili pepper*). Sweet peppers include bell peppers (green, red, yellow, and even purple), pimentos, and those used to make paprika. Substitutes — none.

Pigeon Pea: Small pea in a hairy pod (a member of the legume family, but not a true pea) common in the cooking of Africa, the Caribbean, and India. Yellow or tan when dried. Substitutes — may be used interchangeably with black-eyed peas.

Pignoli: See *pine nut*.

Pili Nut: Almondlike nut of a tropical tree found in the Philippines. Substitutes — almonds, although the flavor is slightly different.

Pine Nut (pignoli, piñon seed): Delicately flavored kernel from any of several species of pine tree. Pine nuts are found in Portugal (most expensive type), China (less costly, with a stronger taste), and the southwestern United States. Common in some Asian, European, Latin American, Middle Eastern, and Native American dishes. Substitutes — walnut pieces can be used, but the flavor is not similar.

Pink Bean (rosada): Small oval meaty bean that is a light tannish pink in color. Substitutes — pinto beans.

Plantain: Starchy type of banana with a thick skin, which can be green, red, or black. There are many varieties, ranging in size from 3 to 10 inches. The pulp is used as a vegetable and must be cooked. It is similar in taste to squash. Substitutes — underripe bananas or acorn squash.

Porcini: See *mushrooms*.

Pozole: See *hominy*.

Pulses: Term used especially in India for edible legume seeds, including peas, beans, lentils, and chickpeas. Substitutes — some legumes are interchangeable.

Rambutan: Bristly, juicy, orange or bright red fruit used in Filipino cooking; related to the litchi. Substitutes — none.

Red Bean: Small, dark red bean native to Mexico and the southwestern United States. Substitutes — kidney beans.

Rice: Grain native to India. Over 2,500 varieties are available worldwide, including basmati rice (small grain with a flavor similar to popcorn, very popular in India and the Middle East); brown rice (unmilled rice with the bran layer intact, can be short-, medium-, or long-grain); glutinous rice (also called sweet or pearl rice, very short grain and very sticky when cooked); long-grain rice (white, polished, grains that flake when cooked); and short-grain rice (slightly sticky when cooked, popular in Japan). Substitutes — long-grain rices may be used interchangeably.

Saewu-Jeot: See *shrimp paste*.

Saffron: Dried stamens of the crocus flower. It has a delicate, slightly bitter flavor and bright red-orange color. Available as threads or powder. Substitutes — 1 part turmeric may be used for every 2 parts saffron listed, although the color and flavor will be slightly different.

Salal: Thick-skinned, black berries of a native American plant in the heath family (*Gaultheria shallon*). Substitutes — none.

Salmon Roe: See *caviar*.

Salt Pork: White fat from the side of the hog, streaked with pork meat, cured in salt. Substitutes — unsmoked bacon.

Sapodilla: See *zapote*.

Sassafras (filé powder): Native American herb used to thicken soups and stews. Substitutes — thyme (which has a similar flavor, but does not thicken dishes) or okra (which does not have the same flavor, but will act as a thickener).

Sea Cucumber (sea slug): Brown or black saltwater mollusk up to 1 foot in length. They lack a shell, but have a leathery skin and look something like smooth, dark cucumbers. Sold dried, they are rehydrated for Chinese dishes, becoming soft and jellylike with a mild flavor. Substitutes — none.

Sea Urchin Roe (uni): Small, delicate eggs of the spiny sea urchin, popular in Japan. Substitutes — none.

Seaweed: Many types of dried seaweed are used in Chinese, Korean, and Japanese dishes, including aonoriko (powdered green seaweed), kombu (kelp sheets), and nori (paper-thin sheets of dark green seaweed). Substitutes — none.

Sesame Seeds (benne seeds): Seeds of an herbaceous plant native to Indonesia. Two types are available, tan colored (white when hulled) and black (slightly bitter). Commonly grown for their oil. Light sesame oil is pressed from raw seeds, dark oil from toasted seeds; the dark oil has a strong taste and is used as a flavoring. Substitutes — none for seeds and dark sesame oil; peanut oil for light sesame oil, although the flavor is not the same.

Shallot: Very small bulb covered with a reddish, papery skin, related to onions but with a milder, sweeter flavor. Substitutes — 2 tablespoons chopped scallions (white end only) for each shallot.

Shea Nut: Nut from the African shea tree, grown for its thick oil, called shea butter. Substitutes — coconut oil or palm oil.

Shiitake Mushrooms: See *mushrooms*.

Short-Grain Rice: See *rice*.

Shrimp Paste: Strongly flavored, fermented Asian sauce or paste made from small, dried shrimp or similar crustaceans. Many types are available (bagoong-alamang is the Filipino variety, saewu-jeot is the Korean type). Substitutes — 1 part anchovy paste for every 2 parts shrimp paste called for.

Snail (escargot): Small, edible land snail (a common variety of garden snail, cleansed with a commercial feed). Popular in France. Substitutes — none.

Snow Pea (Chinese pea pod, sugar pea): Flat, edible pod with small, immature peas. Substitutes — none.

Sorghum (guinea corn): Cereal common to tropical regions of Africa with seeds produced on a stalk (often used as animal feed in the United States). Substitutes—millet (use one-quarter the amount of water to prepare).

Sorrel (dock, sourgrass): Small, sour green. Substitutes—spinach (especially the more bitter varieties). Adding a little lemon juice gives a similar sourness.

Sour Orange: Bitter or Seville orange used in Central American, Caribbean, and European cooking. Inedible when raw; flavorful when cooked. Juice most commonly used. Substitutes—2 parts of sweet orange juice mixed with 1 part lemon juice.

Soursop (guanabana): Large (often 12 inches long), rough-skinned fruit with cottony, fluffy flesh that can be white, pink, or light orange. Often made into juice or conserves. Substitutes—pears have a similar taste, although the texture is not the same.

Soy Milk: Soybeans that are boiled, puréed, then strained and boiled again to produce a white milklike drink. Substitutes—none.

Soy Sauce (shoyu): Thin, salty, brown sauce made from fermented soybeans. Several types are available. Chinese soy sauces tend to be lighter in flavor than the stronger, darker Japanese shoyu. Substitutes—none.

Soybean: Small, high-protein bean common in Asia. Many varieties of different colors, including black, green, red, and yellow, are available. They are used fresh, dried, and sprouted, most often processed into sauces, condiments, and other products (see *hoisin sauce, oyster sauce, miso, soy milk, soy sauce, and bean curd*). Substitutes—none.

Star Anise: Eight-armed pods from a plant in the magnolia family, with an aniselike flavor. Native to China. Substitutes—small amounts of anise extract or five-spice powder will approximate the taste.

Star Fruit (carambola): Small, deeply ribbed, oval fruit with thin skin that is shaped like a star when sliced. Green and sour when unripe, it turns yellow and slightly sweet (though still tart) when ripe. The unripe fruit is used in Indian and Chinese dishes; when ripe it is eaten fresh. Substitutes—none.

Straw Mushrooms: See *mushrooms*.

Sumac: Sour, red Middle Eastern spice made from the ground berries of a nontoxic variety of the sumac plant. Substitutes—paprika can be sprinkled for color, but the flavor differs. A little lemon juice can be added for astringency.

Sweet Peppers: See *peppers*.

Szechuan Pepper (fagara): Aromatic berries with a hot flavor popular in some Chinese and Japanese dishes. Substitutes—none.

Tamarind: Tart pulp from the pod of the tamarind bean. Available in the pod, as a paste, in a brick, or as a liquid concentrate. Substitutes—equal amounts of unripe star fruit or twice the amount of lemon juice.

Tannier (tannia): See *taro* and *malanga*; both are referred to as tannier.

Taro: (eddo, dasheen): Starchy underground vegetable similar to cassava with brown hairy skin and white to grayish flesh, common in the Caribbean and Polynesia. In Hawaii, the boiled, fermented taro paste called poi is a staple in the traditional diet. The large leaves are also eaten (see *callaloo*). Substitutes—cassava.

Tarpon: Large, silver fish of the herring family found off the coasts of Mexico and Central America. Substitutes—none.

Ti: Tropical plant popular in Polynesia (not related to tea). Ti leaves are used to wrap food packets, and the root is eaten and brewed for a beverage. Substitutes—bamboo or banana leaves, corn husks, or parchment for ti leaves; none for the root.

Tilapia: Small freshwater fish with sweet, firm, white flesh. Substitutes—flounder, sole, or any rockfish.

Tofu: See *bean curd*.

Tomatillo: Small, light green tomatolike fruit surrounded by a green or tan papery husk, common in Mexico. The flesh is slightly tart and is eaten cooked, usually in sauces and condiments. Available fresh or canned. Substitutes—green, unripe tomatoes, although flavor will differ.

Truffle: Black (French) or white (Italian) fungus found underground. Truffles vary from the size of small marbles to that of tennis balls and are distinctively flavored, similar to a wild mushroom. Available fresh or canned. Substitutes—none.

Tuna: See *cactus*.

Ugli Fruit: Citrus fruit that is a cross between an orange and a grapefruit, with a very bumpy yellow-orange skin and a sweet orangelike flavor. Especially popular in Jamaica. Substitutes—sweet oranges.

Wasabi: Light green Japanese horseradish with a powerful pungency. Available fresh or powdered. Substitutes—none.

Water Chestnut: Aquatic, walnut-sized tuber with fibrous brown peel and crunchy, sweet, ivory-colored flesh. Available fresh or canned. Substitutes—none.

Watermelon Seeds: See *egusi*.

White Bean: Three types of white bean are widely used: cannellini (see *kidney bean*); Great Northern beans, which are large, soft, and mild tasting; and the smaller, firmer navy beans. Substitutes—white beans can be used interchangeably.

White Radish: See *daikon*.

White Yam: African yam with rough brown skin and starchy white flesh (not related to the orange sweet potato called yam in the United States). It may grow quite large, up to 100 pounds. Substitutes—waxy potatoes.

Wild Rice: Seeds of a native American grass. Substitutes—long-grain rice or basmati rice, although the flavor is not the same.

Winged Bean: Edible legume (*Psophocarpus tetragonolobus*) called the "soybean of the tropics." All parts of the plant are consumed, including the shoots, leaves, flowers, pods and seeds, and tuberous root. The pods are large, 12" to 24" long, and feature wing-like flanges. Substitutes—equal amounts of spinach may be used for leaves; green beans for young pods; and soybeans for the seeds.

Winter Melon: Round, green-skinned member of the squash family with translucent white flesh. Similar in taste to zucchini, it is used cooked in Chinese dishes. Substitutes—zucchini.

Worcestershire Sauce: Sauce developed by the British firm of Lea and Perrins including anchovies, garlic, onions, molasses, sugar or corn sweetener, tamarind, and vinegar, among other ingredients. Substitutes—none.

Yautia: See *malanga.*

Yuca: See *cassava.*

Zapote (sapodilla, black sapote, naseberry): Drab-colored fruit of the sapodilla tree (which is the source of chicle used in chewing gum) with yellow, red, or black, granular, mildly sweet flesh. The zapote is a member of the persimmon family. Substitutes—none.

✦ *Bibliography* ✦

Abdullah, Syed. 1966. *House of India Cookbook*. Chicago: Follett Publishing Co.

Adam, Hans K. 1967. *German Cookery*. Cleveland: World Publishing.

Alejandro, Reynaldo. 1982. *The Philippine Cookbook*. New York: Coward McCann.

Anderson, Jean. 1986. *The Food of Portugal*. New York: William Morrow.

Anderson, Jean, and Ellaine Hanna. 1975. *The Doubleday Cookbook*. Garden City, NY: Doubleday.

Andrews, Colman. 1988. *Catalan Cuisine*. New York: Atheneum.

Atwood, Mary S. 1969. *A Taste of India*. Boston: Houghton Mifflin Co.

Aulicino, Armand. 1976. *The New French Cooking*. New York: Grosset & Dunlap.

Bach, Ngo, and Gloria Zimmerman. 1979. *The Classic Cuisine of Vietnam*. Woodbury, NY: Barron's.

Bailey, Adrian. 1969. *The Cooking of the British Isles*. New York: Time-Life Books.

Banai, Margalit. 1972. *What's Cooking in Israel?* New York: Thomas Y. Crowell.

Barrett, Otis W. 1928. *The Tropical Crops*. New York: Macmillan.

Bayless, Rick, and Deann G. Bayless. 1987. *Authentic Mexican*. New York: William Morrow.

Bazore, Katherine. 1947. *Hawaiian and Pacific Foods: A Cook Book of Culinary Customs and Recipes Adapted for the American Hostess*. New York: M. Barrows.

Beck, Simone, and Patricia Simon. 1972. *Simca's Cuisine*. New York: Knopf.

Better Homes and Gardens. 1975. *Heritage Cook Book*. Des Moines, IA: Meredith.

Black, Collette. 1963. *French Provincial Cookery*. New York: Crowell-Collier Press.

Boyd, Lizzie. 1979. *British Cookery*. Woodstock, NY: The Overlook Press.

Brennan, Jennifer. 1984. *The Cuisines of Asia: Nine Great Oriental Cuisines by Technique*. New York: St. Martin's/Marek.

Brissinden, Rosemary. 1970. *South East Asian Food*. Harmondsworth, England: Penguin Books.

Brown, Dale. 1968. *The Cooking of Scandinavia*. New York: Time-Life Books.

Bugialli, Giuliano. 1977. *The Fine Art of Italian Cooking*. New York: Quadrangle/New York Times Book Co.

Bugialli, Giuliano. 1984. *Giuliano Bugialli's Foods of Italy*. New York: Stewart, Tabori & Chang.

Butel, Jane. 1980. *Tex-Mex Cookbook*. New York: Harmony Books.

Cadwallader, Sharon. 1987. *Savoring Mexico: Classic Recipes of Traditional Cuisine from All Regions of Mexico*. San Francisco: Chronicle Books.

Cameron, Sheila M. 1966. *The Highlander's Cookbook*. New York: Gramercy Publishing.

Casas, Penelope. 1982. *The Foods and Wines of Spain*. New York: Knopf.

Castle, Coralie, and Margaret Gin. 1972. *Peasant Cooking of Many Lands*. San Francisco: 101 Productions.

Chance, Jeanne Louise Duzant. 1985. *Ma Chance's French Caribbean Creole Cooking*. New York: Putnam.

Chang, Wonona W., Irving B. Chang, Lillian G. Kutscher, and Austin H. Kutscher. *The Northern Chinese Cookbook*. New York: Crown Publishers.

Chantiles, Vilma L. 1975. *The Food of Greece*. New York: Atheneum.

Chen, Pearl Kong, Tien Chi Chen, and Rose Y. Tseng. 1983. *Everything You Want to Know about Chinese Cooking*. Woodbury, NY: Barron's.

Child, Julia. 1968. *The French Chef Cookbook*. New York: Knopf.

Child, Julia. 1978. *Julia Child and Company*. New York: Knopf.

Child, Julia, Louisette Bertholle, and Simone Beck. 1974. *Mastering the Art of French Cooking* (vol. I). New York: Knopf.

Chin, H. F., and H. S. Yong. 1980. *Malaysian Fruits in Colour*. Kuala Lumpur: Tropical Press.

Cho, Joong Ok. 1981. *Home-style Korean Cooking in Pictures*. New York: Kodansha International USA (distributed through Harper & Row).

Chung, Henry. 1978. *Henry Chung's Hunan Style Chinese Cookbook*. New York: Harmony Books.

Claiborne, Craig. 1971. *The New York Times International Cookbook*. New York: Harper & Row.

Claiborne, Craig, and Pierre Franey. 1970. *Classic French Cuisine*. New York: Time-Life Books.

Clark, Sydney. 1961. *All the Best in Central America*. New York: Dodd, Mead & Co.

Condon, Richard, and Wendy Bennett. 1973. *The Mexican Stove*. Garden City, NY: Doubleday.

Coombs, Anna O. 1958. *The New Smörgåsbord Cookbook*. New York: Hill and Wang.

Corey, Helen. 1962. *The Art of Syrian Cookery*. Garden City, NY: Doubleday.

Cost, Bruce. 1988. *Bruce Cost's Asian Ingredients*. New York: William Morrow.

Coyle, L. Patrick Jr. 1982. *The World Encyclopedia of Food*. New York: Facts on File.

Culinary Arts Institute. 1976. *Polish Cooking*. Chicago: Culinary Arts Institute.

Culinary Arts Institute. 1980. *The Greek Cookbook*. New York: Delair.

Cunningham, Marion, with Jeri Laber. 1979. *The Fannie Farmer Cookbook* (12th edition). New York: Knopf.

Day, Avanelle, and Lillie Stuckey. 1964. *The Spice Cookbook*. New York: David White Co.

De Vore, Sally, and Thelma White. 1978. *The Appetites of Man*. Garden City, NY: Anchor Books.

Delfs, Robert A. 1974. *The Good Food of Szechuan*. Tokyo: Kodansha International.

Derecskey, Susan. 1972. *The Hungarian Cookbook*. New York: Harper & Row.

DeWitt, Dave, and Nancy Gerlach. 1984. *The Fiery Cuisines*. New York: St. Martin's Press.

Elliot, Douglas B. 1976. *Roots: An Underground Botany and Forager's Guide*. Old Greenwich, CT: Chatham Press.

Ensminger, Audrey H., M. E. Ensminger, James E. Konlande, and John R. K. Robson. 1963. *Foods and Nutrition Encyclopedia*. Clovis, CA: Pegus Press.

Eren, Neset. 1969. *The Art of Turkish Cooking*. Garden City, NY: Doubleday.
Espy, Hilda C. 1970. *Another World: Central America*. New York: Viking.

Farah, Madelain. 1981. *Lebanese Cuisine*. Portland, OR: M. Farah.
Feibelman, Peter S. 1969. *The Cooking of Spain and Portugal*. New York: Time-Life Books.
Feibleman, Peter S. 1971. *American Cooking: Creole and Acadian*. New York: Time-Life Books.
Feldman, Annette. (ed.). 1971. *Enjoy*. Iowa Falls, IA: Eden Chapter, Hassadah (General Publishing Building).
Field, Carol. 1985. *The Italian Baker*. New York: Harper & Row.
Fisher, M. F. K. 1969. *The Cooking of Provincial France*. New York: Time-Life Books.
FitzGibbon, Theodora. 1968. *A Taste of Ireland: Irish Traditional Food*. New York: Avenel Books.
Folsom, LeRoi A. 1974. *The Professional Chef* (4th edition). New York: Van Nostrand Reinhold.
Frederikson, Karin. 1967. *The Great Scandinavian Cook Book*. New York: Crown.

Giusti-Lanham, Hedy, and Andrea Dodi. 1978. *The Cuisine of Venice*. Woodbury, NY: Barron's.
Glassman, Paul. 1988. *Costa Rica*. Champlain, NY: Passport Press.
Goldstein, Darra. 1983. *A La Russe*. New York: Random House.
Goodheart, Robert S., and Maurice E. Shils. 1980. *Modern Nutrition in Health and Disease*. Philadelphia: Lea & Febiger.
Greig, M. A. Undated. *Cajun Cuisine at Its Best*. St. Martinville, LA: M. A. Greig.

Hahn, Emily. 1968. *The Cooking of China*. New York: Time-Life Books.
Hanle, Zack. 1987. The exciting flavors of Costa Rica. *Bon Appetit*, vol. 32 (3).
Hazan, Marcella. 1976. *The Classic Italian Cook Book: The Art of Italian Cooking and the Italian Art of Eating*. New York: Knopf.
Hazelton, Nika S. 1964. *The Art of Danish Cooking*. Garden City, NY: Doubleday.
Hazelton, Nika S. 1965. *The Art of Scandinavian Cooking*. New York: Macmillan.
Hazelton, Nika S. 1969. *The Cooking of Germany*. New York: Time-Life Books.
Hazelton, Nika S. 1987. *Classic Scandinavian Cooking*. New York: Scribner's Sons.
Heberle, Marianna O. 1985. *Polish Cooking*. Tucson, AZ: HP Books.
Hedrick, U. P. (ed.). 1972. *Sturtevant's Edible Plants of the World*. New York: Dover.
Heller, Edna E. 1968. *The Art of Pennsylvania Dutch Cooking*. Garden City, NY: Doubleday.
Howe, Robin. 1971. *Far Eastern Cookery*. New York: Drake Publishers.
Hudson, Charles. 1976. *The Southeastern Indians*. Knoxville: University of Tennessee Press.
Hultman, Tami. 1985. *The Africa News Cookbook*. New York: Viking.
Hush, Joanne, and Peter Wong. 1976. *The Chinese Menu Cookbook*. New York: Holt, Rinehart and Winston.
Hutchison, Ruth Shepard. 1958. *The New Pennsylvania Dutch Cook Book*. New York: Harper & Row.

Jaffrey, Madhur. 1975. *An Invitation to Indian Cooking*. New York: Vintage Books.
Jaffrey, Madhur. 1987. *Madhur Jaffrey's Indian Cooking*. London, England: BBC Books.
Johnson, Alice B. 1964. *The Complete Scandinavian Cookbook*. New York: Macmillan.
Jones, Evan. 1975. *American Food*. New York: E. P. Dutton.

Kaufman, William I., and Mary U. Cooper. 1962. *The Art of Creole Cookery*. Garden City, NY: Doubleday.
Kavena, Juanita T. 1980. *Hopi Cookery*. Tucson, AZ: University of Arizona Press.

Kaye, Dena. 1984. A blend of ancient and modern: Florida teacher explores the Maya Culture through its cuisine. *Bon Appetit*, vol. 29 (9).

Käkönen, Ulla. 1974. *Natural Cooking the Finnish Way*. New York: Quadrangle.

Keegan, Marcia. 1987. *Southwest Indian Cookbook*. Weehawken, NJ: Clear Light Publications.

Kennedy, Diana. 1975. *The Tortilla Book*. New York: Harper & Row.

Kennedy, Diana. 1978. *Recipes from the Regional Cooks of Mexico*. New York: Harper & Row.

Kimball, Yeffe, and Jean Anderson. 1986. *The Art of American Indian Cooking*. New York: Simon & Schuster.

Kittler, Pamela Goyan, and Kathryn Sucher. 1989. *Food and Culture in America*. New York: Van Nostrand Reinhold.

Knopf, Edwin H., and Mildred O. Knopf. 1964. *The Food of Italy and How To Prepare It*. New York: Knopf.

Koehler, Margaret H. 1973. *Recipes from the Portuguese of Provincetown*. Riverside, CT: Chatham Press.

Koh, Frances M. 1985. *Creative Korean Cooking*. Minneapolis: East-West Press.

Lang, George. 1971. *The Cuisine of Hungary*. New York: Atheneum.

Law, Ruth. 1982. *Dim Sum, Fast and Festive Chinese Cooking*. Chicago: Contemporary Books.

Leonard, Jonathan Norton. 1968. *Latin American Cooking*. New York: Time-Life Books.

Leonard, Jonathan Norton. 1971. *American Cooking: The Great West*. New York: Time-Life Books.

Lin, Hsiang J., and Tsuifeng Lin. 1972. *Chinese Gastronomy*. New York: Pyramid Publications.

Ludlow, Rose Budd. 1986. *Total Health and Food Power*. Santa Barbara, CA: Woodbridge Press.

Marks, Copeland. 1985. *False Tongues and Sunday Bread: A Guatemalan and Mayan Cookbook*. New York: M. Evans.

Marks, Copeland: 1986. *The Varied Kitchens of India: Cuisines of the Anglo-Indians of Calcutta, Bengalis, Jews of Calcutta, Kashmiris, Parsis, and Tibetans of Darjeeling*. New York: M. Evans.

McCall's Introduction to French Cooking. 1971. New York: McCall Publishing.

McCormick, Malachi. 1988. *Irish Country Cooking*. New York: Clarkson N. Potter.

McGee, Harold. 1984. *On Food and Cooking*. New York: Scribner's Sons.

McKendry, Maxime. 1983. *Seven Hundred Years of English Cooking*. New York: Exeter Books.

Merinoff, Linda. 1987. *The Savory Sausage*. New York: Poseidon Press.

Miller, Gloria B. 1970. *The Thousand Recipe Chinese Cookbook*. New York: Grosset & Dunlap.

Miller, Jill Nhu Huong. 1968. *Vietnamese Cookery*. Rutland, VT: C. E. Tuttle.

Millon, Marc, and Kim Millon. 1985. *The Taste of Britain*. Salem, NH: Salem House.

Mitchell, Leonard Jan. 1952. *Lüchow's German Cookbook: The Story and the Favorite Dishes of America's Most Famous German Restaurant*. Garden City, NY: Doubleday.

Montagne, Prosper. 1961. *Larousse Gastronomique: The Encyclopedia of Food, Wine, and Cookery*. New York: Crown Publishers.

Mulherin, Jennifer. 1988. *Spices and Natural Flavorings*. New York: Macmillan.

Nahoum, Aldo. 1970. *The Art of Israeli Cooking*. New York: Holt, Rinehart & Winston.

Nakamura, Julia V. 1985. *Japanese Recipes for the American Cook*. Hicksville, NY: Exposition Press.

Nelson, Kay Shaw. 1977. *The Eastern European Cookbook*. New York: Dover Publications.

Nickles, Harry G. 1969. *Middle Eastern Cooking*. New York: Time-Life Books.

Niethammer, Carolyn. 1974. *American Indian Food and Lore*. New York: Macmillan.

Ortiz, Elisabeth Lambert. 1967. *The Complete Book of Mexican Cooking*. New York: M. Evans.

Ortiz, Elisabeth Lambert, with Mitsuko Endo. 1976. *The Complete Book of Japanese Cooking*. New York: M. Evans.

Papashvily, Helen Waite, and George Papashvily. 1969. *Russian Cooking*. New York: Time-Life Books.

Popenoe, Wilson. 1974. *Manual of Tropical and Subtropical Fruits*. New York: Hafner Press.

Prudhomme, Paul. 1984. *Chef Paul Prudhomme's Louisiana Kitchen*. New York: William Morrow.

Prudhomme, Paul, and the eleven Prudhomme brothers and sisters. 1987. *The Prudhomme Family Cookbook: Old-time Louisiana Recipes*. New York: William Morrow.

Reavis, Charles. 1981. *Home Sausage Making*. Charlotte, VT: Garden Way.

Richie, Donald. 1985. *A Taste of Japan*. Tokyo: Kodansha International.

Roden, Claudia. 1987. *Mediterranean Cookery*. New York: Knopf.

Romagnoli, Margaret, and G. Franco Romagnoli. 1975. *The Romagnolis' Table: Italian Family Recipes*. Boston: Little, Brown.

Root, Waverly. 1968. *The Cooking of Italy*. New York: Time-Life Books.

Rosengarten, Frederic Jr. 1969. *The Book of Spices*. Wynnewood, PA: Livingston.

Rudzinski, Russell. 1969. *Japanese Country Cookbook*. San Francisco: Nitty Gritty Productions.

Sacharoff, Shanta N. 1972. *Flavors of India*. San Francisco: 101 Productions.

Sahni, Julie. 1980. *Classic Indian Cooking*. New York: William Morrow & Co.

Sandler, Bea. 1970. *The African Cookbook*. Cleveland: World Publishing.

Sarvis, Shirley. 1967. *A Taste of Portugal*. New York: Charles Scribner's Sons.

Schindler, Roana, and Gene Schindler. 1970. *Hawaii Kai Cookbook*. New York: Hearthside Press.

Schneider, Elizabeth. 1986. *Uncommon Fruits and Vegetables*. New York: Harper & Row.

Schryver, Alice. 1975. *Oriental Cooking*. New York: Grosset & Dunlap.

Sheridan, Monica. 1965. *The Art of Irish Cooking*. Garden City, NY: Doubleday.

Shugart, Grave S., Mary Molt, and Maxine F. Wilson. 1985. *Food for Fifty*. New York: John Wiley & Sons.

Simon, Andre L. 1981. *A Concise Encyclopedia of Gastronomy*. Woodstock, NY: Overlook.

Singh, Dharamjit. 1970. *Indian Cookery*. Harmondsworth, England: Penguin Books.

Slater, Mary. 1965. *Cooking the Caribbean Way*. London: Paul Hamlyn.

Solomon, Charmaine. 1976. *The Complete Asian Cookbook*. New York: McGraw-Hill.

Soper, Musia (ed.). 1962. *Encyclopedia of European Cooking*. London: Spring Books.

Steinberg, Rafael. 1969. *The Cooking of Japan*. New York: Time-Life Books.

Steinberg, Rafael. 1970. *Pacific and Southeast Asian Cooking*. New York: Time-Life Books.

Stewart, Martha. 1985. *Martha Stewart's Pies and Tarts*. New York: C. N. Potter.

Stewart, Martha, with Elizabeth Hawes. 1982. *Entertaining*. New York: C. N. Potter.

Stobart, T. 1980. *The Cook's Encyclopedia*. New York: Harper & Row.

Stone, Sally, and Martin Stone. 1985. *Classic Mexican Cooking*. New York: Wallaby Books.

Sunset Italian Cook Book. 1972. Menlo Park, CA: Lane Publishing.

Tannahill, Reay. 1973. *Food in History*. New York: Stein and Day.

Tsuji, Shizuo. 1980. *Japanese Cooking: A Simple Art*. New York: Kodansha International USA (distributed through Harper & Row).

Valldejuli, Carmen A. 1977. *Puerto Rican Cookery*. Gretna, LA: Pelican Publishing.
Van Der Post, Laurens. 1970. *African Cooking*. New York: Time-Life Books.
Van Der Post, Laurens. 1978. *First Catch Your Eland*. New York: William Morrow.
Verrill, A. Hyatt. 1937. *Foods America Gave the World*. Boston: L. C. Page.
Viherjuuri, Matti, Anna Maija Tanttu, and Juha Tanttu. 1983. *Finlandia Gastronomica* (5th edition). Helsinki: Otava.
Volokh, Anne. 1983. *The Art of Russian Cuisine*. New York: Macmillan.
Von Welantz, Diana, and Paul Von Welantz. 1982. *The Von Welantz Guide to Ethnic Ingredients*. New York: Warner Books.

Wagner, Candy, and Sandra Marquez. 1983. *Cooking Texas Style: A Heritage of Traditional Recipes*. Austin, TX: University of Texas Press.
Waldo, Myra. 1967. *The International Encyclopedia of Cooking* (vol. 2). New York: Macmillan.
Waldo, Myra. 1973. *The Complete Round-the-World Cookbook*. Garden City, NY: Doubleday.
Walter, Eugene. 1971. *American Cooking: Southern Style*. New York: Time-Life Books.
Wason, Betty. 1963. *The Art of Spanish Cooking*. Garden City, NY: Doubleday.
Weaver, William Woys. 1983. *Sauerkraut Yankees: Pennsylvania-German Foods and Foodways*. Philadelphia: University of Pennsylvania Press.
Wechberg, Joseph. 1968. *The Cooking of Vienna's Empire*. New York: Time-Life Books.
Weiner, Michael A. 1972. *Earth Medicine—Earth Foods*. New York: Macmillan.
Wilson, Ellen Gibson. 1971. *A West African Cookbook*. M. Evans.
Wilson, Justin. 1979. *Cookin' Cajun*. Gretna, LA: Pelican Publishing.
Wolfe, Linda. 1970. *The Cooking of the Caribbean Islands*. New York: Time-Life Books.
Wong, Ella-Mei. 1981. *Yum Cha*. London: Angus & Robertson.

Yardley, Maili. 1970. *Hawaii Cooks*. Tokyo: Charles E. Tuttle Co.
Yianilos, T. K. 1970. *The Complete Greek Cookbook*. New York: Funk and Wagnalls.
Young, Joyce L. 1987. *Tropic Cooking*. Berkeley, CA: Ten Speed Press.

Zane, Eva. 1970. *Greek Cooking for the Gods*. San Francisco: 101 Productions.

Acknowledgments

The recipes for Sopa de Pesce, Adobado de Carne de Cerdo, Tomato Salad, and Coconut Candy in Chapter 2 were adapted from Marks, Copeland, 1985, *False Tongues and Sunday Bread*. New York: M. Evans and Co.

The recipes for Funnel Cake, Scrapple, Apple Rings, and Potato Cakes in Chapter 6 were adapted from Hutchinson, Ruth, 1958, *The New Pennsylvania Dutch Cook Book*. New York: Harper & Row.

The recipes for Ginger Beer, Coconut Soup, Rice Balls, Chicken in Peanut Sauce, and Adalu in Chapter 20 were adapted from Wilson, Ellen Gibson, 1971, *A West African Cookbook*. New York: M. Evans and Co.,

◆ *Index* ◆

Note: Boldface numbers indicate pictured recipes.

Yogurt (*continued*)
   sauce, 92
   with tomato and cucumber (raita), 113
Yuca, 5, 150
Yucatan, 149
Yunnan, 26

Zabaglione, 119
Zakuski, 39, 44
Zapote, 17, 150
Zarzuela, 204
Zucchini, 52
Zuppa di pesce, **114**, 118, 125